CUTTING OFF THE SERPENT'S HEAD

Tightening Control in Tibet, 1994-1995

Tibet Information Network

Human Rights Watch/Asia

Human Rights Watch
New York • Washington • Los Angeles • London • Brussels

ISBN 1-56432-166-5
Library of Congress Catalog Card Number 96-76096

Cover photograph copyright © Tibet Information Network. People's Armed Police patrol through crowds gathered outside Tashilhunpo on July 12, 1995 while monks inside protest against denunciation of abbot.

Permission to reprint map on inside front cover granted by Atelier Golok, copyright © 1993.

TIBET INFORMATION NETWORK

The Tibet Information Network (TIN) is an independent news and research service that collects and distributes information about what is happening in Tibet. TIN monitors social, economic, political, environmental, and human rights conditions in Tibet, and then publishes the information in an easily accessible form. It collects its information by using sources inside and outside Tibet, by conducting projects among refugees, and by monitoring established Chinese and international sources.

TIN aims to present information that is accurate, reliable, and free from bias. Its material is available to subscribers who, in return for an annual fee, receive news and research publications. The service is used by individuals and institutions, including journalists, governments, academics, China-watchers, and human rights organizations. TIN was started in 1987 and is based in London. It has no political affiliations or objectives and endeavors to provide a reliable and dispassionate news service for an area of increasing significance.

TIN services include: News Updates providing detailed coverage of news events; Background Briefing Papers on key social and political issues; full texts of key interviews and original documents; translations of articles from Tibetan newspapers; and briefings for delegations and analysts. A selection of TIN information is translated into Tibetan, Japanese, German, French, and Danish. TIN's office in the U.S. distributes information to subscribers in North America.

Addresses for the Tibet Information Network:
TIN UK: 7 Beck Road, London E8 4RE, UK
Tel: (44) 181-533-5458 fax: (44) 181-985-4751
E-mail: tin@gn.apc.org

TIN USA: PO Box 2270, Jackson, WY 83001, USA
Tel/fax: (307) 733-4670
E-mail: tinusa@igc.apc.org

HUMAN RIGHTS WATCH

CONTENTS

A NOTE ON THE TITLE

The title is taken from *A Golden Bridge Leading Into a New Era*, (*Dus rabs gsar par skyod-pa'i gser zam*), a propaganda manual published by the Propaganda Committee of the TAR Communist Party as "reference materials to publicize the spirit of the Third Forum on Work in Tibet" (Tibetan People's Publishing House, October 1, 1994):

> As the saying goes, to kill a serpent, we must first chop off its head. If we don't do that, we cannot succeed in the struggle against separatism. .... it is not a matter of religious belief nor a matter of the question of autonomy, it is a matter of securing the unity of our country and opposing separatism. It is a matter of antagonistic contradiction with the enemy, and it represents the concentrated form of the class struggle in Tibet at the present time. It is the continuing struggle of the Chinese people against imperialism, the struggle against the invading force of the imperialists ... Any separatist activities and convictions must be continuously crushed, according to the law. We must heighten our vigilance, and watch out for those few who are holding to a reactionary standpoint, and who are launching vengeful counterattacks and harming our cadres at the grassroots level. They must be struck down and punished severely... We have the correct leadership of the Party and the solid and unchangeable support of the People's Army and the Public Security plus the garrison command. Whoever sabotages the solidarity of the nationalities and wants to separate China will be completely opposed by the Tibetan people and the people of the whole country, and will definitely be smashed and will become criminals who have committed the most heinous crimes.

ACKNOWLEDGMENTS

This report was written by Robert Barnett of the Tibet Information Network. It is based on research conducted by a TIN team most of whose members, in order to allow their work to continue, cannot be named. They dedicated many months of intensive work to collecting primary information, interviewing escapees, translating documents, and then keying in, analyzing and cross-checking the data received. One leading member of the research team created an exhaustive database and statistical analysis of all references to political prisoners, and another did a survey of official press statements on policy in the period. Three others carried out and translated some 200 interviews in a project in India which lasted well over a year.

Most of the researchers worked, unpaid, under extremely difficult conditions. In particular many of the Tibetans involved in this work contributed vital information at serious risk to themselves and their families. It remains illegal under current Chinese legal practice for Tibetans to communicate news or opinions of the kind studied in this report, and several prisoners, such as Dr Jampa Ngodrup, Ngawang Gyaltsen, Ngawang Pelkar and Yeshe Ngawang, are serving long prison sentences for attempting to pass such news to the outside world. Other Tibetans famous for taking the risk to monitor the situation, such as Yulo Rinpoche and most notably Gendun Rinchen, have now been released from prison, although Yulo Rinpoche remains under restrictions. Without the courage and determination of all these people to carry out this research and to maintain a commitment to high standards of accuracy and balance, especially those involved in monitoring arrests in the field, this report would not have been possible.

The majority of the interviews in India were carried out for TIN by Francisca van Holthoon, with initial translations in Dharamsala by Tendar and others, thanks to the co-operation kindly provided there by the exile Tibetan administration. Editing in London was done by Joanna Ross and others. Administrative support was provided in the London office by Claire Sparksman and Nathalie Warren, and in the TIN USA office by Alana Guarnieri.

Mickey Spiegel of Human Rights Watch/Asia wrote the last three sections of Part 2 and Appendix II, and did extensive cross-checking of prisoner lists. The report was edited by Sidney Jones, Mickey Spiegel and Cynthia Brown, and produced with the assistance of Paul Lall, all of Human Rights Watch.

The research for this report would not have been possible without the generous financial support of Dialoog, Harrison Ford, Wilde Ganzen, Melissa Mathison, Vicki Riskin and Fred Segal.

GLOSSARY

A-ni (Tibetan) - nun.

Anquan bu (Chinese) - Ministry of State Security. Tibetan: *rgyal-khab dbe-'jags las-khung* (gyalkhab denjak lekhung).

Barkor (Tibetan *bar-skor*) - literally the "middle circuit," the road or alleyway used for circumambulation around the Jokhang Temple in Lhasa, and the main site for *korwa* (q.v.) in Lhasa.

Bonpo (Tibetan: *dpon-po*) - the traditional animist religion of Tibet, originating from before the arrival of Buddhism, and still practiced in many areas.

CCP - the Chinese Communist Party, founded in Shanghai in July 1921. The Chinese term is *zhongguo gong chan dang*; in Tibetan the term is not translated but is rendered phonetically as *krung-go gung bran tang*.

counterrevolutionary - legal/political term for an enemy of the state or for any act "committed with the goal of overthrowing the political power of the dictatorship of the proletariat and the socialist system" (Chinese Criminal Code, 1980, Article 90). Chinese: *fan ge ming*, Tibetan: *gsar-brjer ngo-rgol* (sar-je ngo-gol).

CPPCC - the Chinese People's Political Consultative Conference. First convened in 1949, the CPPCC is an institution consisting of representatives of non-Party organizations which support the Party. In nationality areas it includes leading religious figures and former aristocrats who support the Party ("patriotic upper strata"). It is the main public organ for the United Front (*q.v.*). and meets regularly to express support and sometimes comment on Party policies. Tibetan: *Krung-go mi-dmangs chab-srid gros mol tshogs-'du*, or, more simply, *chab srid gros* (chab si droe).

Cultural Revolution - the campaign initiated by Mao Zedong in order to regain control of the Party by ordering the youth to "bombard the headquarters" (purge opponents within the Party) and to eradicate "the Four Olds" (old ideas, old culture, old customs, old habits). The Chinese authorities now describe it as "the Ten Bad Years," referring to the period from 1966-1976. In Tibet it is sometimes considered to have continued until 1979. Tibetan: *rigs-nas gsar-brje (rig-ne sar-je)*.

dang'an (Chinese) - the file or archive containing information held by the state on each individual's social and political history, usually retained in the security section.

Democratic Management Committee - administrative organs established in monasteries in Tibet from 1962 onwards. See *u-yon lhan-khang*.

Dharamsala - hill station in Himachal Pradesh, Northern India, currently the seat of the Dalai Lama and of the Tibetan government in exile.

Dharma (Sanskrit) - religion or truth; can also refer to the nature of reality. Used as a synonym for Buddhism or for Buddhist teachings. Tibetan: *chos* (choe).

ganbu (Chinese) - cadre; usually refers to any member of the Party who holds a responsible position, but technically also applies to a non-Party member who holds a responsible position in the government. Tibetan: *las byed-pa* (le che pa).

Gelugpa (Tibetan *dge-lugs-pa*) - the dominant school of Tibetan Buddhism, sometimes called the "yellow hat" school. Founded in the fifteenth century by Tsongkhapa, and mainly associated with the Dalai Lamas.

geshe (Tibetan: *dge-bshes*) - monk or lama who has completed the highest course in metaphysics and other academic monastic studies in the Gelugpa school; similar to a doctor of theology.

Gongan Ju (Chinese) - Public Security Bureau (PSB); local-level police force. Tibetan: *sbyi sde chu* (chi de chu).

gonpa (Tibetan *dgon-pa*) - monastery.

hu kou (Chinese)- residence registration document. Tibetan: *them-mtho*; also used for ration permit.

Kagyu or **Kagyupa** (Tibetan *bka'-rgyud-pa*) - the school of Buddhism originating in the eleventh century, and associated with the Karmapas, whose traditional seat is at Tsurphu, 50 miles west of Lhasa.

kanshousuo (Chinese) - detention center, Tibetan: *lta-srung-khang.*

korwa (Tibetan *skor-ba*) - circuit; the practice of walking around a Buddhist temple or religious site in a clockwise direction, a form of religious practice.

kusho (Tibetan *sku-bzhogs, sku-zhabs*) - term of respect for a learned or distinguished person; similar to the English "sir."

Jo-khang (Tibetan) - the most sacred temple in Tibet, situated in the Tibetan quarter or Old City of Lhasa, usually referred to in Tibetan as the *Tsug-lha-khang*.

lama - the Tibetan term for a respected religious teacher, equivalent to the Sanskrit term *guru*. A lama is not necessarily a monk, although monasticism is preferred for all lamas in the Gelugpa school. Chinese politicians use the term incorrectly to refer to any monk.

laogai (Chinese) - reform-through-labor center which houses judicially-sentenced prisoners. Also used informally to refer to the entire penal system (Tibetan: *ngal rtsol bsgyur bkod)*. A *laojiao* (short for ***laodong jiaoyang***) is a re-education-through-labor camp housing administratively sentenced prisoners.

las don ru khag (ledun rukha) (Tibetan) - literally a work team. Refers to a specially formed and temporary unit of Party members sent to conduct investigations or give political re-education in a particular institution or locality. Chinese: *gongzuo dui*.

le che pa - see *ganbu*.

mu (Chinese) - a measure of land area, equal to 1/15th (0.0667) of a hectare, or 67 sq. meters (i.e., 1500 mu = 1 sq km.)**.**

paichusuo (Chinese) - local police station.

PAP - People's Armed Police. See *Wujing.*

PCC - Party Central Committee. Chinese: *dang zhong yang*, Tibetan: *tang krung yang.*

peaceful evolution - Party term for a western strategy to undermine communism by gradually introducing western ideas. Tibetan: *zhi-wa'i rim 'gyur* (shiwei rim gyur), Chinese: *heping yanbian*.

peaceful liberation - Party term for the PLA's 1959 entry into what is now termed the Tibet Autonomous Region. Tibetan: *zhi-wa'i bcings-bkrol* (shiwei ching drol).

prefecture - the administrative area below the level of a province or region and above the level of a county. Chinese: *diqu*. The TAR is divided into five prefectures, each of which is divided into seven or more counties. A "Tibetan autonomous prefecture" (Chinese: *xizang zizhizhou*) is a prefecture outside the Tibetan Autonomous Region but still considered to include a predominantly Tibetan population.

procuracy - Chinese governmental organization responsible for investigating and prosecuting criminal cases. Tibetan: *zhib chu*, Chinese: *jianchayuan*.

PSB - Public Security Bureau. See *Gongan Ju*.

reactionary - thinking which is backward or resistant to correct political ideas. Tibetan: *log spyod-pa* (lok choe pa). Chinese: *fan dong pai*.

reform and opening up - the guiding policy of the Party initiated by Deng Xiaoping in 1978 and allowing the development of the "household responsibility system" and the "socialist market economy," but not encouraging political liberalization. Tibetan: *'gyur-bcos sgo-bye srid chus* (gyur choe go-che si chue). Chinese: *gaige kaifang*.

Rinpoche (Tibetan *rin-po-che*) - literally precious, a term of respect added to a lama's name.

shourongsuo (Chinese) - shelter and investigation center, a local detention center/jail for holding short-term offenders or vagrants.

splittism - Party term for the movement for Tibetan independence or any secessionist movement. Tibetan: *kha-bral ring-lugs* (khadrel ringluk).

TAR - the Tibet Autonomous Region, the Tibetan area west of the Yangzi river and south of the Kunlun mountains. This is the only area recognized by modern-day China as "Tibet." The area was formally constituted as an "autonomous region" in 1965. Tibetan: *Bod rang-skyong ljongs*; Chinese: *Xizang Zizhiqu*.

them-mtho - see *hu kou*.

ting (Chinese) - government department or office at the level of a province or autonomous region; below a *bu* (Ministry, at state level, Tibetan: *pu'u*) and above a *ju* (local office or department, Tibetan: *chu*). Tibetan: *thing*.

tsampa (Tibetan *rtsam-pa*) - roasted barley flour, the staple foodstuff in Tibet and the national dish. The Chinese refer to it as *qingke*.

tulku or **trulku** (Tibetan *sprul-sku*) - literally, "manifestation body." An incarnate lama, i.e. a person who has achieved a level of spiritual ability which allows him or her to choose to be reborn as a human in order to help others. The Chinese translate the term incorrectly as "living Buddha."

turen or **turing** (Tibetan *kru-ring*) - modern Tibetan term for the appointed foreman or leader of a committee, from the Chinese term *zhuren*.

U-Tsang (Tibetan *dbus-gtsang*) - the traditional name for the two areas of central Tibet including Lhasa and Shigatse respectively.

u-yon lhan-khang (Tibetan): committee, based on the Chinese term *hui yuan*. Sometimes used as a short form of *sa-ngas u-yon lhan-khang* (sa-ne u-yon lhen-khang), the neighborhood committee (the grassroots level administrative unit for local residents who are not members of a work unit). In a monastery, for example, it is used to refer to the "Democratic Management Committee."

United Front - the organ of the Party devoted to forming broad 'alliance' with non-Party and often with non-Chinese sectors, particularly by co-opting "patriotic upper strata" to get them to acknowledge the supremacy of the Party. See also CPPCC. Chinese: *tong zhan bu*, Tibetan: *'thab-phyogs gcig-sgyur* (thab-chog chiggyur).

Wujing (Chinese) - People's Armed Police, a paramilitary unit formed in 1983.

xian (Chinese) - county, the middle level administrative unit. Tibetan: *shen* or *rdzong*.

xiang (Chinese) - the lower level administrative unit, formerly covering a township, but in rural areas covering a group of villages. Tibetan: *shang*.

Xizang (Chinese) - the Chinese term for Tibet, referring only to the area now covered by the Tibet Autonomous Region.

zangzu (Chinese) - the Chinese term for the Tibetan ethnic group.

zhuxi (Chinese) - chairman, governor (Tibetan: *kru'ushi*). The equivalent in the Party is the Party is the s*huji,* Party secretary (Tibetan: *hru-chi*)

ABBREVIATIONS

CPPCC	Chinese People's Political Consultative Conference
FBIS	Foreign Broadcast Information Service
NPC	National People's Congress
PAP	People's Armed Police
PLA	People's Liberation Army
PRC	People's Republic of China
PSB	Public Security Bureau
SWB	Summary of World Broadcasts (BBC)
TAR	Tibet Autonomous Region
TIN	Tibet Information Network

PART 1: THE POLITICAL CONTEXT

I. SUMMARY AND INTRODUCTION

This report, based entirely on primary sources, documents the emerging trends in political repression in Tibet, an area which for the purposes of this report includes both the mountainous plateau now called the Tibetan Autonomous Region (TAR) and the Tibetan-inhabited parts of the neighboring Chinese provinces of Qinghai, Sichuan, Gansu and Yunnan.[1] It examines new Chinese government strategies for dealing with dissent and focuses in particular on the impact of a crucial conference held in Beijing in July 1994 known as the Third National Forum on Work in Tibet or "the Third Forum" for short. The Third Forum produced the most fundamental revision of policies on Tibet since the relaxation of hard-line Maoist policies in 1979 and led directly, among other things, to a dramatic increase in political imprisonment which is exhaustively documented in the report.

The main findings of the study are that political dissent in Tibet is spreading to rural areas and to wider sections of the community; that the number of political prisoners in Tibet substantially increased in 1994-1995; that the Third Forum has resulted in increasingly repressive policies, many of which are designed to identify potential dissidents in the broader population through various mechanisms of surveillance and screening; and that the dispute over the selection of the Panchen Lama, Tibet's second most senior religious leader, has been used to increase restrictions on religion and to set up denunciation campaigns against religious leaders in a way not seen for some fifteen years. The conclusions can be summarized as follows:

---

[1] This is the definition used by Hugh Richardson, the last British representative in Tibet, to describe what he called "ethnographic Tibet," corresponding to the Chinese term "the Five [Tibetan] Autonomous Areas and Regions" (Chinese: *wu shen qu*, Tibetan: *zhing-chen dang rang-skyong-ljongs lnga*). Since 1951 this area has been formally incorporated within the People's Republic of China. The Chinese authorities use the term "Tibet" to refer to the Tibet Autonomous Region only, which is the western half of ethnographic Tibet and the area ruled by Lhasa at the time of invasion. The Tibetan exile government claims additional areas beyond ethnographic Tibet such as Xining. The use of these terms does not indicate any political position by the Tibet Information Network, which is not a political organization, or Human Rights Watch, which takes no stand on this issue.

1

Political Imprisonment

•   As of January 1996 the names of 610 Tibetans in detention for opposition to Chinese rule had been documented. The whereabouts of an additional eighty political detainees remain unknown. This means that there are now more political detainees in Chinese prisons in Tibet than at any time since lists were first compiled by observers in 1990.[2] The difficulty of obtaining information from Tibet means that it is hard to make definitive comparisons for the whole of the Tibetan area, but there are relatively complete statistics available for Tibet's main prison in Lhasa, known as Drapchi. These show that the number of political prisoners in Drapchi was 274 in August 1995, a three-fold increase in the number held there compared with five years earlier.

•   Protest, and therefore political imprisonment, has increased in rural areas of central Tibet. In Tibet's second city, Shigatse, major dissent emerged for the first time, following the dispute over the selection of the new Panchen Lama in May 1995. That dissent prompted an increase in security activity and political arrests.

•   An increase in political detentions in Tibet followed the end of efforts by the U.S. administration in May 1994 to link human rights conditions and Most Favored Nation (MFN) trade status for China. Similar gestures by other western governments, notably France and Germany, to downplay human rights concerns took place around the same time. While it is difficult to determine cause and effect, many Tibetans are convinced that the increased repression was a direct result of the easing of international pressure on China.

•   Suppression of dissent appears to have increased in 1995. There were, for example, more political arrests in the first three months of that year than in the

---

[2] The first detailed published list was in Asia Watch, *Evading Scrutiny* (New York: Human Rights Watch, 1988), taken from a list supplied by the exile Tibetan government, which gave 256 names of political prisoners. At that time there were an estimated 2,000 to 3,000 prisoners, most of whom were held for periods of about six months and who were released by 1990. The first list since the end of that period of more or less indiscriminate detentions was printed in "Reports from Tibet, August-October 1990," *TIN News Review*, November 10, 1990, which gave the names of seventy-seven political offenders then in the male section of Drapchi prison; a later list gave the names of twenty-three female political prisoners held there ("List of Tibetan Women Held in TAR Prison No.1," *TIN News Update*, February 21, 1992). Both *TIN News Update* and *TIN News Review* are publications of the Tibet Information Network.

whole of 1994.³ Following a series of pro-independence demonstrations by Buddhist monks and nuns in the first three months of 1995 (the period leading up to the Tibetan New Year), conditions of heightened security and surveillance were imposed on the capital, Lhasa. These were extended after the March anniversary, apparently as part of security preparations to prevent dissent during the run-up to the September 1995 celebrations marking the thirtieth anniversary of the granting of "regional autonomy" status to central and western Tibet.

Impact of the Third Forum's Policy Revisions

In July 1994, the Third Forum opened in Beijing. It was attended by China's top leaders, who gave high-level approval for a number of repressive policies in Tibet. These included:

• curtailing the spread of religious activity, including increased control and surveillance of monasteries. The Third Forum resulted in the upgrading of security work undertaken by administrative bodies, beyond their existing duties as informants and political educators. The Religious Affairs Bureau, for example, created a new body of "temple registration officials" who are seen as potential enforcement officers for new regulations involving monasteries.

• identifying Tibetan cadres and officials suspected of harboring nationalist sympathies, implying an eventual purge of Tibetan leaders. The formal recognition that the local Tibetan leadership is politically unreliable signaled a steady move away from the 1980s policy of making concessions to Tibetan cultural and economic concerns in return for political loyalty. The Third Forum called for an increase in the transfer of Chinese cadres and former soldiers to the TAR, and a China-wide propaganda campaign began in November 1994 to promote such transfer.

• launching an unusually aggressive campaign against the Dalai Lama, Tibet's exiled leader and main religious figure. The campaign included prohibitions on the possession of Dalai Lama photographs or other religious symbols by government employees. These orders appear to have been worded in a deliberately

---

³ Throughout the report the term "arrest" is used in the same sense as detention, to describe the taking of a person into custody by the police or other security force. In Chinese official documents the term "arrest" is only used to describe the formal laying of charges against a detainee, a procedure which may take place months after detention, if at all.

ambiguous way in order to increase their intimidatory effect while at the same time allowing the leadership to distance themselves from any negative response. The campaign reached a new peak in November 1995 with the announcement that the Dalai Lama's influence was to be eradicated not only from politics but also from religion, suggesting a plan to restructure Buddhist belief. In March 1996 a statement was published in the Chinese press questioning whether he is a reincarnated lama.

•   full endorsement of the policy of high-speed economic growth in the TAR. This policy, first implemented in this form in 1992, was framed in ideological terms that indicated an end to positive involvement for Tibetans in the economy. It is generally understood to have led to an increased influx of Chinese entrepreneurs and migrant workers and has become a source of discontent and unrest in the Tibetan community.

•   an initiative to increase the ideological content of school education and define socialist thinking as the objective of all education. The initiative was part of a "patriotic education" campaign launched in Tibet in September 1994 to attack support among Tibetan youths for the independence movement. The campaign was parallel to a similar drive being carried out in China.

Dispute over the Panchen Lama

       In May 1995 the Dalai Lama announced that a six-year-old boy living in northern Tibet was the reincarnation of the tenth Panchen Lama, who at his death in January 1989 was the most significant of the Tibetan leaders to have remained in Tibet after the Dalai Lama's flight to India in 1959. The reaction of the Chinese authorities to this announcement led to the most serious political dispute with the Dalai Lama in two decades and showed the impact of the Third Forum policies on decision-making on Tibetan issues. The reaction included:

•   taking direct control of the selection of religious leaders and initiating an artificial schism within Tibetan Buddhism. This was done by forbidding Tibetans from recognizing the child identified by the Tibetan search team and the Dalai Lama. The unusual intensity of Chinese intervention in this case is evident from the fact that the selection process for the Panchen Lama was appropriated directly by the Communist Party rather than by an organ of the Chinese government.

• dismissing the leaders of the main monastery involved in the dispute and replacing them with government appointees, despite a stated commitment to the principle of elected management in monasteries.

• detaining two leading lamas and approximately sixty monks and lay people accused of opposing China's takeover of the Panchen Lama selection procedure.

• setting up denunciation campaigns against the Dalai Lama and against the abbot in charge of the search team and putting pressure on Tibetan leaders and officials to join in the process of public denunciation.

• exploiting the two children involved for ideological purposes. The child identified by the Dalai Lama and his family have been in some form of custody since May 1995, and in November both the child and his parents were publicly vilified by the Chinese government through the official media. The child appointed by the government has been required to appear in public and to make political statements supporting the state, despite the right to freedom from exploitation to which children are entitled in international law.[4]

A Note on Methodology
The study is based on about 1,000 statements and submissions received by the Tibet Information Network (TIN) from Tibetans over the last five years which give information about the imprisonment of dissidents, mostly gathered from detailed interviews with escapees and former prisoners. The material has been organized into a database in which each submission has been checked and cross-checked against other sources. In addition, where available, official Chinese sources have been used, most of them not publicly available. The main work for this study was carried out over a two-year period by a TIN team consisting of an interviewer, a translator, a database collator, and two analysts, all with specialist knowledge of the area. Further cross-checking and editing took place at Human Rights Watch.

---

[4] China ratified the International Convention on the Rights of the Child in 1992.

II. THE BACKGROUND TO SUPPRESSION IN TIBET, 1993-1995

In 1993 protest in Tibet entered a new phase, leading to a minor crisis for the Chinese authorities, who over the previous four years had only had to cope with small demonstrations involving less than a dozen monks or nuns, almost always calling for independence. On May 24, 1993 the Tibetan capital of Lhasa saw the first large-scale popular demonstration on the streets since martial law was imposed in 1989.

The protest, which involved at least 1,000 people, was significant not only for its size, but because it was composed of lay people rather than monks. In addition, it raised issues which had not previously sparked demonstrations: food prices, medical fees and school charges. Initially this seems to have left the police uncertain as to how to respond. Unlike pro-independence protests, which are broken up as soon as they begin, the food prices demonstration of May 1993 was allowed to continue for about six hours because the demonstrators' slogans were confined to non-political issues. When, late in the afternoon, the protestors finally began to shout calls for independence, the security forces immediately intervened, using tear gas to break up the crowds and inflicting severe injuries in a number of cases.[5]

Afterwards a series of party meetings was convened to decide on the appropriate ideological response. The meetings continued for two days before a decision was reached which declared that the food price complaints had been partly genuine and partly manipulated by the pro-independence movement.[6] As the mayor of Lhasa put it three months later:

> Some people could not understand why the prices had gone up and felt the situation difficult to cope with. They had certain complaints about the price increase. Then the splittists seized that opportunity to stir up troubles from behind the scenes. As a result, some masses joined the demonstration on May 24 ... The great majority of participants did not have any political purpose.

---

[5] See "Accounts of Lhasa Demonstration, May 1993," in "Reports from Tibet, October 1992-1993," *TIN News Review*, October 1993.

[6] See TIN Document No. mk27my-e.

They participated in the demonstration only because they could not follow the change from a long-term planned economy to a spiritual civilization market economy. ... But ... there were splittists lurking in the procession. [7]

A number of arrests followed, but it was only a year later that the implications of this decision were to become clear.

The year 1993 was noteworthy not only for large economic protests in the capital but for the emergence of political protests in rural areas. A series of such protests took place in the rural areas of Nyemo, Meldro Gyama, Phenpo, and Chideshol, all within about 150 kilometers of Lhasa, destroying any assumptions that the authorities might have had about the political quiescence of Tibetan farming communities.[8] The unrest at Kyimshi, in the Chideshol valley south of the capital, was ended only when a force of reportedly 1,700 soldiers surrounded the village and carried out house-to-house searches.[9]

In June and July 1993 a number of pastoral communities in the area of Sog county and other parts of Nagchu prefecture, some 350 kilometers to the north of Lhasa, resorted to direct action in evicting recent Chinese settlers, forming teams to carry out their own "arrests" of illegal hunters and poachers and ransacking Chinese shops.[10] In the same months, hundreds of kilometers east of Lhasa, there

---

[7] Lobsang Dondrup, *Wen Wei Po*, August 18, 1993; Summary of World Broadcasts (SWB), August 20, 1993.

[8] See, for example, "Rural Protests in Meldrogungkar, Tibet," *TIN News Update*, July 11, 1993, which describes a series of pro-independence village demonstrations in Taktse and Meldro Gyama in February, and in villages near Rinchenling in April. Details of unrest in Lhundrup Nemo and Nyemo appear in "Tibet Protests Spread to Peasants, Students, Workers," *TIN News Update*, July 31, 1993.

[9] "Troops Take Over Tibetan Village: Villagers Appeal to UN," *TIN News Update*, August 11, 1993.

[10] "1993 Protests in Northern Tibet Confirmed," *TIN News Update*, November 30, 1994, citing an article printed in *Tibet Daily* on November 8, 1994. Sixty Tibetans are said by unofficial sources to have been arrested, including eleven local officials, after troops, probably from the People's Armed Police, surrounded the villages involved in the protests.

was a wave of protests among Tibetans in southern Qinghai province, apparently in response to the visit of China's President Jiang Zemin to the area.[11]

In November 1993, in the first political trial in Tibet acknowledged by the Chinese media for nearly three years, a monk was given a four-year sentence for putting up a leaflet containing "reactionary slogans" on the door of a government office in Chamdo Pomda, about 700 kilometers east of Lhasa.[12] His sentence was relatively light compared to those of prisoners arrested later, but the announcement of the decision suggested an increasing confidence by the Chinese authorities about their right to take punitive actions against Tibet dissidents. The Chinese had since May been under relatively strong pressure from diplomats of the European Union and from human rights organizations, which had made strong representations about two Tibetans arrested that month on the eve of a high-level visit to Lhasa by a delegation of European ambassadors. Eight months later, the two men were released more or less unharmed, an apparent rare concession to outside pressure.[13]

---

[11] "Wave of Arrests in Eastern Tibet," *TIN News Update*, October 6, 1993. Early reports suggested that up to sixty arrests were made, of whom the names of twelve are known, in connection with dissident leaflets distributed mainly in the Tsholho (Chinese: Hainan) area of Qinghai shortly before Jiang's inspection tour of the province from July 16 to 21. Jiang's visit to the area, like the protests, was timed to coincide with the celebration of the fortieth anniversary of the declaration that certain prefectures in Qinghai were autonomous. The detainees, unlike most groups of protestors in central Tibet, included well-known intellectuals, teachers and officials.

[12] This report, the first official acknowledgment of a trial or arrest since March 1991, concerned a monk named Jampa (called Gyaga by the Chinese press) who was found guilty of "counterrevolutionary propaganda and incitement" at a trial held "recently" by the Intermediate People's Court of Chamdo Prefecture, according to an announcement by the Tibet People's Broadcasting Service on November 21. A translation of the statement was published by the BBC Monitoring Service's Summary of World Broadcasts on November 23, 1994. Jampa was accused of putting leaflets up "on the house number plate of the township's family planning service station" in Pomda. "The trial of this specific case served as an example in educating the masses," said the radio broadcast. See "Pomda Man Gets Four Years for Writing Slogans," *TIN News Update*, November 24, 1993.

[13] See "Chinese Release Gendun Rinchen," *TIN News Update*, January 13, 1994. The two men were Gendun Rinchen, a tour guide, and Lobsang Yonten, a former monk, who had been preparing a letter about Tibetan human rights for the delegation when they were detained on May 11 and 13, 1993, about forty-eight hours before the European Community delegation arrived.

But in fact the concession, if it was one, was token. By the end of 1993 the Chinese authorities had reason to feel more confident: from April to June (1993) they had scored their most notable success in six years of fighting the independence movement by identifying and arresting up to fifty members of the Tibetan underground in Lhasa. Since 1987 there had been approximately 3,500 political arrests, but most of these had been of people caught taking part in street protests; many of the organizers and planners within the independence movement had remained at liberty, and were thus able to continue to organize protests and in some cases to distribute news to the outside world. By mid-1993 the security forces in Tibet had sufficiently improved their information-gathering to carry out preemptive house arrests instead of reacting to street protests.

This wave of arrests reflected an increase in investment and resources for the security forces, helped by mistakes made both by Tibetan activists and by visiting western journalists. The 1993 arrests are believed to have destroyed many of the underground groups in Lhasa and fragmented their lines of communication with the outside world. Indeed, it was two years before news of most of the 1993 arrests became known outside Tibet. (The research for this report revealed the names of 289 political prisoners detained in 1993, 150 more than had been previously recorded for that year.)

The extent of the achievement by the security forces in Tibet seems to have been communicated to Beijing, where, in October 1993, a Chinese deputy foreign minister felt confident enough of his government's control over information flow to tell the European Union that Damchoe Pemo, a women activist who had suffered a miscarriage in custody after her arrest in May 1993, had been freed from prison. Two years later it was discovered that she was still in custody five months after the Foreign Ministry statement.[14]

---

[14] Damchoe Pemo, also called Dawa Choezom, was arrested on May 20, 1993 on suspicion of involvement in an underground pro-independence organization (see "Pregnant Mother Loses Child in Detention - Update," Tibet Information Network, *TIN News Update*, August 4, 1994). On October 29, 1993, Chinese Vice-Foreign Minister Jiang Enzhu, since appointed Chinese ambassador to the United Kingdom, told the European Community that she had been released (See "Gendun Rinchen - 110 Sign Petition to UN from Tibet,"*TIN News Update*, December 10, 1993). There are first-hand reports of her being in Seitru prison in Lhasa in December 1993, and unconfirmed reports that she was still there in March 1994. There has been no news of her since then. A similar incident took place in October 1994 when the EU was informed by the Chinese authorities that a fifteen-year-old nun, Gyaltsen Pelsang (lay name: Nyima or Migmar), had been released from prison. In fact she remained in Gutsa detention center until February 9, 1995 (see "Tibetan Girl Held for 1 Year After Release Announced," *TIN News Update*, April 9, 1995).

The authorities followed their success in arresting underground activist leaders by imposing stricter security measures on the streets and in prisons. Twelve nuns accused of taking part in a brief demonstration in June were given sentences of up to seven years, and re-education teams were moved into their nunneries.[15] In October 1993 fourteen women prisoners had their sentences doubled or tripled after they were found making a tape recording of pro-independence songs in their cells.[16] At the same time, longer prison sentences were being handed out by courts and police stations around Tibet, so that by the end of 1992 the average sentence for dissidents was just under six years, nearly twice the average in the previous year.[17]

In May 1994 the security forces responded to economic protests in a new way, a consequence of Party decisions taken after the food prices demonstration of May 1993. This coincided with the effective end of international pressure on China, symbolized by President Clinton's decision in May 1994 to unconditionally renew Most Favored Nation trading status for China. On May 27, the same day that President Clinton's decision was announced, taxes on Tibetan street traders and shopkeepers were unexpectedly increased. Later that day a demonstration outside Lhasa's municipal government compound by local traders in protest at the new taxes was broken up by members of the paramilitary People's Armed Police. Although the protest remained both small and nonviolent, the police arrested and assaulted a number of the participants.

In ideological terms this marked a notable shift for the Chinese authorities, who up until that point, in line with conventional Maoist doctrine, had based all such decisions on a clear distinction between so-called antagonistic and non-antagonistic contradictions.[18] Repressive policies had been applied only to the first category, involving alleged offenses "against the people," meaning acts which threaten such fundamentals of state power as the integrity of the state and the supremacy of the Communist Party. Complaints about living standards, income and government bureaucracy were classed as non-antagonistic contradictions, or

---

[15] "Nuns Sentenced to 7 Years for June 'Incident,'" *TIN News Update*, January 10, 1994.

[16] "Nun's Sentence Increased to 17 Years for Singing Songs," *TIN News Update*, February 20, 1994.

[17] See section on "Sentences" in Part 2.

[18] See Mao Zedong, *On Contradictions Among the People*, Beijing, January 1957.

offenses "within the people," to be resolved by discussion and education. They thus were rarely countered by the use of force or arrest by the security forces.

The response to the tax protest of May 27, 1994 was the first time in recent years that the security forces in Tibet had treated a purely economic complaint as an antagonistic contradiction — that is, as a fundamental protest against Party rule. It was thus the first time that they had responded to such an incident in the same way as with political protests, by arresting and beating the participants.[19] The decision to treat the tax protest as political rather than economic dissent was therefore of considerable importance in ideological terms and must have been made by Party leaders in Lhasa acting on instructions from Beijing. In official statements a new phrase—"hot topics"—was coined to describe concerns such as price rises and tax increases which were now susceptible to manipulation by dissidents and thus to being interpreted as antagonistic contradictions:

> Under the new situation, the Dalai Lama clique and international hostile forces are strengthening their collusion, constantly readjusting their tactics and changing methods in their intensified activities to split the motherland. They continue to send agents and spies into China to expand their underground reactionary organizations and to intensify political, ideological and religious infiltration. They ... are using every means to compete with us in winning over the next generation. Exploiting "hot" topics in society, they incite the masses, sow dissension among various nationalities and create incidents in an attempt to undermine political stability and unity and to interfere with reform, opening to the outside world and economic construction.[20]

---

[19] Before this date there had been several demonstrations that were allowed to take place without any police interference: a student protest calling for human rights on December 30, 1988; student protests supporting the pro-democracy movement in May 1989; protests against kerosene ration price increases in 1990 and against fertilizer dumping in 1991; and the early part of the food price demonstrations on May 24, 1993.

[20] "The 1994 Work Report of the Government of the Tibetan Autonomous Region," *Tibet Daily*, SWB, July 1, 1994. The Work Report was delivered by Gyaltsen Norbu, chairman of the Tibet Autonomous Regional People's Government, at the second session of the sixth Tibet Autonomous Regional People's Congress on May 15.

This represented a new and important expansion of the concept of unacceptable dissent. The May 1994 incident was the first indication that this ideological ruling did indeed mean that previously tolerated economic protests would be met by force, as if they were covert political attacks.

III. EASING OF INTERNATIONAL PRESSURE AND NEW CHINESE ASSERTIVENESS

The signs of a gradual expansion of security concerns in Tibet in 1993 and early 1994 were not isolated phenomena. Reports of rural unrest based on economic concerns and of aggressive responses by the security forces were also emerging at this time from what the Chinese government refers to as "inland China." In the township of Renshou in rural Sichuan, up to 10,000 people rioted for several days in June 1993 when they were charged taxes toward road construction; politicians accepted that the taxes had been unreasonable but still imprisoned the peasants' leader, Xiang Wenqing, on the grounds that he had "stirred up trouble" by "manipulating" reports in the official press.[21] The growing gulf between urban and rural incomes, coupled with rising prices, increasing limitations on access to free education and medicine, rising unemployment, and growing public discontent with corruption among officials, were seen as threats to stability throughout China.[22] Although trade with the outside world was growing, its benefits were not distributed evenly, and at the same time as China's supreme ruler, Deng Xiaoping, was reaching the end of his political life, Taiwan was starting to become more assertive in its foreign policy. There were therefore a range of reasons for the Chinese leadership to become more conservative in its responses to unrest at this period; its moves to enhance internal security included new laws, on state security and public security, which are discussed in more detail below. But at the same time another phenomenon was taking place: western governments were beginning to step back from their post-Tiananmen policy of putting pressure on China to improve its human rights practices.

Between November 1993 and April 1994, three senior western leaders—German Chancellor Kohl, French Prime Minister Balladur, and U.S. Secretary of State Christopher—visited Beijing as they sought to resolve disagreements over the relationship between human rights and trade with China.

---

[21] See "Thousands of Peasants Riot in Sichuan," Reuters, Beijing, June 12, 1993, and "China is Sowing Discontent with 'Taxes' on Peasants," Sheryl WuDunn, *New York Times*, May 19, 1993.

[22] Peasant threats to "rise up" in protest at village level corruption in Anhui were documented in the article,"China's Villagers Vent Hatred at Leaders They Say Are Corrupt; Party Braces for Trouble As Peasant Protests Mount," Lena H. Sun, *Washington Post*, April 28, 1994.

But by late March, three months before the date by which President Clinton was obliged to come to a decision on MFN, it was already apparent that the Chinese authorities had decided not to yield to western pressure. Their decision was symbolized by the rearrest of China's leading dissident, Wei Jingsheng, during Prime Minister Balladur's visit and days before the arrival in Beijing of Secretary of State Christopher.

That arrest brought no effective response from the international community, and on May 26 President Clinton renewed MFN despite Beijing's failure to meet the criteria he had announced the previous year. Renewal did not bring more openness from the Chinese side: it was six months before the Chinese authorities even acknowledged that they were holding Wei Jingsheng, and in December 1995, he was sentenced to fourteen years in prison, not counting time in detention, for conspiring to overthrow the regime.

Renewed Publishing of Information on Arrests

Immediately after the American decision to end the linkage between MFN and human rights, the Chinese authorities did make one change in their practice toward dissidents by ending a policy of silence about arrests. Just over a month after the U.S. decision, Tibetan TV, an official Chinese broadcasting service, announced that a provincial tribunal at Chamdo in eastern Tibet had handed down sentences of twelve and fifteen years in prison to a group of monks convicted of "counterrevolutionary crimes" such as putting up posters calling for Tibetan independence.[23]

The announcement was noteworthy not just for the severity of the sentences but also because it represented a renewed frankness by the Chinese authorities about political trials in Tibet. Before March 1991 the official news media in Tibet had carried frequent reports of trials and arrests of pro-independence activists, always described as counterrevolutionaries; such reports were a major source of information for the international community. After March 1991 the Chinese media began a policy of silence about trials and arrests in Tibet, perhaps because of the international criticism China had received as a result of the reporting.[24]

---

[23] Statement in Chinese broadcast on Tibet TV, Lhasa, July 26, 1994; SWB, July 29, 1994.

[24] In the two and a half years that the Chinese press refrained from publishing news of political arrests in Tibet, at least 317 Tibetans dissidents are believed to have been arrested, according to TIN records.

The official silence had been first broken by the report in November 1993 of the four-year sentence imposed on Jampa, the Chamdo monk who had written leaflets with "reactionary slogans," described above. At about the same time, the Chinese authorities began to release more information about imprisonments, although not necessarily for public distribution. Less than a month after the MFN decision, Chinese diplomats finally handed to U.S. State Department officials its response to a list of 108 Tibetan political prisoners about whom the Clinton administration had first sought information in October 1993.[25]

Secretary of State Christopher had raised the question of the 108 prisoners with Chinese Foreign Minister Qian Qichen in Paris in January 1994 and again during his visit to Beijing in March of that year. He met with no success either time. His efforts had, in fact, been belittled by the Chinese authorities on several occasions. "When western personalities have given such name lists to us, we have tried to verify the contents and sources with them, but they themselves could not tell us where the information came from," said Shen Guofang, spokesman for China's Foreign Ministry, speaking "not without ridicule" of the "so-called list presented by Christopher," which one Chinese paper described as "fabricated."[26] Ragdi (spelled Raidi in Chinese), a deputy Party secretary in the TAR and the top Tibetan official in the Tibetan Communist Party, had also ridiculed the list. "I don't know where they get the name list from," he told a news conference in Beijing that March. He added that fewer than twenty of the names presented by Christopher were still in custody.[27] This claim was to prove wrong.

The information given in the Chinese response consisted of no more than four words in each case—"not yet criminally sentenced" was the most common denominator—but it showed that Chinese authorities had known all along about many, if not most, of the prisoners. It provided confirmation for the first time that fifty-six Tibetans were indeed in custody, as had been alleged by unofficial Tibetan sources, and it implicitly accepted that their offenses involved political activities

---

[25] The original list submitted by the U.S. in October 1993 is said to have consisted of 108 names, but the Chinese reply referred to a list of 107 names, and in fact only gave information about 106. The discrepancies are presumably due to clerical errors. See "Chinese Confirm 56 Arrests," *TIN News Update*, August 30, 1994.

[26] *Ta Kung Pao* (a pro-Chinese paper published in Hong Kong); SWB, April 19, 1994.

[27] "Raidi Says Fewer Than 20 on U.S. List," Press Trust of India, SWB; March 19, 1994.

of some sort. More significantly, the entire list of 108 names presented by the Americans consisted of Tibetans detained in 1993, so the Chinese response provided important evidence that a major political crackdown had taken place in that year, as maintained by monitoring organizations.

A similar instance of the government providing evidence of a crackdown took place in June 1995, when the Chinese authorities in Tibet published for the first time the number of counterrevolutionaries arrested in a given year. The procurator announced that 164 people had been formally charged with involvement in forty-four counterrevolutionary cases in 1994.[28] It marked at least a temporary end to the Chinese policy of silence over political arrests in Tibet, but what it indicated seems to have been Beijing's growing confidence rather than any spirit of concessions in international human rights concerns.

China's new confidence toward the outside world also took on an aggressive tone. In early 1994 statements about Tibet policy began, for the first time since 1979 to our knowledge, to blame western countries for the unrest in Tibet and in other areas of China inhabited by non-Chinese nationalities. There had been references in the past to some sort of international conspiracy against China, but the term "foreign hostile forces" had been used, a phrase which could have referred as much to the exile Tibetans as to foreign powers. In December 1993 a Party statement about the threat of secession in Inner Mongolia had warned against "the westernization and polarization of international hostile elements" but was still reluctant to identify the countries involved.[29] Two months later, the head of propaganda in Tibet made a statement referring confidently to the ending of international sanctions after the 1989 Tiananmen crackdown and specifically stating that western countries were supporting separatists: "Although China has

---

[28] This is the first time that the Chinese authorities have given an annual total of arrests connected with the "splittist" movement. Foreign observers had only managed to document 113 cases of political arrest during 1994, few of which involved the formalities of charge and trial, unlike the cases referred to here. "Work Report of the TAR Peoples' Procuratorate, delivered at the Sixth TAR Peoples' Congress," *Tibet Daily*; SWB, July 11, 1995.

[29] "We should particularly guard against...advocating the westernisation and polarisation of international hostile elements, [and should] prevent domestic and foreign hostile forces from using nationalities and religious issues to engage in sabotage... and never tolerate or abet them." Wang Qun, Inner Mongolia Party Secretary, in a report to the Regional Party Committee on December 22, 1993, (published in the *Inner Mongolia Daily*, December 31, 1993; SWB, February 10, 1994).

broken the western economic blockade and sanctions, western countries have stepped up activities to westernize and divide us."[30]

But it was only with the publication of the Third Forum's decisions that it became routine for the Chinese government to declare that western governments—and specifically the United States—were the source of the pro-independence movement in Tibet: "Since the ending of the cold war, the West, led by America, is continuously bringing forth the 'Tibet issue' as their best weapon to 'Westernize China' and to 'split' China," said the Third Forum in its statement on the strategic context of its decisions.[31] As the full drift of the Third Forum decisions became clearer over the following months, the anti-western rhetoric became stronger, and the western "forces" were said to be using the Dalai Lama as their agent to carry out acts of sabotage.[32] By the end of 1994, while the intensity

---

[30] Chen Hanchang, standing committee member of the Regional Party Committee and director of the Propaganda Department, on an inspection tour of Nagchu on February 7 and 8, 1994, according to a broadcast by Tibet TV on February 9. The statement was published by SWB on February 11, 1994 under the title "Tibet Propaganda Chief Warns Against 'Westernization' Attempts by West." He had expressed similar views in a speech reproduced in the *Tibet Daily* (Chinese language edition), November 12, 1993 (SWB, December 8, 1993), under the title "Further Deepen the Study of the Theory of Building Socialism with Chinese Characteristics."

[31] The public parts of the decisions of the Third Forum were issued in a document known as *A Golden Bridge into the New Era* (*Dus rabs gsar par skyod-pa'i gser zam*) by the Propaganda Committee of the TAR Communist Party (Tibetan People's Publishing House, October 1, 1994). The book is divided into fourteen sections, of which Section 12 deals with nationality and religious policies and Section 13 with autonomy. The book consists of ninety-six pages plus a cover, a title page and two colophons in Chinese and Tibetan respectively. Sections 12 and 13 were reprinted in the Tibetan language edition of the *Tibet Daily*, with small variations, on November 25, 1994. The remark about western involvement appeared on p.3 of the introductory section entitled "Understanding the Importance of Work in Tibet from a High Standard All-round Strategy Point of View."

[32] See, for example, the front-page article in *Tibet Daily* (Tibetan language edition), March 7, 1995, and *Tibet Daily* (Chinese language edition), March 10, 1995: "Western countries, headed by the United States, started to carry out a general strategy of initiating a peaceful evolution in socialist countries and began to intensify their offensives against China ... the Tibet issue became the main justification for exercising pressure and the Dalai clique's usefulness soared." The article shows some pride in the collapse of the U.S. attempts to link trade with human rights: "The West dares not go to the extreme of doing what it wants in exploiting the Dalai clique because of China's political stability,

of these criticisms had greatly increased, the western forces were no longer being identified as governments, perhaps for diplomatic reasons:

> Is the Dalai a religious leader or a tool employed against China by hostile forces in the West? We will get a clearer answer to that from an examination of the Dalai's ties to western nations. ... Since the mid-eighties, hostile forces in the West have constantly employed "national self-determination" to promote reactionary propaganda for "self-determination in Tibet ... The Dalai clique is ... playing a sabotage role which Western hostile forces have failed to play. ... To sum up, the Dalai ... has bartered away his honor for Western hostile forces' patronage. What can the Dalai do without the support of hostile Western forces?[33]

Another sign of growing Chinese confidence toward external criticism of its human rights performance came in a statement made in January 1995 by an unnamed Chinese official about negotiations with the International Committee of the Red Cross (ICRC) over visits to political prisoners. Discussions between China and the ICRC on access to Chinese prisoners had taken place sporadically since 1991. In November 1993 Foreign Minister Qian Qichen had indicated on his way to the Asia-Pacific Economic Cooperation (APEC) summit in Seattle that the Chinese government would give "positive consideration" to an ICRC request to visit prisons. That statement appears in retrospect to have been one of the government's last concessions toward American demands concerning human rights: progress toward ICRC access to Chinese prisons had been one of the criteria the U.S. president was to use in making a decision about MFN. Two important rounds of discussions took place between China and the ICRC after the APEC meeting, in January and April 1994, and there were additional exchanges until March 1995

---

economic development, and combined national strength, which is quickly strengthening, as well as restraint caused by the West's overall strategy toward China. For example, not one single country has openly recognized Tibetan independence or the government in exile; and recently the United States could not help separating China's human rights from its most-favoured-nation trading status. All this shows that the West has problems which are beyond its ability to solve and that its support for and exploitation of the Dalai Lama are restricted."

[33] Li Bing,"Dalai is a tool of hostile forces in the West," *Tibet Daily* (Chinese language edition), December 11, 1995, p. 2; SWB, January 3, 1996.

when they abruptly stopped. By then, however, the need to respond to U.S. pressure in order to secure MFN status was no longer relevant, and the unnamed official informed the western press that China would not be reaching any agreement with the ICRC.[34]

---

[34] Jeffrey Parker, "China Says No to Free Red Cross Prison Visits," Reuters, January 27, 1995.

IV. THE THIRD FORUM

The Third National Forum on Work in Tibet was held in Beijing from July 20 to 23, 1994.[35] It was attended by China's most senior leaders and was proclaimed the most important meeting of its kind since 1984, when the Chinese reformer Hu Yaobang had convened a policy meeting known as the Second Forum on Work in Tibet. The main purpose of the Third Forum was to issue a mandate from the central authorities for the implementation of policies of fast-track economic growth which had effectively been pursued in the TAR since June 1992.

These policies were described by the authorities as development measures for the uplifting of a backward province and were initially presented as overtures toward international investment in Tibet. But the Chinese authorities have made conspicuously little effort to attract foreign capital, clearly preferring overseas or inland Chinese investment. Accordingly, these development initiatives have been somewhat differently perceived by Tibetans, for many of whom such policies represent a forced process of attempting to assimilate the resource-rich hinterland into the booming mainland economy. Signs that the policies were not merely driven by economic priorities emerged in the newspaper attacks on Tibetan members of the Communist Party who argued that economic development in Tibet should be moderated in line with the region's "special characteristics," not least of which was the characteristic that its population consisted mainly of Tibetans.[36]

---

[35] The First Forum was the title retrospectively applied to the convention in April 1980 which immediately preceded Hu Yaobang's watershed visit to Tibet on May 23 of that year, in which he announced the historic six-point reforms which brought to an end the commune system, removed the majority of Chinese cadres, announced a tax amnesty in the countryside and reestablished Tibetan rights to religious and cultural pursuits. See Wang Yao, "Hu Yaobang's Visit to Tibet, May 22-31: An Important Development in the Chinese Government's Tibet Policy," in Robert Barnett and S. Akiner, eds., *Resistance and Reform in Tibet* (Hursts/ University of Indiana Press, 1994).

[36] See "Crackdown on Party Moderates," *TIN News Update*, April 25, 1994. The moderates, who included Chinese cadres, were in a more powerful position before Chen's appointment in 1992. See, for example, Zhang Shuring and Guo Wutian, "On the Regional Characteristics of Party Construction in Tibet," *Tibet Daily* (Chinese Language edition), January 7, 1991. At one point the article states, "The special characteristics of the Tibetan region must be recognised and there must be special measures and flexible methods... " This type of argument was decisively attacked, and labelled as "leftist," in a series of press statements by Chen and other leaders in the period from April to June 1992.

These attacks, which in 1992 were led by the new party secretary of the TAR, Chen Kuiyuan, signaled an end to special concessions being made for Tibetan language and culture in the race to develop the Tibetan economy along Chinese lines. In May 1994 the attacks were resumed in more strident terms at the central level and published in the *People's Daily*, the main newspaper of the Communist Party:

> Is Tibet willing to accept the label of "being special" and stand at the rear of reform and opening up? [...] Backwardness is not terrifying. Being geographically closed is not terrifying. What is terrifying is rigid and conservative thinking and the psychology of idleness.[37]

The perception that the reforms were designed to incorporate Tibet within the structure of China's economic needs was confirmed when the decisions of the Third Forum were published, together with lengthy commentaries, in the official press in late 1994. The Third Forum had decided that:

> Tibet's reform must conform with the framework for ongoing reform of the entire nation in the process of establishing a socialist market economy; ... Tibet's economic structure must converge with that of the entire nation ... establishing an inseparable organic link between Tibet's economy and the national economy.[38]

In particular these reforms were seen by some Tibetans as seeking to encourage the movement of Chinese traders and workers into Tibet. When in 1984

---

[37] *Renmin Ribao (People's Daily)*, May 16, 1994. A month earlier Chen Kuiyuan had also relaunched his 1992 theory that opponents of the reforms were leftist: "A major obstacle to socialist economic construction and the implementation of profound reforms in Tibet is leftist ideas and outmoded ways of thinking. By leftist ideas we mean sticking to an economic mode that is outdated, [that] runs counter to the conditions in China and stands in the way of the development of productive forces. After living and working for many years under this mode, we have got used to it and find it quite hard to free ourselves from its influence. Emancipation of the mind requires hard work over a long period of time. This is particularly true of Tibet, which is economically backward and has a closed market and where contacts and exchanges with the outside world are few and far between." (Tibet Radio, April 18, 1994; SWB, April 20, 1994.)

[38] Ragdi, quoted in *Tibet Daily*, September 6, 1994.

the Second Forum had announced that forty-three major construction projects would be set up in Tibet with support from inland Chinese provinces, Tibetans had complained that these projects were a veiled device to import Chinese into central Tibet. In fact in some cases entire work units are said to have been transported to Tibet as part of the "Help Tibet Prosper" campaign, but the Chinese authorities argued strongly that the labor that came with those projects was skilled or technical personnel on temporary placements, as was indeed often the case. By April 1992 however, the pattern of government statements about Chinese migration into the TAR had changed and for the first time a policy emerged which appeared to encourage the movement of unskilled non-Tibetans into the area. The first signs of this change in policy were instructions to government offices to convert the ground floor areas of any roadside properties to small shops that could be rented out to retailers; in the following year 5,300 "individually run enterprises" were set up in Lhasa alone, an increase of 56 percent over 1992, and twenty-three new "markets" or shopping arcades were built in the Tibet region, bringing the total in the TAR to ninety-nine.[39] By the end of 1993 the number of individually-owned enterprises had shot up from 489 in 1980, when communes were disbanded, to 41,830[40] and the total amount of retail sales in the private sector had risen to 1.9 billion yuan, a rise of 13.1 percent over the previous year.[41]

None of the official accounts suggested at this stage that the new shops were being bought up by entrepreneurs from China, but foreign visitors to Lhasa described an increase in the non-Tibetan population, especially small shopkeepers and traders. The U.S. Department of State, in its February 1994 report on human rights conditions in China, reported a major increase in migrants in this period. "Tens of thousands of non-Tibetan entrepreneurs without residence permits have

---

[39]   *Tibet Daily*, February 4, 1994. In June and July 1993 alone, "over 500 individual industrial and commercial entrepreneurs" established new businesses in Lhasa. The boom also took place in other Tibetan towns. "Several bustling commercial streets were also found in such central cities and towns as Xigaze [Shigatse] and Zetang [Tsethang]", said the *People's Daily* on May 16, 1994.

[40]   *Tibet Daily*, January 31, 1994.

[41]   Tibet Radio, February 13, 1994. This was much higher than the general growth in the economy, which averaged 8.1 percent that year, and was very lucrative for the local government. The TAR authorities received 26 million yuan in revenue from individually run enterprises in 1993.

come to Lhasa, capital of Tibet, to engage in business," said the report, although it did not give any source for its figures.

By the time that the Third Forum opened in Beijing, a number of administrative steps had already been taken to ease the development of non-Tibetan businesses in central Tibet. These included the ending of intra-provincial border controls between the TAR and its neighboring provinces in December 1992, a gesture which was taken as implying that there would be no further restrictions on Chinese migration into the area. New regulations for obtaining trading licenses were implemented in November 1993 so that "anyone can apply for an operating license as long as he has an identity card and a letter of recommendation from relevant authorities," according to an official statement.[42] The *Tibet Daily* announced that, "Individually run enterprises have flourished in Tibet since the procedure for applying for a business permit was simplified, making it unnecessary to ask favors of friends,"[43] and Tibet Radio noted that as a result of the new registration policies "those from other parts of the country were allowed to engage in wholesale or retail trading of whatever commodities the state had decontrolled."

Up to the time of the Third Forum, however, officials felt it necessary to insist that the Chinese migrants in Tibet were technicians who were providing specialist skills unavailable among the indigenous community. The Third Forum, besides establishing sixty-two more construction projects which would introduce more labor from China into central Tibet, gave final political authorization to the highly contentious policy of encouraging non-Tibetan entrepreneurialism in the region:

> The focal point of the policy of opening the door wider in Tibet should be towards the inner part of the country. While depending on our region's own good aspects of policy and production resources, we should combine these with the good aspects of the inner part of the country, its intellectuals, technicians, management personnel and communications. Mutual economical support and exchange in every field should be broadened. We should encourage traders, investment, economic units and individuals to enter our region to run different sorts of enterprises. We should turn our good production resources into

---

[42] Tibet Radio, February 3, 1994.

[43] *Tibet Daily*, February 4, 1994.

economic [advantages] and join our region's economy with the nation's vast market. [44]

By the end of 1994 Chen and Ragdi no longer felt it necessary to deny that there was a policy of encouraging Chinese traders to move to Tibet and openly referred for the first time to the fact that these migrants were traders rather than technicians or administrators.[45] Behind this shift in presentation was an even more major change, from the point of view of Tibetans: it meant that the positive discrimination practices which had been at the basis of China's policy towards its non-Chinese nationalities had effectively come to an end. The restrictions on trading licenses and residence in Tibet had been designed at least in part to encourage local Tibetans to take those opportunities and to enter the commercial world on preferential terms. The Third Forum in effect ruled that such concessions should be discarded and that Tibetans should compete on the open market without assistance or encouragement from the state.

As is usual in the formulation of policy in Tibet, issues relating to security and the suppression of dissent were also high on the agenda, and some well-placed Tibetans have said privately that the real objectives of the Third Forum were not economic, as presented in the official publications on the conference, but political. These analysts argue that the main purpose of the Third Forum was to provide the highest level of political legitimation for the use of force and of other measures not previously sanctioned at such a level, in the suppression of the pro-independence movement in Tibet. They identify three principal areas in which the Third Forum demanded that new policies of repression be introduced immediately: stricter

---

[44] Speech given by Ragdi on September 5, 1994 at the Seventh Plenum of the Sixth Standing Committee Session of the TAR Communist Party and distributed internally as "Document No 5."

[45] "All localities ... should welcome the opening of various restaurants and stores by people from the hinterland. They should particularly encourage development projects which invite the participation of Tibetans. They should not be afraid that people from the hinterland are taking their money or jobs away. Under a socialist market economy, Tibet develops its economy and the Tibetan people learn the skills to earn money when a hinterlander makes money in Tibet." Chen Kuiyuan, in *Tibet Daily*, November 28, 1994; SWB, December 5, 1994. Ragdi, Chen's deputy, had made a statement in a much milder form on the same issue earlier in the year: "People in all sovereign countries often move from one region to another. Therefore what then is wrong of the Han to do the same?" *China's Tibet*, Vol.5, No.3, 1994.

control of religious institutions, an ideological campaign to remove the influence of the Dalai Lama, and increased monitoring of Tibetan Communist Party cadres.

Religion

The authorities had since the mid-1980s made attempts to limit the growth of religion in Tibet, but these policies had rarely been implemented, even after the outbreak of unrest at monasteries in Lhasa in 1987. The Third Forum represented the decision by China's most powerful leaders to authorize their representatives in Tibet to impose these limits at any cost, short of provoking further unrest. But in doing so they antagonized communities which had so far not taken part in protest, accelerated the tendency to ideological conflict, and increased the security role played by government officials.

The guidelines on religious policy, announced at the Third Forum and later published by the TAR Party in a publication called *A Golden Bridge Leading Into a New Era*, had expressed deep concern at the continued popularity of Tibetan Buddhism. For the first time since China's liberalization era began some fifteen years earlier, the Party publicly ordered a halt to any further spread of Buddhist institutions or of the monastic population in Tibet:

> There are too many places where monasteries have been opened without permission from the authorities, and having too much religious activity ... the waste of materials, manpower and money has been tremendous, ... sometimes leading to interference in administration, law, education, marriages, birth control, productivity and daily life.[46]

The argument of the documents, however, is not a genuine attempt to criticize monks for wasting social resources. What really concerns the authorities is the perceived relationship between the clergy and the continuing activism of the pro-independence movement:

> A number of religious institutions have been used at times by a few people who harbor sinister motives to plot against us and have become counterrevolutionary bases ... The influence of our enemies in foreign countries, especially the "Dalai clique," was slipping into the monasteries of our region more than ever. They

---

[46] *A Golden Bridge Leading to a New Era*, p. 37.

assume that to get hold of a monastery is the equivalent of [getting hold of] a district of the Communist Party.[47]

The logic of this argument is not as obvious as it might appear. Between the implementation of a post-Tiananmen security policy called the Comprehensive Management scheme (also known as "active" policing) in 1990 and the convening of the Third Forum four and a half years later, there had been about 100 confirmed reports of demonstrations calling for independence in Tibet as well as over twenty-five others which are not confirmed.[48] Almost all of these were, as the language of *A Golden Bridge...* suggests, initiated and carried out by members of the Tibetan clergy. But few if any of these protests in Lhasa lasted more than a few minutes, and none is known to have involved more than a dozen or fifteen people. In other words, the protests carried out by religious figures were frequent but insignificant in terms of size: the large-scale incidents of this period were entirely lay affairs. In fact, more than five years had passed since a protest initiated by monks and nuns had led to even a medium-sized nationalist protest. And yet the Third Forum's identification of Tibetan monasteries with fomenting opposition to the state was more aggressive than ever before.

To explain this insistence on the religious element of Tibetan protest, we have to look to the countryside. For while large-scale demonstrations in the towns were clearly lay affairs, there were important rural incidents during the 1990-1994 period which showed the potential impact of monastic dissent. Much less is known about rural unrest because of the difficulty of obtaining information from such areas and because rapid containment of any outbreak of rural unrest is much easier to effect than in a town; incidents are less likely to spread beyond a small cluster of villages before the area can be sealed off. But it is clear that there were rural

---

[47] *A Golden Bridge...*, Section 12.

[48] The "Comprehensive Management of Public Security" (*shehui zhi'an zonghe zhili*) was a restructuring of security operations in Tibet which replaced the more aggressive methods, associated with the People's Armed Police, of "passive" policing, which essentially meant carrying out more or less random arrests and waiting for a protest to begin and then beating or shooting the participants. "Active" policing introduced in 1990 ended the practice of random arrest and imposed on all areas of the administration a responsibility to take part in security operations, mainly by maintaining vigilance and detecting political (or criminal) offenders. See "Comprehensive Security in Tibet," in "Reports from Tibet: March-August 1991," *TIN News Review*, August 30, 1991, and "Security Policy in the TAR, 1992-94: Analysis of a Speech," *TIN Background Briefing Paper No.24*, March 1995. See also below, Section VII.

incidents which constituted serious threats to the administration. One of these was the eruption of unrest in the *xiang* or group of villages called Kyimshi, in the upper Chideshol valley in southern Tibet in late May 1993. The Kyimshi protests appear to have involved the entire community, including the local monastery of Sungrabling. The villages were soon sealed off by the military and there were at least thirty-five arrests from Kyimshi alone; dissent also flared in the neighboring monastery of Dunphu Choekhor, as well as at least one nearby nunnery, Choebup.[49] Other rural flashpoints in April and June 1993—notably Rinchenling in Meldrogongkar and Nemo in Phenpo Lhundrup—were triggered by lay people and had little, if any, religious involvement.

But the incident at Kyimshi may well have been seen by the authorities as a warning of the risks of allowing nationalist discontent to spread to rural communities where they could become focused on the monasteries and nunneries. There is a further reason why the authorities may have decided to concentrate on quelling religious activism: there seems to have been more unrest in rural monasteries and nunneries in 1993 and 1994 than was reported to external observers. This is implicit in the emergence from late 1993 onwards of frequent statements by the Chinese authorities accusing the independence movement of spreading its ideas to the countryside, and, as we shall see, the events of 1995 to a great extent were to confirm their fears.

Thus the thrust of the religious policy guidelines issued by the Third Forum was to give approval at the highest level for stricter control over the monastic institutions. The term used in the publicly available texts is "strengthening the administration of temples," a phrase which in effect means that the lay authorities were ordered to increase the extent of official intervention in the running of religious institutions. This was to be achieved principally through the control of "Democratic Management Committees," supposedly elected organs installed within each monastery to replace the traditional authority of abbots and lamas. In 1962, as part of the Chinese response to the Tibetan uprising of 1959, the committees had been created and granted responsibility by the state authorities over admission, rules, curriculum and discipline within the monasteries and nunneries. The Third Forum reverted to traditional Leninist practice in insisting on the reassertion of rigorous control over the selection of candidates for the committees:

---

[49] See "Troops take over Tibet Village: Villagers Appeal to UN," *TIN News Update*, August 11, 1993. Of the thirty-five arrests during the operation, twenty-seven involved monks and nuns: seven monks from Sungrabling monastery, eighteen from Dunphu Choekhor monastery, and two nuns from Choebup.

We must enhance the administration of the monasteries,
especially of those troublesome ones ... We must choose well the
members of the Democratic Management Committees so that it
is patriotic devotees ... who have authority over the
monasteries.[50]

The device is purely political in its rationale, unlike other control
mechanisms, most of which have at least some pragmatic justification: limiting the
number of monks, for example, makes economic sense and has even been
welcomed by some lamas, many of whom no longer have the resources needed to
sustain large communities. Control over the selection of committee members,
however, is not the only political aspect of the religious program ordered by the
Third Forum. It also ordered officials to continue the process of directly reshaping
the thinking of all monks and nuns through political education, and, in what is a
new strain of political rhetoric, began to speak about reforming the religion itself
to meet the demands of socialism:

We must enhance the knowledge of the monks and nuns about
patriotism and law. Tibetan Buddhism must self-reform ... they
must adapt themselves to suit the development and stabilization
of Tibet ... Religious tenets and practices which do not comply
with a socialist society should be changed.[51]

The practical implications of these instructions were not immediately clear
from the often ambiguous statements revealed by the official media but emerged
gradually in the months that followed the meeting in Beijing. Essentially, the Third
Forum called for four practical steps to be taken in each religious institution:

---

[50] *A Golden Bridge...*, p.39. The functioning of Democratic Management
Committees is described in some detail in the award citation given to Tashilhunpo
monastery in October 1994 to mark its achievement in patriotism. The document,
"Tashilhunpo's Record of Patriotism," is reprinted as "Commendatory Document No.1: The
Resplendent Model of Safe-guarding the Unification of the Motherland by Displaying the
Spirit of Patriotism" in "Documents and Statements from Tibet, 1995," *TIN Background
Briefing Paper No.26*, December 1995.

[51] *A Golden Bridge...*, p.81.

•vetting the political position of each member of each Democratic Management Committee and appointing only pro-Chinese monks to those committees.

•enforcing a ban on the construction of any religious buildings except with official permission.

•enforcing limits set some years earlier on the numbers of monks or nuns allowed in each institution.

•obliging each monk and nun to give declarations of their absolute support for the leadership of the Communist Party and the integrity of the motherland.

As we shall see later, the Third Forum also made a fifth and more sensitive demand of each monk and nun. Each was required to "politically draw a clear line of demarcation with the Dalai clique"—in other words to give a formal declaration of his or her opposition to the Dalai Lama and his policies.[52]

It seems that the authorities attempted to carry out these five steps by sending work teams, groups of Party educators known in Chinese as *gongzuo dui* or in Tibetan as *ledun rukhag*, to each monastery or nunnery. In retrospect it appears that the work teams that, as we saw earlier, had been sent out to nunneries around Lhasa in late 1993 and early 1994, before the Third Forum was convened, had been testing some of the proposals which the Third Forum was later to confirm as state policy. As far as we can see from the accounts available, the first wave of work teams to apply the new policies seems to have been sent to monasteries in the weeks immediately after the Third Forum to inform people of the new demands, many of which in fact were existing demands that had never been enforced.

About three months later, in November and December 1994, the teams appear to have been sent out again to assess the extent of obedience to the demands imposed on the first visit: to see, for example, whether unregistered monks had been expelled or underage novices sent back to their families. In some cases, the teams began to implement the fifth instruction, the process of extracting declarations of allegiance to the Party and the motherland, or of opposition to the Dalai Lama. It is still not completely clear when or whether the political education teams imposed punishments for failure to obey the orders, but a number of demonstrations in late 1994 and early 1995, notably those staged by monks from Sang Ngag Khar monastery in Taktse, appear to have been a response of monks and nuns to the demands made on them during these visits by the teams.

---

[52] *A Golden Bridge...*, Section 12.

What made the new program exceptional was not the content of the orders, as most of the rules and policies demanded by the Third Forum had existed for several years, but the level of political authority that supported the work teams and the degree of enforcement that was being demanded of them. Most campaigns in modern China are weary affairs which lose momentum as they reach the outlying areas of the country, but this was a campaign coming directly from the central leadership and aimed specifically at Tibet rather than at China as a whole. In addition, it combined relatively pragmatic demands with deeply ideological propositions. Such efforts had been applied in Tibet in the late 1980s, but only to monasteries which had taken part in protests; this time all religious institutions were subjected to the same political demands, irrespective of their political record.

In addition, the new regime involved administrative departments, notably the Religious Affairs Bureau which shares responsibility for controlling monasteries with local governments and local Party cells, in implementing new policies of control at the grassroots level. As far as we can tell from the available accounts, the officials were being called on to act not only as informants and ideological educators, their existing role, but also as enforcers of the policies which they were prescribing. In the case of the religious administration organs, new regulations were introduced to support their greater intervention in everyday religious affairs.[53] Their new role as enforcers rather than as administrators was symbolized by the announcement in June 1995 that a new category of official was to be created under their supervision—the temple registration official. Registration was necessary to give religious places legal status and to "improve the management of religious affairs," a senior official announced. The process of registration should

---

[53] The decision to register places of worship was a China-wide policy, contained in regulations issued by the State Council in 1994, and was part of a growing body of legislation controlling religion in the country. "China will beef up its rule of law in handling religious affairs," Ismail Amat was quoted as saying in January 1996. Amat listed the registration of religious sites as "on top of the three major tasks for religious work this year" but singled out pro-independence activists as targets for punishment: "those who make use of religion to interfere with administrative, judicial, martial, educational and other social affairs, especially those who take advantage of religious reasons to split the country, must be severely cracked down upon according to law," he said (Xinhua, January 14, 1994; SWB, January 15, 1996). By mid-1995 the TAR had already promulgated at least three sets of regulations on religious activities, including *Regulations on the Democratic Management of Lamaseries, the Management of Religious Affairs in Tibet, and a Detailed Rule on the Reincarnation of the Living Buddha.* "Local officials say that enforcement of the regulations will separate political actions from religious affairs, and ensure freedom of religious belief among local people," Xinhua reported on April 29, 1995; SWB, May 1, 1995.

be used to publicize the Party's policies on religion, he added.[54] The new officials were quickly dubbed "temple police" in popular parlance. In effect, at least in the eyes of some observers, the Third Forum had shifted monastic security work from the police to the administrative organs of the government and created a kind of police force which the local Religious Affairs offices would operate in the monasteries and nunneries.

Anti-Dalai Lama Campaign

A further indication of the character of the new religious policy established by the Third Forum was the announcement of a campaign against Tibet's exiled spiritual leader, the Dalai Lama. Despite the frequent repudiation of his political status and views, the Dalai Lama's religious authority had not been challenged by the Chinese authorities since the liberalization era began. Chinese propaganda experts have always tended toward caution in the extent to which they permit personal criticism of the Tibetan leader, especially since 1987, when major unrest was set off by press attacks on the Dalai Lama.[55] It is thus almost certain that any increase in the level of rhetoric against him would have been authorized by senior politicians and would have been part of a carefully prepared propaganda strategy.

In particular, politicians in Tibet are careful to distinguish between attacks on the "clique" (in Tibetan, *ru-tsog*) that is supposed to surround and advise the Dalai Lama, and *ad hominem* attacks on the leader himself. The latter are usually indicated in Chinese official language by the use of "the Dalai" to describe the Tibetan leader instead of the full term "the Dalai Lama." As far as we know, despite frequent attacks on the Dalai clique, there had been no personal attacks on the Dalai Lama since the Cultural Revolution, apart from the brief and ill-judged burst of invective in September 1987. Thus the Third Forum demand that Tibetans denounce this highly revered figure in order to demonstrate their loyalty as Chinese citizens represented a significant upgrading of the official campaign to suppress

---

[54] Jipu Pingcuocideng [Kyibug Phuntsog Tseten], vice-chairman of the TAR government, quoted in *Tibet Daily; SWB*, July 21, 1995.

[55] See "Western Account of Lhasa Demonstrations," *Tibetan Review* (New Delhi), November 1987. The Chinese press criticized the Dalai Lama personally, using the pejorative term "Dalai," because of a political speech he gave to the U.S. Congress in September 1987, the first time he had publicly involved the international community in the Tibet question since Sino-Tibetan negotiations collapsed in 1984.

dissent and a strong indication of the new assertiveness and confidence of the state in handling internal opposition.

The campaign initiated by the Third Forum against the Dalai Lama first emerged in official documents in September 1994. It was exceptionally aggressive, even violent, in its choice of language. According to *A Golden Bridge...*:

> Although sometimes Dalai speaks softly and says nice things to deceive the masses, he has never ceased his splittist activities. Even up to today he has never changed his standpoint of trying to gain Tibet's independence. We must always have a clear view of Dalai and reveal his double-faced true color as much as possible. The focal point in our region's fight to oppose splittism is to oppose the Dalai clique. As the saying goes, to kill a serpent, we must first cut off its head. If we don't do that, we cannot succeed in the struggle against splittism.[56]

Vitriolic attacks on the Dalai Lama subsequently appeared in materials used for political education[57] and in January 1995, the campaign was publicly launched in the official media. By this time what was unusual was not the violence of the language used, but the fact that it criticized the Dalai Lama on religious rather than political grounds. For the first time since 1979, the polemic attacked his religious standing and suitability for leadership:

---

[56] The phrase about cutting off the serpent's head appears in the internal document entitled "Seize this Good Opportunity of Having 'The Third Forum' [and] Achieve in an All-Round Way a New Aspect on Work in Tibet," a speech given by Ragdi on September 5, 1994 at the Seventh Plenum of the Sixth Standing Committee Session of the TAR Communist Party. It was printed for internal circulation as Document No. 5 of that meeting (see Appendix C), which was called so that Ragdi could brief the Tibetan cadres in Lhasa on the decisions reached by the Third Forum. An official public summary of this speech by Ragdi was printed in the Chinese language version of *Tibet Daily* on September 6, 1994; an English translation was published by the BBC in SWB, September 26, 1994. All the sections on cutting off the serpent's head (and on encouraging Chinese migration into Tibet) were omitted from the public version.

[57] The phrase about cutting off the serpent's head is used prominently in *A Golden Bridge...*, which is the official source-book for speeches and education sessions on the decisions of the Third Forum.

The purpose of Buddhism is to deliver all living creatures in a peaceful manner. Now that Dalai and his clique have violated the religious doctrine and even have spread rumours to fool and incite one people against the other, in what way can he be regarded as a spiritual leader? ... As for Dalai [as opposed to the clique], he has always incorporated "Tibetan Independence" into the doctrines which he preaches in his sermons, ... wildly attempting to use godly strength to poison and bewitch the masses ... Such flagrant deceptiveness and demagoguery constitute a blasphemy to Buddhism.[58]

The campaign was not purely confined to propaganda statements but included a number of practical steps. It was combined with the new directives being imposed on monasteries and nunneries, in the form of the fifth stage discussed above—the demand that the monks and nuns should separate themselves from the Dalai Lama's supporters:

We must emphasize that we must look squarely at the reality that the Dalai clique is using religion for its splittist activities; we must expose the fact that Dalai is using the mask of religion to cover up his political features; and we must firmly stop the Dalai clique from influencing lamas and nuns in Tibet in any way. The broad masses of people, lamas and nuns, no matter whether or not they are Party members or cadres, must politically draw a clear line of demarcation with the Dalai clique.[59]

---

[58] From the article "Clearly Understand the True Nature of the Dalai Clique, Oppose Splittism and Safeguard Stability" published in the Chinese language version of *Tibet Daily*, March 10, 1995 (see "Tibet Authorities to Crack Down on Religion, Splittism," SWB, March 28, 1995). A version of the same article had appeared in the Tibetan language edition of the *Tibet Daily* three days earlier. The Chinese language version, which is read by foreign diplomats in Beijing, was signed by an unknown writer using the name Xuan Wen, a convention which is used to suggest that the article does not necessarily represent the final views of the Party. The Tibetan language version article, which it could be assumed would not reach the outside world, was unsigned and so was intended to indicate to Tibetans that its views represented the Party's official position.

[59] This section is reproduced more or less identically in *A Golden Bridge...* on October 1, 1994, in the *Tibet Daily* (Chinese language version), November 25, 1994, in the *Tibet Daily* (Tibetan language version) on March 7, 1995 and in the *Tibet Daily* (Chinese

This demand in practice meant that work teams or management committees had to obtain from each monk and nun a written or oral declaration that they would not support the political position and claims of the Dalai Lama or his followers. The demand is worded in such a way that it criticizes the Dalai Lama personally but does not explicitly require Tibetans to oppose the Dalai Lama as an individual or as their religious leader; instead they are ordered to separate themselves from the "clique," and it is specified that the separation related to politics rather than religious matters. Given the general tone of these instructions to Party cadres, which elsewhere include extensive attacks on the Dalai as an individual and as a religious figure, we can assume that this ambiguity is not an oversight, but a reflection of the sense of caution amongst Chinese propagandists about how far they can push their demands without triggering off major unrest. Certain questions remain unanswered in these instructions—whether, for example, it would be enough for monks and nuns to state allegiance to the Party and the motherland, or whether they are required to make explicit condemnations of the Dalai clique. The ambiguity leaves decisions about difficult policy implementation to be decided by cadres at the local level and thus leaves the senior leadership free to deny responsibility if things go wrong. It is also in effect an invitation to grassroots cadres to be more energetic in carrying out the spirit of the instructions than required by the instructions themselves.

This at least was the situation by March 1995. As it happened, the Panchen Lama dispute was to change the tone and thrust of the anti-Dalai Lama rhetoric and to allow the leadership to raise significantly the level of invective against the Tibetan leader.

Attacks on Tibetan Cadres

It was not merely monks and nuns who were required to draw a line between themselves and the Dalai clique: the "broad masses of the people" were also told to declare their loyalty to China. But in practice there is probably no way

---

language version) on March 10, 1995. In Ragdi's speech to the Party Conference on September 5, 1994 the same instructions appear, but in greater detail and with more precise distinctions. His speech demands that only the cadres, monks, and nuns should draw a line between themselves and the Dalai clique, not the "broad masses of the people" mentioned in the public texts. As in the public texts, Ragdi makes it clear that he is seeking to attack political links with the Dalai clique, not religious links with the Dalai Lama: "The Communist cadres and the vast masses of monks and nuns in the monasteries should be determined to differentiate themselves from the Dalai clique in the political field." Document No. 5, p. 31.

that Chinese officials could have effectively forced every individual to give such declarations; it would be understood, and it is implicit in the wording of the instructions, that in most cases the demand would apply in practice to cadres and government staff, whose lives are organized in a way that makes such demands easy to administer. A fundamental objective of the Third Forum was to do just this: to apply a test of loyalty to the Tibetan cadres.

The clearest indication of the primacy of this objective to the Third Forum planners is given in Ragdi's speech of September 5, 1994. Once he has covered the economic issues, he divides his summary of the Third Forum decisions into eleven categories or major instructions for future work, of which the first is "enhancing the administration of monasteries" and the second is "by enhancing the internal administration, we should purify the cadre contingent."[60] His explanation of this text is worth quoting at length:

> In recent years the Dalai clique has had a corrosive influence on some of our region's cadre contingent and intellectuals, and it was looking for their supporters to rebel against us.
> [1] Some of our Party members believe in religion and have participated in religious activities.
> [2] Some cadres and leaders put up religious symbols inside or outside their locations and have prayer rooms and altars in their houses, and hang up the Dalai's pictures.
> [3] Some cadres were hoodwinked by the publicity of the Dalai clique about nationalism, and they see people and events from the stand of nationalism.
> [4] Some cadres act as secret enemy agents and have joined counterrevolutionary organizations. They collect confidential information for the Dalai clique and participate in splittist activities.

---

[60] Like all major policies of the Third Forum, this section was reproduced in a number of key public statements. This section appears in the *Tibet Daily*'s attack on the Dalai Lama published on March 10, 1995, in which it appears under the sub-heading "Tighten political discipline and purify the ranks of cadres." In that article it was listed as the third of four items under the heading "We should take powerful measures to ensure stability." The previous two "powerful measures" were: "We must firmly stop and crack down on infiltration" and "Control over monasteries, monks and nuns must be strengthened according to the law."

[5] Some teachers use their classroom platform to spread the idea of "Tibetan independence" without hesitation.

[6] Some cadres don't have a firm standpoint, and when splittists cause disturbances they don't dare to fight against it.

[7] Some cadres and leading members have sent their children abroad to be educated in schools run by the Dalai clique to leave a leeway for themselves.

All these things mean that if it is not an ordinary problem of ideological understanding, then it is a problem of nationalism and religion. What it reflects is that some cadres of our region do not have a firm standpoint and that the cadre contingent is not pure. ... The purification of our contingent and our region's development has direct connection with the fight against splittism, and the size of the victory relies on this. ... Every Party and government organization at all levels must do well this investigation and purification work.[61]

Official nervousness about the prevalence of "unpatriotic" cadres, a term which presumably referred to Tibetan rather than Chinese cadres, had been evident as early as 1991.[62] The text makes it clear that the term "cadre" is applied in a much wider sense than the English term "official," and includes non-administrative employees and other professionals in the public sector, notably school teachers. The Third Forum formalized central government approval of suspicions about these employees and implemented a series of practical steps to identify and punish them.

Information has not become available on all the steps that were taken within government offices to implement this purification drive, but two mechanisms were made clear by Ragdi's speech of September 5, 1994, and are

---

[61] Document No. 5, Speech to the TAR Party conference, September 5, 1994. The numbers and separation into paragraphs have been added by us and do not appear in the original.

[62] The first recent public reference to cadre disloyalty was made by an official called Tashi Phuntsog in October 1991. "Some party cadres, including some leading cadres, have mixed in among the local people and no longer believe in Marxism and socialism ... They openly believe in Buddhism and regard the Dalai Lama, a political exile, as their spiritual support," he said, in a signed article in the *Tibet Daily*, cited by Reuters, October 16, 1991.

extensively documented from eyewitness accounts—the ban on possession by government employees of Dalai Lama photographs and the recalling of their children attending exile schools:

> All Party members, especially leading members, are not allowed to put up religious symbols, Dalai photographs and altars in their houses, and shouldn't have prayer rooms. Their children are not allowed to be sent abroad to study in schools run by the Dalai clique.

Ragdi then describes the penalties for Party members who have breached these regulations. Interestingly, he confines himself to describing the penalties that can be administered by the Party itself, as if to underline the concept that the Party is separate from the state and from the public system of punishment, and lists these penalties in ascending order of gravity:

> [1] Those cadres who don't correct their above mistakes after this meeting at once should never be promoted.
> [2] Those who are leaders and are in important positions should be transferred to other places without hesitation.
> [3] Those who have serious problems should be punished according to the Party's Constitution and Government rules.
> [4] Those who have opposed the Party and defected from our country by escaping abroad and who have surrendered themselves to the Dalai clique should be expelled from the Party.
> [5] Those who were involved in splittist and counterrevolutionary activities should be dealt with by the law.[63]

During the last three months of 1994, Tibetan Party members and government workers were accordingly being asked to demonstrate their lack of religious belief, often by submitting to searches of their houses to determine whether they or their families possessed religious shrines, pictures, rosaries or other items of Buddhist devotion. In addition, they were required to recall any of their children studying in schools maintained by the exile government in India and Nepal by the end of the year, or face dismissal; forms had already been distributed around

---

[63] Document No. 5; numbers added.

all government offices several months earlier asking parents to state where their children were attending school.[64]

In both cases the wording of the instructions was again ambiguous. In public texts, although not in Ragdi's internal speech, it was unclear whether the restrictions applied to all displays of religious belief or only to photographs of the Dalai Lama. Some official statements downplayed the issue even further and suggested that the restrictions applied only to the sale of such photographs in public. Even in Ragdi's speech some phrases imply that the new prohibitions apply to the display of religious symbols, while others suggest the ban applies to all forms of religious activity. The various texts are also unclear about whether the bans on religious display and on sending children to India apply only to Party members or to all government employees.

Technically, the answers to these ambiguities are clear: there is a ban on religious activity among Party members, and there is a ban on the display of Dalai Lama photographs in the offices of all government employees, whether or not they are Party members, and in the residences of those employees where they live in government accommodation. In practice, however, the bans seem to have been imposed in a more haphazard way, so that officials who were not Party members found themselves prohibited from the possession or display of religious symbols, and members of the families of Party members were subject to the same bans. Most people understood the bans to apply to any visible religious activity by officials, not merely to the possession of symbols. In some areas the bans were applied to all officials, and there are a significant number of reports of rural areas (notably Nagchu) where officials attempted to apply them to all citizens.[65] This erratic pattern of implementation applied to the ban on sending children to exile schools as much as it did to the ban on the display of religious symbols. At least one of the parents who traveled to India to take his children back from school there was a

---

[64] See "Tibetan Cadres Ordered to Call Back Their Children from Exile Schools," Department of Information and International Relations, Tibetan Government in Exile, October 15, 1994, and "Chinese Extend Ban on Children Going to Exile Schools," *TIN Briefing*, March 20, 1995.

[65] See "Summary of Written Submissions from Tibet Addressed to the UN" in "Restrictions on Religion in Tibet, 1994," *TIN Background Briefing Paper No.25*, March 1995.

businessman, not a government employee, who said that the ban had been extended to him because he was known to have a record of dissident views.[66]

The haphazard and often arbitrary implementation of the bans appear to have been designed as much to intimidate a broad sector of Tibetans as to end the practices the bans were aimed at. It is thus important to note that these bans, which formed the public part of the campaign against cadre disloyalty, were not in fact elimination drives aimed at removing one or other practice, and in fact are unlikely to have been intended to end religious practice among Tibetan cadres. They were in fact identification devices, strategies designed to identify potentially disloyal cadres, and to flush out unpatriotic officials. That is, perhaps, the significance of the terminology used by Ragdi when he referred to the exercise as "this investigation and purification work": the restrictions on religion and on sending children to India were in fact part of the investigation process. Similarly, it is noteworthy that the Third Forum does not appear so far to have ordered the purging of disloyal officials; instead it called for them to be identified, apparently on the basis that identifying them will be sufficient to neutralize their ability to cause damage.

One reason why the authorities may not have felt it necessary to carry out a purge of unpatriotic cadres was that they had at their disposal another option: bringing in more cadres from China. At the same time as raising the specter of dismissal for Tibetan cadres suspected of disloyalty to the Party, the Third Forum guidelines specify the need for the deployment of ethnic Chinese cadres and the settlement of demobilized Chinese military personnel in Tibet:

> We should continue to import Chinese and other nationalities to work in Tibet. We should recruit specially trained students, former PAP troops and demobilized soldiers to be cadres.[67]

Throughout 1995, articles appeared in official Chinese and Tibetan newspapers describing groups of officials and technicians who were volunteering

---

[66] "Chinese Extend Ban on Children Going to Exile Schools," *TIN Briefing*, March 20, 1995.

[67] *A Golden Bridge...*, p.83. See also Jiang Zemin's speech to the Forum, where he speaks of the need for 30 percent of the cadres in Tibet to be Chinese.

to go to work in Tibet.[68] A major propaganda campaign was initiated in November 1994 glorifying Kong Fansen, a prefecture-level Chinese cadre from Shandong who had done several tours of duty in Tibet before dying in a road accident. The campaign called on other Chinese to follow his example and go to work in Tibet.[69] There were indications that the drive for recruits was not limited to volunteers: in one case a deputy mayor of a Chinese city was reportedly sacked for not agreeing to volunteer to work in Tibet.[70]

Education

The education strategy announced at the Third Forum aimed to increase the ideological content of schooling in Tibet, specifically to increase patriotic thinking and to eradicate by force support for religion or the "Dalai clique." In effect, it aimed to control the opinions of school children and teachers and to limit the ideas available to them. Again, like the anti-Dalai Lama campaign and the campaign to restrict religion, its objective was to identify supporters of the dissident movement.

> The Dalai clique targets youngsters in its efforts to incite defections in the vain hope that the goal of secession will be realized several years or decades later if it cannot be achieved at the moment. Accordingly, it has stepped up its efforts to divide and demoralize Tibetan youngsters.[71]

---

[68] See for example, "Former Soldiers to be Given Permanent Posts in Tibet," *TIN News Update*, April 10, 1995.

[69] "He understood that Tibet is an inalienable part of the great motherland's sacred territory and that Tibet cannot develop and prosper without the support of cadres and qualified personnel of various kinds from the interior of the country. So, once the party issued a call, he answered the call and rushed to work in Tibet without any hesitation ... We should learn from Comrade Kong Fansen's lofty character." *People's Daily*, April 7, 1995.

[70] Reuters, May 29, 1995, citing the Hong Kong-based paper *Wen Wei Po* on the case of Zhao Fuqing, vice-mayor of Xiaoshan in Zhejiang province.

[71] Text of article by Yu Dun'riu entitled "Persist in the two-handed approach and intensify the anti-splittist struggle," *Tibet Daily* (Chinese language edition), January 30, 1995, SWB, April 5, 1995. See also the report of a meeting of the autonomous regional committee of the Chinese Youth League (CYL) held March 31, 1995 in Lhasa: "The Dalai clique is colluding with western anti-China forces, stepping up its infiltration of Tibet and

The Third Forum's attacks on education indicate that the Chinese state sees itself as in competition with indigenous Tibetan institutions in winning the loyalty of the young generation. This concern was spelled out by Chen Kuiyuan, the TAR Party secretary, in his speech to the Fifth TAR Meeting on Education in October 1994, where he explained how the guidelines issued by the Third Forum relate to education policy. In the first instance, he described the new education policy in terms of the Third Forum's instructions to halt the spread of religion:

> Splittist elements try to infiltrate the educational circle by using narrow nationalism and religion. Scriptures have entered some schools and become textbooks in the classrooms. Some students have joined the ranks of monks. Some people purposely interpret this phenomenon as a national feature in an attempt to legalise religious interference in educational affairs. ... Therefore, we have arduous tasks in political and ideological work as well as heavy responsibilities in training constructors and successors who possess deep love for the Motherland and socialist undertakings.[72]

A few days later, continuing his tour of Chamdo in eastern Tibet, Party Secretary Chen stated the official position on education in more precise terms. Here he sets out a positive, socialist agenda for education which goes far beyond the insistence on the exclusion of religion. But he goes further than saying that education should be socialist: he says that producing "socialist constructors" should be its only objective, and, surprisingly, he rejects scientific and technical learning as sufficient goals:

> While inspecting Qamdo [Chamdo] Prefectural Primary School and Middle School, Secretary Chen noted: The development of ethnic education should aim at improving the quality of nationalities as a whole. Ethnic education should not only maintain and carry forward a nationality's fine traditions, but also meet the needs of present social development. Ethnic

---

its subversive activities in Tibet. The struggle between them and us to win the support of young people is very intense." (Tibet People's Broadcasting Station, Lhasa, April 2, 1995; SWB, April 5, 1995.)

[72] *Tibet Daily*, October 28, 1994, SWB, November 21, 1994.

education cannot be regarded as successful if it successfully maintains the old culture and traditions, but fails to suit the needs of present social development. The essence of educational work is to cultivate qualified constructors and successors for the socialist cause, and this is the sole basic mission in ethnic education. [...] Currently, there is a practice that merely stresses education in science and culture and overlooks moral education. A man who merely receives education is certainly not a constructor and successor for the socialist cause. He may advocate socialism, but it is also likely that he opposes socialism. He may safeguard the unification of the motherland and national unity, but it is also possible that he will disrupt national unity and engage in activities to split the motherland. The broad masses of comrades on the educational front should have a clear understanding of this fact.[73]

The attack on scientific knowledge is unusual, and goes against standard Chinese demands for improved scientific knowledge to be spread in Tibet, a demand that has always been a basis of the Chinese dispensation in Tibet, including in many of its most left-wing phases. The liberalizations inspired by Hu Yaobang in the early 1980s also encouraged modern education for Tibetans and attracted Party support on the assumption that both religious belief and Tibetan nationalism were a consequence of lack of learning. Chen's reversal of Hu's policy is a comment on the growing perception among officials in Tibet that even highly educated people can retain both religious and nationalist ideas. It was this perception that lay behind the Forum's decision to identify disloyal cadres and to replace them with Chinese, and to restructure educational objectives from the acquisition of scientific knowledge to the attainment of ideological compliance.

In making this attack on teachers and Tibetan education, Chen was drawing directly on the Third Forum's ruling that for teachers as well as for administrators, political correctness is to be considered more important than

---

[73] "Chen Kuiyuan in Qamdo Says Prosperity Will Drive Out Religion," Tibet People's Broadcasting Station, Lhasa, November 28, 1994; SWB, December 5, 1994.

professional competence: "... they should have some professional skills, but most of all, they must be determined revolutionaries," the *Golden Bridge* states. [74]

Like most policies of this period, this one can be traced back to the demands of the Third Forum. It had been spelled out in some detail as the third of the eleven measures listed in Document No.5, where the first was containing religion, and the second was purifying the cadre force. The third was "enhance the work in schools and the education of teenagers" and was described as follows:

> The Dalai clique has enrolled lots of teenagers in their schools abroad to imbue them with "Tibetan independence" and splittist ideas. They are trying lots of methods to train successors to the cause of "Tibetan independence." In our region there are students in schools wearing a red scarf [members of the Young Pioneers] and going to monasteries to supply the butter lamps, and what's more, some have even been deceived by the Dalai clique's counterrevolutionary propaganda, so that they sympathize and take splittist actions. What would happen after some decades: would our teenagers grow up as successors to the cause of socialism or to the cause of splittism? This is an important issue that we ought to consider seriously. ... By exercising the method to recall past suffering and think over the source of present happiness, and by comparing between the old and new society, we should let the young generation have the knowledge of the dark serf system and to see the Dalai clique's true color. Those teachers who spread the "Tibetan independence" idea from the classroom's platform should be reasoned with, and should be cleared away. As for those who have sent their children abroad to be educated in schools run by the Dalai clique, if the parents are citizens, peasants and

---

[74] *A Golden Bridge...*, p.40. This view had already been applied to education in the May 1994 Work Report of the TAR Government: "Schools of all categories at various levels should firmly put the correct political orientation above all else and strive to train qualified personnel who have lofty ideals, moral integrity, a good education and a strong sense of discipline." (*Tibet Daily*, June 6, 1994; SWB, July 1, 1994.) The effort to increase ideological education, emerged during the launching of the Patriotic Education Campaign in September 1994 (see below). This view of education was repeated by Gyaltsen Norbu, the TAR Chairman, at the TAR Education Conference which followed the Third Forum in October 1994; see *Tibet Daily*, October 30, 1994; SWB, November 21, 1994.

herdsmen, we should enhance our work on educating them, but if they are Party members in government departments and are cadres, then we should let them call back their children within a specified period. Those who don't call back their children should be dealt with seriously, and their children's residence cards should be cancelled. Those graduates from Dalai clique's schools who have come to work in Tibet should be controlled strictly; they shouldn't be allowed to work in the Party and government or other important departments. Those who are already working in Tibet should be checked, and should be dealt with in different ways according to different matters.[75]

The education policy imposed by the Third Forum is thus slightly different from the other strategies it advocated for suppression of dissent, in that it is largely an ideological exercise, much in the style of Chinese campaigns in the 1970s. Available reports suggest there were no practical steps to be taken apart from assessing the ideological purity of teaching staff and perhaps purging those who failed to show the correct opinions.

One reason for this relative restraint was that the practical steps, such as establishing new classes and curricula emphasizing "moral education," raising the Chinese flag each day and singing patriotic songs, had already been implemented as part of a national campaign to improve the ideological thinking of school children, especially in primary schools. This three-year "colorful patriotic education" drive which was launched nationwide in September 1994 focused on Tibet in particular, where it was adapted to include an attack on nationalism. Emphasis was to be placed on the "firm opposition to separation, safeguarding the unity of the motherland [and] enhancement of national unity" as well as revitalizing the Tibetan economy, according to *People's Daily*.[76]

---

[75] Ragdi's speech to the TAR Party Committee, Document No.5, September 5, 1995.

[76] "Every Monday morning, the brightly colored five-star red flag is raised at all primary and secondary schools in Lhasa and the singing of the national anthem can be heard all over the city." This is the opening paragraph of the article "Tibet's Education in Patriotism is Varied and Interesting," by Liu Wei, *People's Daily*, September 15, 1994; SWB, October 11, 1994. See "Communists Launch Patriotic Education in Tibet," UPI, September 15, 1994.

Assessing the Impact of the Third Forum

By tracing the implementation of decisions announced at the Third Forum we can discern the emergence of a more repressive trend in Tibet policy—on the one hand an acceleration of economic and demographic policies clearly resented by the indigenous population and, on the other hand, a heightened determination to crack down on institutions and individuals suspected of nationalist sympathies. This in turn helps to account for the growing numbers of Tibetans detained on political charges in the same period. In particular, the call for a halt to any further spread of religious activity, the insistence on denunciation of the Dalai Lama, and the campaign against crypto-nationalist Party members amount to a shift in policy away from the encouragement of expressions of ethnic identity and culture within a "patriotic" framework and toward a more direct association of Tibetan institutions and values with dissent and nationalist aspirations.

V. RESPONSE TO THE NEW POLICIES: A WINTER OF UNREST, 1994-1995

Tibetan reaction to the new policies soon became evident: between December 1994 and March 1995 a wave of protests, demonstrations and confrontations swept across central Tibet. The 127 political arrests during the first three months of 1995, more than there had been in the whole of 1994, arose from ten pro-independence demonstrations, three incidents of protest against Chinese Muslim settlers in Lhasa, four police raids on rural monasteries suspected of organizing such demonstrations (Drigung Emari, Katsel, Phenpo Nalandra, and Gyabdrag) and at least three incidents of political protest at rural monasteries (Drigung Terdrom, Toelung Tsurphu, and Nyemo Donpar).

Apart from the narrowing of religious tolerance, these largely monastic protests may have been influenced by other factors. Some monks, particularly those of the Kagyu school of Tibetan Buddhism, to which the monasteries of Tsurphu and Taglung are affiliated, may have been disturbed by the apparently forced visit to inland China made in October 1994 by the young seventeenth Karmapa, then the most senior religious leader residing in Tibet and leader of the Kagyu school. The visit was accompanied by extensive publicity in the official media which cited the Karmapa's expressions of support for the Chinese state, although they did not mention that he was an eleven-year-old child at the time. The visit coincided with National Day celebrations in Beijing, and the child was presented with gifts by China's premier and quoted as saying that he supported the Party and prayed for Mao Zedong.

A second event that had some impact, at least near Lhasa, was the November 1994 visit to China and Tibet by U.N. Special Rapporteur on Religious Intolerance M. Abdelfattah Amor. This was the first visit China had ever permitted by a U.N. human rights official. Although prevented from having any genuine unofficial contact with Tibetans during his two-day visit to Lhasa, Amor was able to meet with Yulo Dawa Tsering, the veteran political detainee released conditionally on November 4, apparently to coincide with his visit. It is not clear if the meeting was fully endorsed by the authorities, and it is believed to have led to repercussions for the lama, a former abbot and philosophy lecturer at Tibet University who was said as of early 1996 to be confined to his house or at least to Lhasa. In his discussions with the rapporteur the lama confirmed reports that there is a ban on religious activity in prison and that there is a ban on readmission to their monasteries for monks and nuns who have completed prison sentences for political offenses. Both practices were condemned in the rapporteur's subsequent report.[77]

Protests by the monks of Sang Ngag Khar monastery (at Dechen county, some twenty-five kilometers east of Lhasa) in the first week of December were said to have been staged in the mistaken belief that the U.N. rapporteur was still staying in the capital. Sixteen monks are reported to have been arrested as a result of these incidents. Some other monastic protests during this period may also have been intended for the attention of the U.N. delegation.

The spate of protests during the winter of 1994-1995 is remarkable not only for its intensity but also for its apparent confirmation of recent trends in the pattern of Tibetan dissent. These are two in particular. One is the growth of dissent since 1992 in rural areas outside of the capital Lhasa; a secondary but by no means insignificant characteristic of that growth was the wholly unexpected increase in the involvement in protest of monasteries other than those belonging to the dominant Gelugpa sect. The second trend is the tendency for monks and nuns to sustain the momentum of protest following the suppression of popular lay demonstrations or in times of heightened control, as seems to have been the case during 1990-91, after the year of martial law, and in 1994, after the crushing of the many protests involving lay people during the previous year.

Both of these observations, which will be discussed in more detail below, seem to be confirmed by the authorities themselves. The relevant section of the TAR procurator's annual work report for 1994 confirms the scale of the arrests that year:

> The situation concerning splittism and the anti-splittist struggle remained grim and counterrevolutionary cases continued to follow an upward trend. ... 87.53 percent [of these cases] were against 137 lamas [i.e. monks] and nuns.[78]

---

[77] The rapporteur's thirty-five page report on his visit to China and his account of his meeting with Yulu Rinpoche is contained within the document reference E/CN.4/1995/91 issued by the U.N. in February 1995. See also "Tibet's Leading Prisoner Speaks Out; UN Reports on Religion in China," *TIN News Update*, February 10, 1995.

[78] Work Report of the TAR Peoples' Procuratorate, delivered at the Sixth TAR Peoples' Congress on May 20, 1995 and published in *Tibet Daily*, June 13, 1995; SWB July 11, 1995.

But, more importantly, the official reports for 1994 confirm the authorities' perceptions that dissent had spread into the countryside. They also indicate their belief that the expansion of dissent had followed major roads and traffic routes:

> Splittist forces showed a tendency of spreading along communication lines and into key cities and towns, as well as farming and pastoral zones.[79]

The disturbances in the winter of 1994-5 also indicate that the policing of dissent was reaching beyond the major towns. For example, the unrest in some of the smaller, rural monasteries such as Phenpo Shar, Gyabdrag, Taglung Barilbu, and Nyemo Donpar appears to have been a reaction to measures for increased official control described earlier, such as the appointment of unpopular "patriotic" figures on the Democratic Management Committees of each institution and the enforcement of political education sessions. The larger monasteries with established histories of protest—what might be termed "criminal records" in the eyes of the authorities—were already used to such treatment. Local police stations, known in Chinese as *paichusuo*, and carefully selected Democratic Management Committees had been placed in Drepung, Sera, and Ganden (the three largest monasteries in and around Lhasa) since at least 1990.

Events at Phenpo Shar in June 1994, Drigung Emari (also written as Drigung Yamure or Yamari) in January 1995, and Phenpo Nalandra in February 1995 were especially significant because of the heavy-handed way in which the authorities responded to them. In each case several truckloads of troops, either from the People's Armed Police (PAP) or from the People's Liberation Army (PLA), were sent to these relatively small and remote monastic communities. Their objective was to carry out the arrest or punishment of monks or nuns suspected of such offenses as printing pro-independence leaflets (Emari), possessing the Tibetan national flag (Nalandra), or participating in demonstrations (Bumpa Shar).

The amount of force used was not as overwhelming as in Kyimshi or Lhundrup Nemo in June 1993, but those were major incidents which involved the whole village, lay people as well as monks, and which led to a collapse in government control in the area. The 1995 raids were quite different. They were not directed at large lay communities but at a single monastery or nunnery, and were not a response to any major unrest. The use of PAP and PLA paramilitary forces in these arrests indicates the seriousness with which the authorities regarded the

---

[79] Work Report of the TAR Peoples' Procuratorate, see above.

emergence of religious dissent in rural areas and the forceful methods to which they are prepared to resort to crush it.

Further Security Measures: 1995

As the thirtieth anniversary celebrations for the TAR in September 1995 approached, a number of new police mechanisms were introduced. The authorities announced that they had begun to implement a new form of police patrol known as "floating police stations"—basically a Public Security vehicle fitted with sophisticated communications equipment and weapons.[80] Tourists visiting Tibet during July and August 1995 reported the introduction of mobile check-points—police vehicles which set up randomly located road blocks to check cars, trucks, and passengers—on the main roads out of the city. At the same time, helicopters were introduced to patrol China's northwestern borders, notably in Xinjiang, but with some indications that this included part of Tibet's borders with neighboring countries.[81]

The intensification of controls along roads and borders may have been connected to the authorities' perception that dissent is spreading along communication lines from Nepal to Tibet, and from the towns to the countryside, and was accompanied by increased efforts to catch Tibetans carrying illegal documents into Tibet, notably speeches by the Dalai Lama.[82] The determination to stop such documents entering Tibet was indicated by the claims in the Third Forum statements about the amount of dissident literature from the Tibetan exiles that had

---

[80] *Hong Kong Standard*, July 21, 1995.

[81] Jiefang Jun Bao, *Liberation Army Daily*, June 15, 1995; SWB, July 1,1995. The western half of the TAR—the prefectures of Ngari and Nagchu—are administered for military purposes by the (southern) Xinjiang Military District.

[82] In a more direct example of cutting down lines of communication of dissent, the authorities greatly increased their attempts in 1995 to capture dissident literature that was being smuggled into Tibet from exiles in Nepal and India. "Since 1985 ... a large batch of reactionary printing materials, 14,000 audio-video products and 26,000 pornographic products have been tracked down. The [Lhasa customs] office has contributed to removing spiritual pollution." It is not clear whether the term "pornography" is used to include political material. Tibet People's Broadcasting Station, Lhasa, June 16, 1994; SWB, June 22, 1994.

already been intercepted by the authorities: over 2,000 items in 1992 and 15,000 in 1993.[83]

Attempts were also made to stop news of dissent going out of Tibet, rather than coming in, and there were at least three reports of tourists being strip-searched at Lhasa airport on their way out of the country in 1995, the first such reports since tourism was re-established in 1983. The searches were not random: all the tourists involved were either able to speak Tibetan or had close connections with Tibetans, indicating increasingly thorough surveillance of foreigners by the Chinese authorities. At least four Tibetans who were discovered to have given letters to the tourists were detained after the searches.[84]

Where any public statement was made by the authorities about these measures they were described as part of the security preparations needed to prevent or deter any attempt to disrupt the celebrations for the thirtieth anniversary of the TAR. Official rhetoric implied that the protests nine months before the celebrations, which in fact seem to have been linked to the new restrictions on religious activity, were part of a conspiracy by dissidents to use violence to undermine the celebrations:

> This year there were signs of trouble at temples in Maizhokunggar [Meldrogongkar] county and Shannan's [Lhokha's] Gonggar county and on the square of Lhasa's Jokhang temple. Some people posted signed reactionary slogans and openly distributed reactionary leaflets. They were swollen with arrogance. Some splittist forces have even threatened that they will carry out a series of sabotage activities by taking advantage of the celebration of the thirtieth anniversary... public security departments have reminded the masses to heighten

---

[83] Xuan Wen, *Tibet Daily*, March 10, 1995, repeated in Li Bing's article in *Tibet Daily*, December 11, 1995. The 17,000 items are described as "letters and threatening letters to instigate [government and Party] Tibetan staff to rebel" or as "rebellion-instigating letters" (Chinese: *ce fan xin)*.

[84] See "Police Strip-Search Tourists in Hunt for Letters," *TIN News Update*, June 10, 1995, and "US Tourist Stripped in Police Search for Letters," *TIN News Update* August 6, 1995.

vigilance... and be ready to fight against splittism at all times and in all places.[85]

The incidents in Meldrogongkar and Lhokha referred to in this statement were probably the arrests of dissidents in Emari and Chideshol in January 1995, none of whom were associated with sabotage or with violence of any kind, as far as we know. The allegations were not completely without foundation, however, and up to five small bombs exploded in Lhasa during July and August 1995, although there is no evidence as to who had set them off.[86] By August 1995, a major security exercise was in operation to prepare for the celebration, with restrictions being imposed on travel into Lhasa for all Tibetans from outside the capital, especially monks and nuns. According to several reports, visits by Tibetan exiles were also suspended, and all residents of the capital were required to obtain new identity cards, a process which in effect identified any unregistered visitors to the city.

---

[85] Tibet People's Broadcasting Station, Lhasa, January 26, 1995.

[86] In late June and July 1995 there were many reports of at least one and probably two explosions in Lhasa at the base of an obelisk erected to commemorate road construction teams. The monument includes an inscription added later by the Chinese leader Hu Yaobang. Reports in the western press of two more bombs going off at the same monument in August 1995 were a misunderstanding, but a bomb did explode at a fuel depot near Lhasa in late August, and in January 1996 a bomb exploded at the house of a Tibetan lama regarded as pro-Chinese *(South China Morning Post,* January 26, 1996); the report was denied by Chinese officials, according to a PTI dispatch from Beijing on January 28. No one has claimed responsibility for these explosions, and the Chinese authorities have neither admitted that they took place nor blamed the Tibetans for them. Some Tibetan sources claim that the bombs were part of an factional dispute within the Chinese administration. See "Reports of Sabotage in Lhasa," in "Reports from Tibet: April to December 1995," *TIN News Review* No.24, December 1995, p.20.

VI. MAY 1995: THE PANCHEN LAMA DISPUTE

On May 14, 1995, the Dalai Lama announced from exile that he had confirmed the recognition of a child living in Lhari, in northern Tibet, as the reincarnation of the Panchen Lama. The tenth Panchen Lama, besides being the second most senior figure in the main school of Tibetan Buddhism, became the most important Tibetan leader after the Dalai Lama fled to exile in 1959, and was the intermediary on whom the Chinese authorities most relied to obtain the support of the Tibetan people. When he died in January 1989, the Chinese authorities had gone immediately to considerable lengths to accommodate traditional Tibetan wishes concerning the manner in which his successor should be sought, issuing a statement within three days confirming that the search would be carried out under the guidance of the abbot of Tashilhunpo, the Panchen Lama's seat in Shigatse, in the traditional manner.[87] Their stance then was conciliatory, and in July 1993 they went even further and allowed the head of the search team, Chadrel Rinpoche, the abbot of Tashilhunpo, to meet the Dalai Lama's brother in Beijing and to send through him an official request for the Dalai Lama's "guidance" in the search.[88]

Two years later, when the Dalai Lama announced the name of the child he had identified, the Chinese authorities reacted with profound hostility, launching an aggressive campaign which ended in a major schism within the religion.[89] The

---

[87] The first detailed statement said that "the State Council has asked the administrators of the lamasery to arrange the incarnation [sic] procedures ... The Buddhist Association of China and the Association's Tibet Branch will help if necessary," Xinhua, January 30, 1989 in SWB, February 6, 1989. In the same week Xinhua listed a five-stage procedure for discovering the reincarnation, the first three stages of which were entirely traditional Tibetan esoteric practice: "Backgrounder: How are Living Buddhas Reincarnated?," Xinhua, February 5, 1989; SWB, February 9, 1989.

[88] The text of Chadrel Rinpoche's July 1993 letter to the Dalai Lama has not been published by either side, but after delivering it, Gyalo Thondup, the Dalai Lama's elder brother and principal emissary in negotiations, said, "The monastery and the committee led by the Chadrel Rinpoche is seeking His Holiness' guidance of [sic] the search for the reincarnation of the Panchen Lama." He added that China's State Council had endorsed the delivery of the letter (BBC World Service, Dateline East Asia, August 18, 1993).

[89] China attaches exceptional importance to the Panchen Lama issue because its territorial claim to Tibet rests partly on the 1792 agreement between the Emperor Qianlong and the then Tibetan government, which said that the Emperor's representative should be

52

Dalai Lama's announcement may have been preemptive and undiplomatic, but nevertheless the shift in Beijing's attitude to this question between 1993 and 1995 was extreme. That shift provides the clearest example of how deep and how regressive the impact of the Third Forum has been on China's policy toward Tibet.

The Chinese government had three initial reactions to the Panchen Lama dispute. First, within three days, a small number of strategic detentions were carried out: those of Chadrel Rinpoche and his assistant Jampa Chung-la, both of whom were accused of having cooperated with the Dalai Lama concerning the announcement about the child; and that of the child himself, who was moved with his family to an unknown location, almost certainly Beijing, where he remained under some form of unacknowledged custody. Second, once those arrests had been completed, a high-profile campaign was launched from Beijing which required all Tibetan leaders, government officials and leading monks to denounce publicly the Dalai Lama for making his announcement about the child. Third, a three-stage purge took place within the monastery of Tashilhunpo itself: a denunciation campaign against Chadrel Rinpoche was launched within Tashilhunpo monastery, where he had been abbot; thirty-three monks and one lama who had refused to accept the denunciation were arrested and in some cases beaten; and the existing leadership of the monastery was deposed and replaced, without using the nominal election procedure, by lamas who had histories of supporting the Chinese authorities.

These three moves were classic security operations of rapid containment: the elimination of enemy leaders; demanding an oath of loyalty from all potential enemy leaders; and flushing enemy supporters into the open and eliminating them. The replacement of the Tashilhunpo leadership completed the operation by rewarding supporters with leadership positions.

The operation was set in motion with speed and efficiency. The detentions of the leaders were completed by May 17, and on the same day, the government began to obtain statements of support from other Tibetan leaders. The final stage of exposing and replacing dissidents within Tashilhunpo also began three days after the Dalai Lama's announcement: a "work team" of fifty party officials was assembled from the departments of the United Front, Religious Affairs Bureau, and the Public Security Bureau, and on May 17, the team took up residence within the

---

involved in the selection of the Panchen Lama and the Dalai Lama. The text of the 1792 agreement is printed in English by Ya Hanzhang, *Biographies of the Dalai Lamas*, (Beijing: 1991), p.72 ff. On November 13, 1995 and frequently afterwards, the Chinese authorities stated that matter was in the final analysis an issue of sovereignty.

monastery and began screening the monks. Even before the work team moved in, the remaining monastery leaders had been organized to make public statements:

> On May 14, His Holiness announced that he had recognized Gendun Choekyi Nyima as the reincarnation of the Panchen Lama. On May 15, the announcement was disputed by the State Council's Religious [Affairs] Bureau. On May 16, some of the leaders and committee members of the Tashilhunpo Democratic Management Committee [*dmangs dag gnyer au yon lhan khang*] were told to go to the Shigatse local administration offices [*sa gnas srid 'dzin kung hru'u*] and they told those monks, who are pro-Chinese, and who have an exemplary view of politics [*chab srid kyi lta ba mtho ba*], and who are trying to get on well with the Chinese, to read the denunciation speech [*rgol gtam*] written by those local leaders. Also these monks were forced to talk on the TV with words composed according to the Chinese government's wishes.[90]

The role of the work team in the operation at Tashilhunpo was officially to persuade the monks to accept that the Chinese government's preferred method of selecting the reincarnation—a lottery system known as "the Golden Urn"—should be used instead of the divination method used unilaterally by the Dalai Lama. Within two weeks of the team's arrival, the monastery's leaders were themselves carrying out the tasks of re-education, while the work team apparently remained in the background:

> From June 2 to June 3, the Democratic Management Committee held about twenty meetings and read the central government's documents to the monks again and again. The monks were told to think carefully, but were not allowed to discuss their thinking [with each other]. After the meeting the monks were questioned one by one many times ... [91]

---

[90] Statement from a TIN source in Shigatse who asked to remain anonymous. The response of the State Council was not made publicly available until May 17.

[91] See footnote 90.

Delays by the Lamas

But although the containment operation had moved swiftly, it soon ran into delays and had to change strategy accordingly. Within Tashilhunpo many of the monks were resistant to the campaigns with which they were confronted:

> After the meetings [with the Democratic Management Committee on June 2-3] the monks'... answers were that they totally agreed with His Holiness's recognition and they did not agree about using the Golden Urn. So the Chinese government work team got no results with their work. At the beginning of June, there was a meeting at which Ngagchen Rinpoche, who was one of the main people in charge of the search for the reincarnation of the tenth Panchen Rinpoche, stayed behind after the work team members had read out their document and said ... he agreed with the confirmation made by His Holiness, and that he wouldn't accept the idea of using the Golden Urn to choose the reincarnation. So the meeting had to end.[92]

This obliged the Shigatse authorities to become more confrontational, and two months later, after a number of increasingly threatening meetings, they pushed the campaign to its logical conclusion by assembling Tibet's highest leaders in the monastery forecourt to denounce the missing abbot in front of his monks. Ragdi and Gyaltsen Norbu, the two most senior Tibetans in the regional Communist Party, came from Lhasa to attend the meeting, which took place on July 11 and at which Chadrel Rinpoche was to be denounced by name for the first time.[93]

The way in which that meeting was organized gives a good example of how the work team is used as a security tool. As in all work team operations, its re-

---

[92] See footnote 90.

[93] In the gradual build-up to this event, denunciations statements had been read out to the monks but without naming Chadrel Rinpoche specifically: all the monks had been called together on June 10 to hear one of the deputy leaders [*khru'u ren gzhonpa* (Chinese: *fuzhuren*)] of the Democratic Management Committee read out the denunciation document [*skyon 'dzugs shugs chen byed ba'i yig cha*] against Chadrel Rinpoche, "without using his name, but instead referring to [unspecified] bad people," according to one report. In the July 11 meeting the denunciation document was read out, characteristically, by a local Tibetan, Samdrup, Party Secretary of Shigatse prefecture, while the leaders from Lhasa, who had written the document, watched.

education task, in this case persuading monks to accept the Golden Urn system, was secondary to the task of "screening and investigation"—the process of identifying through re-education sessions potential dissidents in the group.[94] In this way it was similar, although on a smaller scale, to the Third Forum device of identifying disloyal cadres throughout the TAR by banning the possession of Dalai Lama photographs. In the case of Tashilhunpo the usefulness of the identification strategy was illustrated in the seating arrangement for the denunciation meeting. This was later described by a Tibetan who attended the meeting:

> When [the monks and officials] arrived for the meeting in the Tashilhunpo courtyard, they found that it had been drawn up like a chessboard, and each person was to sit in an allocated position where their name was written in chalk on the pavement. The arrangement was made in such a way that monks were separated from each other so that communication among themselves during the meeting would be impossible. The monks ignored these seating positions and began shouting,"We are not prisoners or soldiers" and formed their own groups, and sat wherever they chose.[95]

The monks' names were apparently arranged according to political views, presumably identified by the work teams with the help of the monastery staff in the previous two months. The meeting was interrupted frequently by heckling and was not a success for the authorities, but the identification process meant that the security forces did not have to intervene during the meeting itself, which would have led to the leaders losing face. When the People's Armed Police raided the monastery eight hours after the incident they were able to arrest thirty-two dissident monks, whose names they already knew. Two days later the authorities appointed a new set of monks to the leadership positions on the Democratic Management Committee, presumably also on the basis of information supplied or negotiated by

---

[94] "Screening and investigation" methods were reintroduced through work teams in Tibet after the unrest of October 1987 in Lhasa, and there have been periodic operations since then, mainly in monasteries and nunneries, to identify dissidents. An account of the reintroduction of "screening and investigation" in Tibet is given by Ronald Schwartz in his study, *Circle of Protest*, (New York: Columbia University Press, 1994).

[95] This account was given by a monk to a tourist who was in Shigatse in July 1995. Both asked to remain anonymous.

the work teams, and through these appointees they have been more or less been able to control the monastery ever since.[96]

In the TAR as a whole there were also arrests—a total of sixty Tibetans are believed to have been arrested for involvement in the Dalai Lama's recognition of the child reincarnation, including the abbot and the thirty-two monks from Tashilhunpo.[97] But the main strategy was to adapt the identification operations already set in motion by the Third Forum. These offered similar advantages in security terms to the work team's screening within Tashilhunpo, but they also experienced long delays. Initially, the main device was to get leading religious and social figures to make public statements condemning the Dalai Lama's announcement. The first statement of condemnation was made by Ragdi in Lhasa, and the subsequent statements appear to have been arranged so that they would give the impression that the rejection of the announcement was a Tibetan, and in particular a religious, initiative, rather than a Chinese one.[98] This was the order in which statements condemning the Dalai Lama's announcement were published by the main Chinese and Tibetan media:

---

[96] Some outbreaks of dissent did continue to emerge. Two more monks were arrested from Tashilhunpo in the week after the denunciation meeting, and six monks were arrested after staging a demonstration on November 4, 1995. See "Panchen Lama Dispute: New Leaders Installed at Tashilhunpo," *TIN News Update*, October 25, 1995.

[97] "48 Arrests Reported in Reincarnation Dispute," *TIN News Update*, September 14, 1995, and "Chinese Killed as Prisoners Escape," *TIN News Update*, February 18, 1996.

[98] Ragdi is depicted by the official press as the first person to speak on this issue, but this may have been something of a retrospective effort. The first statement issued by the Chinese press was that of the Religious Affairs Bureau in Beijing, at 11:14 GMT on May 17, which is 7:14 p.m. local time. The Foreign Affairs Bureau held back until the next day, preserving the impression that the condemnation of the Dalai Lama's announcement was a religious decision, if not a Tibetan one. Subsequently Tibet Radio issued a report saying that Ragdi had made a statement condemning the Dalai Lama "on the afternoon of May 17," which would have been earlier than the Religious Affairs Bureau, and which may have restored the impression that the decision had been made by Tibetans. Ragdi's statement, however, was very general and only said the Dalai Lama "had kicked up a rumpus over the issue on the reincarnated child of the Panchen Lama to confuse and poison people's minds." (Tibet Radio, May 18, 1995, in SWB, May 24, 1995). It was only after the Beijing statement that he and other Tibetans criticized the announcement in specific terms.

May 17: Ragdi, TAR Party and TAR Congress, in Lhasa
May 17: Religious Affairs Bureau, Beijing
May 18: Head of Tashilhunpo; Mayor of Lhasa; unknown Congress deputies
May 18: Zhao Puchu, head of the Chinese Buddhist Association, Beijing
May 18: Foreign Ministry, Beijing
May 19: Phagpalha Geleg Namgyal and "noted patriotic figures" including most importantly Sengchen Lobsang Gyaltsen, Bilung Rinpoche at Tashilhunpo, Dedrub Rinpoche in Lhasa.
May 20: Gyaltsen Norbu, TAR Party and TAR Government
May 22: TAR Branch of the Chinese Buddhist Association
May 23: Qinghai CPPCC and religious figures
May 24: TAR CPPCC and religious figures
May 25: TAR People's Congress
May 28: Qinghai religious figures
June 1: Shigatse Party Committee
June 8: Shigatse Branch of the Chinese Buddhist Association
June 14: Retring Rinpoche
June 14: Chamdo religious and lay figures
July 6: Joint meeting of the five Tibetan areas (TAR, Qinghai, Yunnan, Sichuan and Gansu)

The list reflects the importance China attaches to presenting nationality policies as autonomous decisions made by the nationality members themselves, and it is evident that considerable pressure was placed on religious and local leaders to deliver these statements so that the Chinese authorities could remain in the background. However, the list also shows a certain amount of delay in obtaining statements from certain figures—notably Retring Rinpoche, who is of "inner Hutuktu" rank, meaning that he is one of less than a dozen lamas in Central Tibet entitled traditionally to carry out the "Golden Urn" procedure. Ngapo Ngawang Rinchen, the most senior Tibetan political figure, appears to have avoided making a public statement at all, by arguing that it was a purely religious affair.[99] In these months, the statements of condemnation did not vary, and, with one exception, they never denied that the child identified by the Dalai Lama was the correct

---

[99]   See, for example, "China's Highest Tibetan Official Excluded from Rival Panchen Lama Selection Meeting," Department of Information and International Relations of the Tibet Government in Exile, Dharamsala, India, November 10, 1995.

reincarnation of the tenth Panchen Lama.[100] This diffidence suggests in retrospect that the Chinese authorities were experiencing some difficulties in finding lamas of sufficiently high status who would agree to carry out the Golden Urn procedure and appoint an alternative candidate.

November 1995: Opting for Confrontation

The delays seem to have caused considerable annoyance to Jiang Zemin and other Chinese leaders and led after six months of stasis to the emergence of a new and much more confrontational strategy. On November 4, a number of Tibetan leaders were ordered to take part in a week-long meeting at which they were required for the first time to declare that the child identified by the Dalai Lama was not the real reincarnation of the Panchen Lama.[101] This meant that a religious schism was inevitable and that for the first time there were to be two competing Panchen Lamas.[102] It also raised the preeminent security issue of what was to be done with the child recognized by the Dalai Lama, now placed in the tragic position of being a potential source of major unrest at any appearance and so

---

[100] The exception was in a statement attributed to Jamyang Shepa Rinpoche of Labrang Tashikyil monastery in Gansu, in the special edition dedicated to the selection issue of the official publication *China's Tibet*, August 1995, p.14. The edition may have been partly withdrawn after publication, since it appears not to have been distributed to subscribers. There were some earlier statements which were read by some translators as rejections of the child but these were ambiguously worded, e.g. "[We] will never recognize the reincarnated child for the Panchen Lama announced illegally by the Dalai Lama [Chinese: *jue bu cheng ren fei fa xuan bu di ban chan zhuan shi ling tong*]." That statement came from the Shigatse Prefectural Party Committee cited by Tibet Radio on June 15, 1995.

[101] The decision of the meeting was announced in *China Daily*, the *People's Daily*, and other official papers on November 13, 1995. The accompanying text focused on Jiang persuading the lamas to speed up their decisions, and the headlines also reflected the sense that the lamas had deliberately delayed a resolution of the dispute: "Tibetan soul search nears end - President calls for early confirmation," said *China Daily's* front page headline on November 13, 1995.

[102] There had, of course, been disputes over Panchen Lama candidates before, notably in the period 1941-51 when the Tibetan government refused for several years to accept a Shigatse- and later Chinese-backed candidate, but these had in the past been reconciled before any official decision on recognition was made.

certain to be kept in some sort of confinement.[103] The whereabouts of the child remain unknown.

The decision to take the most confrontational path—until the November meeting the Chinese had retained the compromise option of at least including the Dalai Lama's child in the lottery procedure—was another indication of the extent to which attitudes had hardened in Beijing since 1993.[104] The details of this November meeting showed how far this rigidity had gone. The staging of the meeting represented in effect a collapse in the usual Chinese attention to presentation in nationality issues: the way the meeting was arranged, held in closed session in a military-owned hotel in Beijing, made it self-evident that the Tibetan leaders had been placed under heavy pressure by the Chinese. There was unusually little attempt to maintain the impression that their decision was freely arrived at, an indication that was reemphasized by official photographs published in the Chinese press showing the lamas standing obediently behind President Jiang with Liu Huaqing, deputy head of the Central Military Commission, in full uniform.[105]

A more telling shift, however, was contained in the nomenclature surrounding the meeting and subsequent events. The meeting was described as the third session of the "Leading Group for Locating the Reincarnation Child of the Panchen Lama," a group that had not been named before the crisis emerged in May 1995. The term "Leading Group" is generally used for Party bodies, rather than government organs, and it soon became clear from other phrases and indicators—the hotel where the meeting was held, for example, is associated with

---

[103] One senior lama at the meeting is reported by unofficial sources to have said that the decision reached by the meeting left the authorities with three alternatives about what to with Gendun Choekyi Nyima, the child identified by the Dalai Lama—either to kill him, banish him or to imprison him without a trial.

[104] See for example, "China softens on Panchen Lama choice," K.R. Shudhaman, writing for Press Trust of India from Beijing, August 23,1995, printed in *Asian Age,* August 24, 1995. Shudhaman quotes "senior Chinese official Zhu Xiao Ming [as] implying that the possibility of accepting the reincarnation [recognized by the Dalai Lama] could not be ruled out."

[105] The photograph was printed in the *People's Daily,* the *China Daily,* and *Tibet Daily* (Chinese language edition) on November 13, 1995. A version of the photograph was printed in the Tibetan language edition of *Tibet Daily* on November 14, 1995, apparently doctored deliberately to show some of the lamas standing in front of Jiang and Liu. See "Tibetan Newspaper Sabotage; Lama's House Bombed," *TIN News Update,* January 28, 1996.

high-level Party meetings—that the Party at its highest level had taken over direct control of the issue instead of leaving the matter to the government, let alone to its specialist agencies like the Religious Affairs Bureau or the Nationalities Commission. It was announced on November 13 that Jiang Zemin and Li Peng had been directly involved in the Panchen Lama issue for some time. Later that month, the official press revealed that within the TAR, direct control of the Panchen Lama issue had been taken over by the TAR Party in April 1994, a year before the dispute emerged into the public arena.[106]

Subsequent ceremonial events—the Golden Urn ceremony and the enthronement of the child recognized by the Chinese authorities—were carefully arranged as if they were traditional Tibetan religious events conducted in the presence of Chinese government officials, with no Party involvement.[107] The events

---

[106] Question 7 of the "Questions and Answers Regarding the Reincarnated Child of the 10th Panchen," compiled by the TAR Nationalities and Religious Affairs Commission, gives the only known indication that the Party in Tibet, acting on instructions from the Party in Beijing, had taken over direct control of the search a year before the issue became a matter of public dispute: "Question 7: When did the central authorities decide to have the autonomous regional Party committee take full charge of the work concerning the reincarnations of the Panchen? Answer: ... In April 1994. The leading group for the search and confirmation of the Panchen's reincarnated child, consulting group, and inner-party coordination group, which were formed earlier, should continue to ... do their best in work under the unified leadership of the autonomous regional Party committee, so as to step up the pace of the search" (Tibet Radio, November 2, 1995, SWB, November 20, 1995). It is clear that the delay was already causing concern in Beijing, and the unusual publicity given here to the role of the regional Party may have been intended to lessen the impression that Lhasa was not involved in the process. This is the only known reference to the existence of the "inner-party coordinating group."

[107] The effort to present the Golden Urn ceremony as a traditional Tibetan religious procedure involved some historical complications. It was held in the Jokhang temple, as prescribed by the 1792 agreement, but in fact the ceremony had never been done there before: the two Panchen Lamas and three Dalai Lama selections chosen in this method had been carried out in front of the portrait of Qianlong in the Potala Palace. There is a disarmingly frank Chinese explanation of this anomaly in Question 44 in "Questions and answers regarding the reincarnated child of the 10th Panchen," *Tibet Daily,* November 9, 1995 in FBIS, November 28, 1995, p.21: The ceremony had been moved to the Potala "to give expression to subordination and to the relationship between the monarch and his officials." In the November 1995 ceremony the selection of the lots from the Golden Urn was made by a Tibetan lama, presumably to diminish the impression of Chinese involvement in the process, but historically the selection was done by the Imperial

surrounding the crucial November 13 announcement by the Leading Group showed little concern for concealing the dominant role of the Party and indicate the sense of urgency and crisis behind the scenes at that time, and the extraordinary importance attached by the Party to regaining control of the Panchen Lama succession process.

Some uncertainties remained in the days following the mid-November switch to a policy of confrontation: there were, it seemed, still some delays in persuading senior lamas to carry out the Golden Urn and Hair-cutting ceremonies, which would have required them directly to contradict the decision of the Dalai Lama. But these issues were resolved with considerable skill. The Chinese authorities retrospectively recognized the promotion of Bomi Rinpoche, a widely-respected lama, to the most senior academic position in the Gelugpa school, giving him sufficient credibility to carry out the ceremony, although he did not have the right status as an incarnation. The Golden Urn ceremony took place in the Jokhang Temple in Lhasa on November 29. From then on, the public was essentially diverted from the central issues by colorful television footage provided by the Chinese media showing lavish ceremonies featuring a small and somewhat bewildered child as the officially approved Panchen Lama. The ceremonies indicated that the authorities had regained control over the succession procedure and served at the same time to divert attention from the security issues involved. Although one would not have known it from the media coverage given, the Golden Urn ceremony was not a public event: it had taken place at about 2:00 a.m., in conditions of great secrecy, behind locked doors and with armed guards on the roofs of the Jokhang Temple, according to local reports. Throughout December, moreover, the month in which the enthronement took place in Shigatse, the TAR seems to have been in effect closed to foreign tourists.

New Denunciation Campaigns

On the same day as the Golden Urn ceremony, there was, however, another and more important development in security and political terms. It was indicated in an announcement that day by Xinhua, the official Chinese news agency, about Gendun Choekyi Nyima, the six-year-old child recognized by the Dalai Lama, who had become the illegal contender for the Panchen Lama's throne.

Commissioner (See *Tibet Daily*, November 9, 1995). It appears that it had never been done by a Tibetan lama before. The officials representing the Chinese authorities at the 1995 Golden Urn ceremony included two from the State Council (Luo Gan and Gyaltsen Norbu, Chairman of the TAR, who had been appointed a "Special Commissioner" for the event), and one from the Religious Affairs Bureau (Ye Xiaowen).

The announcement criticized the child's parents as "notorious for speculation, deceit, and scrambling for fame and profit" and condemned the child for having "once drowned a dog."[108] The announcement was strange, given that it was unnecessary for China's political objectives in regaining control of the succession procedure, and hence of its territorial claims to Tibet, for it to be denouncing small children. Given that for six months China had been relatively restrained on the issue of the child and his family, the decision to condemn them publicly indicated a policy shift and suggested that some sort of punitive action toward them was being planned. The next day, the abbot, Chadrel Rinpoche, who had also not been seen or heard of since May, was named for the first time by the Chinese authorities as a collaborator in the Dalai Lama's plot to split the country through the choice of the new Panchen Lama.[109] This again was not necessary in terms of the territorial claims or other evident political objectives which had been raised by the succession dispute: China did not need to vilify the child or the abbot in order to sustain its right to control the appointments of Panchen Lamas, which it had that day resumed by force anyway. In addition, the denunciation of Chadrel Rinpoche was somewhat embarrassing for the Chinese authorities, since they had until then declared consistently that he was not in custody and was recovering in private from some unspecified illness.[110] More serious, however, was the fact that the abbot was

---

[108]   Xinhua, November 29, 1995, in FBIS, November 29, 1995.

[109]   The first public statement acknowledging that there had been unnamed "persons of responsibility at Zhaxi Lhunbo lamasery" who had collaborated illegally with the "Dalai clique" appeared in the *Tibet Daily* on November 4, 1995. The protocol of condemnation mimicked the procedure followed within Tashilhunpo monastery where unnamed "bad persons" had been criticized on June 10, 1995, with Chadrel Rinpoche being named only a month later. The first public naming of Chadrel (Qazha in Chinese) was issued by Xinhua on November 30, 1995, reprinted in FBIS on the same day. The views of the article were summarized from an article by an unknown writer named Guo Xin. On December 1, Guo Xin's article, giving a much more detail of the denunciation of Chadrel Rinpoche, was published by the *People's Daily* under the title, "It is both illegal and invalid for the Dalai Lama to unilaterally identify the reincarnated soul boy of the Panchen Lama."

[110]   See, for example, the statements given to western journalists on August 21 which denied that either the child or the abbot were in custody. "I can't say where he is, but he is in good shape and his health conditions are getting better," a United Front official said of Chadrel Rinpoche, according to "Reincarnation Muddle Sparks Tibetan Anger," *South China Morning Post*, August 22, 1995. See also "China denies arrest of Panchen Lama," UPI; and "Search for New Panchen Lama Has Not Been Settled," Deutsche Presse Agentur,

defined in the November 29 article not as someone who had made mistakes but as "a criminal." This, the first known public campaign against a senior Tibetan figure, let alone a religious leader, in Tibet since at least 1980, more or less committed the Chinese government to prosecuting him at a future date.

The possible reason for this aggressive decision became clearer as background statements by regional-level Tibetan officials were published by the media that week. On November 24, Phagpalha Geleg Namgyal, a senior religious figure in Tibet and chairman of the TAR branch of the Chinese People's Political Consultative Conference, told "upper strata" Tibetans that they would be judged by their performance in criticizing the Dalai Lama:

> The struggle to expose and criticise the Dalai is a serious political struggle. CPPCC committees at all levels in Tibet must follow the instructions of the party central committee and the regional party committee and boldly call on and organise CPPCC members to relentlessly expose and criticise the Dalai's schemes and crimes of splitting the motherland. All CPPCC members should participate in condemning the Dalai both orally and in writing. No matter what their rank, they must maintain a firm, clear stand. That is because their stand regarding the issue of exposing and criticizing the Dalai is a major political question that serves as the main basis for determining whether the political orientation, stand and viewpoint of CPPCC cadres, particularly high-ranking cadres, including CPPCC members, is correct; whether cadres can distinguish between right and wrong; and whether their political acumen is strong or weak. At the same time it also serves as the main basis for determining whether patriots are worthy of the name. The people will judge

---

both August 21, 1995. The Chinese government attempted rapidly to correct the damage caused in the international media by the denunciation of the child, and a statement was given in the next Foreign Affairs press conference: "The spokesman said that the interference of the Dalai Lama had caused some effects and harm to the search and work in choosing the reincarnated soul boy, but there had been no effects nor any problems with respect to the child himself, whom the Dalai had chosen to be the so-called reincarnated soul boy," said *Wen Wei Po*, a Hong Kong-based paper, on December 1, 1995. The Ministry spokesman seemed to be saying that the child would not be penalized by the state for having been selected, but he did not withdraw the allegations or give any assurances about the child's welfare or whereabouts.

your practical performance in this serious political struggle; they will judge whether you side with the party and the people and play a positive role in matters of great importance at a critical juncture.[111]

This statement to some extent resembled speeches that had been made by Party leaders after the Third Forum the year before. But those speeches had been delivered within the Party and had addressed specific demands to cadres and government officials. Phagpalha Geleg Namgyal's statement on November 24 was made to the members of the CPPCC—which includes all major lamas—not to Party cadres. It was in effect an announcement that a campaign had been initiated to test the political loyalty of all senior figures in Tibetan society, including the religious leaders. This was an important escalation of Third Forum policy implementation: it meant that the Third Forum's strategy of identifying disloyalty among cadres was now to be formally extended to the non-Party sector, that is, to Tibetan society as a whole or at least to its social and religious leaders.

In his announcement to the CPPCC, Phagpalha Geleg Namgyal indicated that there were four main criteria by which the Tibetan leaders would be judged:

[1] exposing and criticizing the Dalai's crimes of undermining the work related to the reincarnation of the Panchen ...
[2] thoroughly exposing and criticizing the crimes of the former responsible persons of the Committee for Democratic Administration at the Zhaxi Lhunbo Lamasery who colluded with the Dalai;
[3] resolutely negating the so-called reincarnated boy arbitrarily confirmed by the Dalai;
[4] persisting in drawing lots from a gold urn and in the principles approved and recognized by the central government.[112]

---

[111] Speech to the 11th Meeting of the Standing Committee of the TAR Committee of the CPPCC, Tibet Television, November 24, 1995; SWB, November 28, 1995. See also "Anti-Abbot Campaign Begins, Aims to Eliminate Dalai Lama Influence," *TIN News Update*, December 5, 1995.

[112] Numbers added editorially.

The second and third items explain why the child Gendun Choekyi Nyima and the abbot Chadrel Rinpoche were publicly vilified by the official media five days later: it had been decided that they would be used as targets for criticism sessions throughout the TAR, and that the loyalty of leading Tibetan figures would be assessed by their performance in those sessions. In other words, the attacks on the child and the abbot, and on the Dalai Lama for his involvement in the Panchen Lama dispute, were no longer part of a specific campaign to reassert China's claim to appoint senior Panchen Lamas, but part of the Third Forum's continuing overriding policy to identify disloyalty among the leadership. By the end of November, the Panchen Lama dispute had thus been transformed from a crisis of sovereignty to what Chinese propagandists refer to as a "carrying device" (*zai ti* in Chinese), an opportunity for re-education to be carried out by the propaganda departments. This would become in turn, as was perhaps its original intent, an opportunity for the security departments to widen their program of screening and investigation.

Removing the Dalai Lama from Religion

Phagpalha Geleg Namgyal's speech included other forms of escalation as well; these were equally significant. He had threatened the CPPCC members, for example, with judgment by "the people," a phrase reminiscent of the Cultural Revolution; he made a point of saying the CPPCC members were to be assessed for their patriotism, a much more serious threat than previously; and he used the pejorative term "Dalai" for the Dalai Lama, a choice which is not unusual for cadres since the anti-Dalai Lama campaign was initiated by the Third Forum in March 1995 but which is rare among religious speakers.[113] More significant however, was the exact phraseology he used to refer to the anti-Dalai Lama campaign: "We must wage a resolute struggle against the Dalai and clear out his influence in all areas."

---

[113] Phagpalha is considered by the Chinese authorities to be a senior religious figure although he has not been a monk or practiced as a religious teacher for some years and has a very secular reputation in Lhasa. His son is serving a prison sentence in Lhasa for murder, although there are unconfirmed reports that he may have been released shortly before this speech was made. Phagpalha is a lama of "inner Hutuktu" rank, i.e. he comes from a line of reincarnations entitled in theory to act as regents in Tibet. It should be noted, however, that even *A Golden Bridge...* attacks mainly the "Dalai clique," referring to "the Dalai" only in the section on religion. Even the vitriolic attack on the Dalai Lama published in *Tibet Daily* on March 10, 1995, which initiated the anti-Dalai Lama campaign, used the term "Dalai" only fifteen times, referring to the Dalai clique fifty-three times.

The Third Forum had instructed that a campaign be launched to "expose the fact that Dalai is using the mask of religion to cover up his political features," but this was a critique of his politics, not of his religious standing. It is true that they had gone on to accuse him of blasphemy and to point out that he was the leader of only one of the four main Buddhist schools. But those statements were rhetorical warnings given by politicians which were not repeated in speeches by religious figures. Most significantly, they were not incorporated in the practical implementation of the campaign, which, despite its rhetoric, had asked monks and nuns only to "politically draw a clear line of demarcation with the Dalai clique," a specific avoidance of a direct challenge to his religious authority. The new slogans introduced at this time by Phagpalha and other figures were more ambitious: they called for the Dalai Lama's influence to be totally removed from religious as well as political areas. Similar language appeared in other speeches that week and subsequently, under the general rubric "eliminate his influence in all areas":

> The Dalai's behavior has not only run counter to the fundamental interests of the people of the whole country, including the people of Tibet, but also runs counter to the dignified and deeply felt religious rituals of Buddhism. ... Therefore, what the Dalai has done is not for love of Tibet and love of religion as he has advertised; but, on the contrary, is an out-and-out calamity for Tibet and religion. Only by adopting a clear-cut stand in waging a struggle against the Dalai clique to totally wipe out his influence can Tibet enjoy long-term stability and can Tibetan Buddhism establish a normal religious order in a better way. [114]

The language of these statements was more aggressive than before and was specifically focused on the religious status of the Dalai Lama. He was described as "the biggest obstacle to the establishment of a normal order for Tibetan Buddhism," and Chadrel Rinpoche and his supporters were described several times that week as "the scum of this holy place of Buddhism," a reference to Tashilhunpo, or as

---

[114] "Warmly greeting the succession of the 10th Panchen," a commentator's article in the *People's Daily*, November 30, 1995. The article was carried by Xinhua the same day in full and in a briefer version the day before.

simply "the scum of Buddhism."[115] An editorial in the *Tibet Daily* celebrating the selection ceremony announced that the "broad masses" had already "eliminated his influence in all aspects."[116] These statements indicated the launching of both a public version of the denunciation campaign against Chadrel Rinpoche and a revised version of the anti-Dalai Lama campaign, originally launched in January 1995, which this time aimed to remove him altogether from Tibetan Buddhism. On December 11, it was announced that the Dalai Lama was "no longer a religious leader."[117]

At the same time a revised position on religious belief was emerging, with the Chinese authorities suggesting that only supporters of the state have the right to be religious believers:

> In the history of China and in all the countries of the world that value their own independence and dignity, religious belief and patriotism have always been unified. A qualified religious believer should, first of all, be a patriot. Any legitimate religion invariably makes patriotism the primary requirement for believers. One can talk about love of religion only if one is a patriot. A person who is unpatriotic and has even rebelled against the country not only cannot be forgiven by the country but also cannot be tolerated by religion.[118]

There was an implicit reminder in this position, written on the day that the new Panchen Lama was chosen, that religious freedoms in Chinese law were contingent and could be withdrawn: "If [the Dalai Lama's] words are followed, Tibetan Buddhism will be led onto a path of going against the interests of the people and

---

[115] Questions 13 and 54 in "Questions and answers regarding the reincarnated child of the 10th Panchen," *Tibet Daily*, November 10, 1995; FBIS, November 30, 1995 and SWB, November 28, 1995.

[116] "Warmly greet the complete success of the grand Buddhist event of reincarnation of the 10th Panchen Lama," *Tibet Daily*, November 30, 1995; SWB, December 20, 1995.

[117] Li Bing, "Dalai is a tool of hostile forces in the West," *Tibet Daily* (Chinese language edition), Lhasa, December 11, 1995, p.2.

[118] *People's Daily*, November 30, 1995.

the laws of the country, thereby endangering its due position and future in Chinese society," said Xinhua on December 2.[119]

Assessing the Year to January 1996

The complex evolution of security policy in 1995 was a result of the confluence of the Third Forum operations with the Panchen Lama dispute. The Dalai Lama's recognition of the child in May 1995 provided opportunities for the policies of the Third Forum to be implemented with greater speed and with less diffidence. By the end of 1995, as the responses of the authorities to both the Third Forum and the Dalai Lama's May announcement unfolded, they revealed the existence of three increasingly aggressive policy objectives, besides those already in motion from the year before: one was to destroy the religious standing of the Dalai Lama, another was to use the denunciation of Chadrel Rinpoche to assess the patriotism of all senior figures in Tibetan society, including religious leaders, and a third was to make the freedom of religious belief contingent on political loyalty.

But in looking at the pattern of policy formation, which is the main part of what is accessible to outside observers, it is easy to forget the situation on the ground, which offers the only accurate indicators of the extent of policy implementation. Since so little information is available about whether denunciation meetings are being carried out across the region, as the policy documents suggest, we have to turn to the evidence suggested by the reports of arrests and detentions. These are discussed in detail in the following section.

In assessing the situation on the ground in 1995, one other report should be considered. Just before the denunciation campaign began in Tashilhunpo in June 1995, the garrison at Shigatse was reinforced, reportedly by 5,000 or more troops. There were already four military camps in or around the city, and a new one was set up to accommodate the reinforcements; it was set up with some speed, with the soldiers still sleeping under canvas in July, directly beside the western wall of Tashilhunpo monastery. This was followed by a marked increase in military profile and in security checks in the town during the June campaign. Some sources say that, in the build-up to the campaign in Shigatse, control of the garrison was shifted to the civilian leaders of the TAR government and its Congress, Gyaltsen Norbu and Ragdi, both of them Tibetans. Such a move could have been designed to implicate them in any decision to deploy the troops. Shigatse had been the base for the PLA's campaign against the Tibetan guerrillas in the 1960s, but the garrison had been greatly reduced in 1975, by which time the U.S. had ceased funding the guerrillas and the PLA had required more troops on the Xinjiang border with the

---

[119] Xinhua, SWB, December 2, 1995.

Soviet Union.[120] The 1995 decision to increase the military garrison to suppress potential internal unrest had historic implications for the Chinese leadership, since Shigatse had remained free from disturbances throughout the 1980s. Overnight it had become a potential source of major unrest, a factor that was acknowledged by the leaders themselves:

> This year has been an exceptional year for Xigaze [Shigatse] city. The all-out efforts by the Dalai clique to block and sabotage efforts to search and confirm the reincarnation of a Tibetan boy as the Panchen Lama have made, for a while, Xigaze a focus of anti-splittism struggle.[121]

As far as we know the soldiers were not required to go into action to support the security forces in Shigatse during the 1995 campaign, and the street patrols and arrests were carried out by members of the People's Armed Police. But the military build-up serves as a reminder that the relatively small indicators of security activity which become known to international observers are only the visible part of a much larger operation which is fundamentally a military exercise and which remains the basis of security operations in Tibet today, much as it was when the Chinese army arrived in Tibet forty years ago. The character of security operations in Tibet has a civilian profile, and, as a result of the Comprehensive Management campaigns from 1990 and the Third Forum decisions from 1994, the involvement of civilian officials in security has been greatly increased. But the rapid deployment of the military in Shigatse in June 1995 is a reminder that the civilian profile of security operations in Tibet remains essentially a cosmetic elaboration of the military presence there.

---

[120] Military operations in this sector of Tibet relating to India, which led to open conflict in 1987, are run from Nyingtri or Bayi in Kongpo-Nyingtri (Linzhi).

[121] *Tibet Daily*, October 13, 1995; SWB, November 7, 1995. An editorial in the *Tibet Daily* three days later gave more detail of the political crisis in Shigatse in mid-1995. According to a summary published by FBIS, the editorial described Shigatse as having been in the midst of a difficult anti-splittist struggle and as having been on the leading edge of the anti-splittist struggle. The article said that the city had not been disrupted but had exhibited social stability and public contentment. See *Tibet Daily*, October 16, 1995; FBIS, November 29, 1995.

VII. THE THIRD FORUM AND SECURITY POLICY

The impact of the Third Forum on dissent must be seen in the light of security policy in Tibet more generally. The history of security in the region is complicated. There has been a marked drop in the level of force used by the authorities since 1987—the practice of arbitrary executions and the "revolving-door" strategy of mass arrests, for example, both ceased when the military replaced the People's Armed Police as the lead agency in security operations in Tibetan towns in March 1989: it was, paradoxically, the military which provided the period of calm that enabled the authorities to introduce a less brutal policing system. During the thirteen months of martial law that followed the arrival of the army, security policy was shifted from what was called a "passive" mode, which in the west would be called reactive, to an "active" mode, which we would call pro-active. At its simplest this system, known as the "Comprehensive Management of Public Security," meant developing networks of informants who could indicate likely outbreaks of unrest before they happened, rather than using lethal force to suppress incidents once they had emerged.[122]

Incidents involving extensive use of force did of course take place between 1990 and 1994, but special forces, known as *fang bao* ("rebellion suppression") units with training in riot control methods had been set up in Lhasa to deal with urban unrest and at least in theory should have been able to respond with more discipline and competence than the People's Armed Police units had done in the late 1980s. [123] But in policy terms, the security forces in Tibet were responding in those years on an *ad hoc* basis to instances of unrest: there was no unified implementation of a policy imposed by the leadership and operative on all areas of government, and the repression (as distinct from the monitoring) of the

---

[122] See note 48 above.

[123] We do not know in which incidents one or other of the *fang bao* units were deployed. Almost certainly it was a *fang bao* unit which was used to quell the food prices protest of May 1993. Photographs show the units in action, with relatively sophisticated riot helmets and shields. Other photographs taken by tourists, however, show that many of the tear gas cartridges were fired by plainclothes policemen, who must have been from some other unit. In any case the use of tear gas equipment was disastrous: at least one child and a man were seriously injured by shrapnel from the tear gas cartridges, which were cast off material bought from the former Yugoslavia, and a policeman was killed in his car when a tear gas grenade exploded in his hand.

71

independence movement before 1994 was a responsibility which was in effect confined to and fought over by the various local security forces. This observation is supported by the erratic character of the implementation of security policies in Tibet before 1994. For example, the constant bargaining between the administration and the police over the admission of foreign tourists to the area has led to continuing uncertainty as to whether foreigners can travel in Tibet or not, with the result that even individual travelers, let alone group tourists, have never been totally excluded from Tibet at any time in this period. In essence, security policy in Tibet before 1994 had been fragmented by the rivalry between the different agencies involved, with some fighting to assert their own superiority in suppressing the independence movement, and others aiming to enhance the prospects of economic development in the region.[124]

The Comprehensive Management scheme in the early 1990s was essentially an attempt to remotivate managers and staff in the Chinese administration to act as informants so that they would continue to provide information to aid the security services. One of the objectives that the Third Forum appears to have attempted in Tibet was to add to this strategy the use of repressive mechanisms by that same corps of administrators, so that they would shift from being passive informants or supporters of the security forces to being active enforcers of repressive policies in their own right.

The Third Forum security policies also included an increase in aggressive activities of a certain kind, particularly in the countryside, where complete containment is possible—for example, the use of paramilitary forces in raids on rural monasteries to carry out arrests or searches. The Nemo and Kyimshi incidents in 1993 had shown that the security forces knew how to seal off an area with speed, but the rapid deployment of road checks and armed patrols in Shigatse and the closing of the town to tourists after the Dalai Lama's recognition of the new Panchen Lama in May 1995 suggested that in special circumstances the security forces could be prepared to even cut towns off from the outside world.

In urban areas, however, it is clear that in general more subtle security techniques were introduced in 1995. The most significant of these was the use of "recurrent disappearance." This is the simple device of detaining suspects repeatedly for short periods, often about two days each week. They are in long

---

[124] The most detailed account of rivalry within the security forces was given by Tang Daxian, a journalist who worked in Lhasa, who claimed that the intelligence networks of the various agencies were spying on each other. See Tang Daxian, "Lhasa under the Bayonet - Events in Lhasa March 2nd-10th 1989," published in abridged form in the *Observer* (London), August 12, 1990.

enough to be effectively interrogated but are often sufficiently intimidated when they come out that they refrain from informing anyone about their detention, in case they are punished further. This technique is typically used for people who are otherwise likely to be able to communicate news to the outside world, usually lay people who are seen as possible organizers or conduits for information, and again it is a technique which interrogators use either to intimidate or to persuade people to become informers. It is associated inevitably with the use of more sophisticated torture techniques: the use of recurrent disappearance means that torture should leave no visible traces. It is thus not surprising that there is an increase in use of such methods as exposure to extremes of temperature, making people stand in cold water, or making them sit in awkward positions for long periods.

The increased pattern of harassment and surveillance of ordinary citizens suggests that there was an increased role for the elite State Security Bureau in the policing of Tibetan dissent; the bureau is more often identified with such strategies as developing informers rather than imprisoning suspects. The 1994 State Security laws had specified for the first time that "individual foreigners" can qualify as "participants or major suspects who join in activities that hamper state security."[125] In 1995, the security forces accordingly improved their surveillance of foreigners and were able to identify and search on departure the four Tibetan-speaking foreign tourists who were carrying letters from Tibetans. Even the search procedures became more sophisticated: by mid-1995 the security forces at Lhasa airport had been able to reduce the time they needed to search a foreign suspect, including filming and documenting the search and getting signed confessions from the tourist, from five days to less than an hour.

The effort put into intercepting outgoing mail was a reflection of the growing concern of the authorities over the flow of information both in and out of Tibet, evident from the new legislation on state secrets and the efforts to intercept literature being sent into Tibet by the exiles.[126] This was paralleled by efforts to

---

[125] "Rules for the Implementation of the State Security Law," Article 8, point 6, June 4, 1994.

[126] This was in line with the instructions in the fourth section of Ragdi's speech on necessary measures to be implemented, where it followed the instructions concerning following religion, cadres, and education. The section began, "(4) Check up on counterrevolutionary documents and materials of publicity with great determination" and explained, "In recent years some people were singing counterrevolutionary songs in public. Some people were selling Dalai photographs and badges. Some people bring from abroad counterrevolutionary published materials and materials like cassettes and tapes and they

limit the flow of people across the borders by increasing patrols and imposing stiffer punishment for asylum seekers, as the Third Forum had ordered.[127] Whether the effect of these measures was direct or merely intimidatory, Tibet became in the period after the Third Forum a more closed society, in which the passing of officially unacceptable information became increasingly dangerous.

The security policies of the Third Forum seem to have been based on an assumption about security which also showed increasing sophistication, going well beyond the reliance on force that characterized the 1980s. This assumption is that identifying potential dissidents is as effective a means of control as detaining them, perhaps in part because one of its effects is to intimidate potential dissenters. All the other Third Forum policies appear to be derived from this approach to security. The strategy of identifying disloyal cadres was specifically of this kind, but many of the other measures so far enacted are essentially variants of the same approach. The shift in educational priorities, for example, implied that those who had acquired cultural or scientific knowledge should be vetted to check that they were also "socialist constructors," and the 1993 survey identified parents whose children were in school in India. The early stages of the religion policy singled out government employees who had Dalai Lama photographs or religious objects in their offices or homes and isolated any monks or nuns who would not give declarations separating themselves from the Tibetan exiles. The anti-Dalai Lama campaign and its derivatives—the campaign against his identification of the Panchen Lama and the denunciation campaign against Chadrel Rinpoche—similarly established a series of meetings at which participants were required to give statements supporting the government line. Even the economic orthodoxy established by the Third Forum is of this kind: any deviation from

---

record them or make copies to distribute in great numbers. The Public Security Bureau, Commercial and Cultural Departments, etc., should check up on these things seriously, and confiscate them as soon as they appear, without any hesitation. They should cancel the license and fine those who sell these things. Those who encourage teenagers to sing counterrevolutionary songs should be punished severely according to the law. Those who make, hang up and distribute counterrevolutionary publications, and those who shout counterrevolutionary slogans should be punished severely in time, according to the relevant stipulations in the law. We must strike them back through mass media and reinforce this struggle in the ideological field." Ragdi's Speech to the TAR Party Committee, Document No.5, September 5, 1994.

[127] "By putting more effort into construction along the borders and by tightening control along the borders, we must block the way for Dalai intruders to sneak into our region." Document No.5, September 5, 1994.

commitment to its policy of high-speed reforms and sinicization of the economy is also interpreted as a sign of opposition to the Party, since the policy is directly associated with Deng Xiaoping.[128]

Thus these measures, in setting up various mechanisms to justify house searches, surveys, and denunciation meetings of different kinds, when taken in total represent a nexus of demands and investigations from which any defaulting would serve to identify potential dissidents. Although it is not yet clear if a purge will take place, the identification of potential targets must now be well advanced.

The result of the Third Forum appears to have been a new security policy designed not necessarily to lead to more incidents involving force by the authorities, such as shootings or beatings in pre-1990 style, but to establish a broad sweep of repressive measures across the entire spectrum of policy implementation, many of which would be carried out by other organs of the administrations besides the security agencies. This is also what the study of events in 1995 detects, in such measures as the setting up of temple registration officials and the survey of officials' children being educated abroad: the emergence of a range of measures in areas of the administration which support or reinforce the activities of the security services, with the objective of isolating and eliminating dissident activity.

---

[128] This is a consequence of the April-June 1992 debate on Deng's "Spring Tide" in which the leaders in Tibet who dissented from supporting the reforms were labeled leftists by Chen Kuiyuan and others. There has been no public expression of disagreement with the Dengist reform policy in Tibet since then, as far as we know, and the Third Forum documents were able to take acceptance of the economic reform theory as read, without having to threaten repercussions for dissent in that area.

VIII. CONCLUSIONS

Popular dissent and disaffection has increased in Tibet during the 1990s, despite the imposition of draconian security measures intended to defeat it. The discernible changes in Chinese policy in Tibet suggest a readiness to abandon the relatively benign allowances of the 1980s, such as the tolerance of religious practice and other expressions of ethnic identity within a "patriotic" context, where they might threaten or limit security operations. Until the Third Forum, makers of security policy had been required to make allowances for these concessional policies in drawing up their plans; in 1994, given their failure to defuse the protest movement in Tibet, these concessions were effectively withdrawn as fundamental aspects of Chinese policy in Tibet. The period 1994-1995 saw the vigorous implementation of, on the one hand, economic and immigration policies and, on the other hand, restrictions on religious activity and on education which override the implied concessions of Tibet's autonomous status. The new policies, which in part aimed at identifying and isolating nationalist Tibetan cadres, amount to a significant erosion of the policies established in the liberalization era.

This new readiness by the central government to discard or at least to downgrade the remaining restraints on assimilationist policy objectives in Tibet appears in part to have been facilitated by the failure in early 1994 of the international community and particularly the U.S. to sustain pressure on China concerning human rights issues.

As these new policies start to take hold more people, and more different kinds of people and institutions, are being drawn into opposing the state, sometimes as a result of a Chinese refusal to accept popular criticism rather than as a result of the authorities' initial policy objectives. Rural disaffection and protest has spread as the effects of fast-paced economic development—inflation, resource extraction, less controlled immigration—begin to be felt in the countryside, as more restrictions are imposed on rural monasteries and as local officials are disempowered or replaced, often by Chinese officials. China's long-standing claim that Tibetan dissent is the work of a small number of extremists manipulated by foreign interests is increasingly untenable. In its drive to crush dissent, the Chinese state is widening the range of discontent, increasingly criminalizing the process of political criticism, and imprisoning more ordinary Tibetans than at any time since the late 1980s.

76

PART 2:
EXAMPLES OF COERCIVE PRACTICES

The most evident impact of the change in Chinese policy on Tibet has been on the nature and scope of political imprisonment, the focus of much of this section. Most of those arrests involve violations of freedom of expression, assembly, and association. But other forms of human rights violations have continued or intensified, including torture, compulsory labor, and restrictions on freedom of religion. Illustrative cases of these violations are included in the following section. A statistical summary of prisoner data is attached as Appendix A, and cases of all known arrests and prison-related deaths in 1995 are listed, with an index, as Appendix B.

I. POLITICAL IMPRISONMENT IN TIBET, 1994-1995

The easing of international pressure, the policy decisions of the Third Forum, and the repercussions of the Panchen Lama dispute resulted in a new and harsher security environment in Tibet. That in turn has resulted in more political arrests. In March 1996, TIN and Human Rights Watch/Asia completed a study of all available primary material concerning political arrests and detentions in Tibet. The material was assessed, sorted and checked and then entered into a database, producing a list of the names and other available details of each known political prisoner. The full list of over 1,200 individual cases will be published later in the year, but summary statistical information, together with analysis of the data, is included here.

This section explains how to read the data on prisoners presented below and looks in more detail at what they indicate. As collecting information from Tibet has become more difficult in the last two years, the figures presented here represent a partial picture of the situation; there are certainly more political detainees in Tibet whose identities have never been confirmed by independent observers and more incidents of unrest, especially in remote areas, which have never been recorded.[129] It should also be stressed that the figures for 1994 and 1995 given here are incomplete, as there seems to be a delay of about eighteen months or two years

---

[129] "Since 1989, the Dalai has instigated more than 120 large and small disturbances, constantly spreading splittist activities to rural and pastoral areas, and to party and government organizations," Li Bing, *Tibet Daily*, December 11, 1995. TIN had reported 116 confirmed incidents and received unconfirmed reports of forty others in this period.

before representative figures can be arrived at. In mid-1995 when much of the research for this report was compiled, most of the incoming information concerned arrests which had taken place in 1993 but which had not previously been reported. In addition, the figures so far received for 1995 show an upward trend in political detentions.

The term "political detainee" or "political prisoner" used here is not accepted by the Chinese authorities, who maintain that no one can be detained solely on account of their views or opinions.[130] However this statement is not wholly consistent with Chinese legislation: crimes of counterrevolution — with which virtually all the tried prisoners listed here have been charged — are defined in Chapter 1 of the Chinese Criminal Code (1980) as "all acts endangering the PRC committed with the goal of overthrowing the political power of the dictatorship of the proletariat and the socialist system" (Article 90). This includes plotting to "dismember the state" (Article 92) and "inciting the masses to resist or sabotage the implementation of the state's laws or decrees" (Article 102, Paragraph 1). As noted elsewhere, the updating of State Security Laws and Public Security Laws in 1993-4 has strengthened the legal grounds of detention for offenses such as "spreading rumors" and "stealing state secrets,"[131] and in March 1995 the authorities

---

[130] "In China, ideas alone in the absence of action which violates the criminal law, do not constitute a crime. Nobody will be sentenced to punishment merely because he holds dissenting political views. So-called political prisoners do not exist in China." *Human Rights in China*, (Beijing: Information Office of the State Council of the PRC, November 1991), Section IV part 4, p.35.

[131] In December 1992 China's Ministers of State Security and Public Security called for a new law against leaking of information by "hostile foreign forces" (Xinhua, December 12, 1992). The State Security Law of the PRC was adopted by the Thirtieth Session of the Seventh NPC Standing Committee on February 22, 1993. This reaffirmed the "Supplementary Provisions of the Standing Committee of the NPC relating to Punishment for the Offense of Disclosing State Secrets," passed on September 5, 1988, which were supplementary to the 1988 Law on Guarding State Secrets. In an editorial on October 11, 1993, the *People's Daily* reported a stepping up of the nation-wide campaign against leaking state secrets. The "Rules for the Implementation of the State Security Law" were adopted by the State Council on May 10 and were promulgated for implementation by State Council Decree No 157 on June 4, 1994, the anniversary of the crushing of the pro-democracy movement in 1989.

introduced specific adaptations of these instructions for Tibet.[132] Examination of recent trial documents from Tibet even before this date shows that, for example, privately compiled lists of prisoners are considered "state secrets" [133] and that, at least in cases heard by administrative detention committees, suggesting people wear traditional Tibetan clothes can be considered "inciting the masses ... with an intention to split the motherland."[134] Prisoners accused of "counterrevolutionary offenses" in Tibet, who in almost all cases have neither used nor threatened to use violence, can therefore be reasonably described as political prisoners. So far eighteen prisoners out of the more than 1,000 cases described by Tibetans as political detentions have been involved in acts of violence. A study of 879 of the cases assembled for this report, where sufficient information was available to describe the circumstances leading to arrest, shows that the two largest categories of offense are demonstrating and distributing leaflets. Nearly ten percent of the detainees, however, have been detained for offenses having to do with communicating news or information either within Tibet or to the outside world.

---

[132] In a Tibet TV interview on March 27, 1995, Li Hui, deputy director of the TAR State Security Department, led a drive to promote the State Security regulations, according to SWB, April 1, 1995. The rules were "necessary to counter 'splittism,'" Li said. Among the activities listed as "restricted" under the rules are those to "fabricate and distort facts or publish or distribute untrue writings to hamper state security"; "hamper state security under the pretext of religion"; and "create national disputes or stir up national splittism to hamper state security." A month earlier Li Hui had announced that more than 20,000 booklets on the law had been distributed in the TAR although he noted that "a few ... at some units handling external relations have... gone so far as to create obstructions" to training staff in the new law (SWB, March 7, 1995).

[133] See, for example, the case of Jampa Ngodrup, a doctor sentenced to thirteen years for "leaking state secrets," namely a list of detainees. Lhasa Intermediate Court Sentencing Document 40 (1990), December 25, 1990; TIN Ref 3(ZF).

[134] Dorje Wangdu was given a three-year sentence for this offense, according to an administrative order issued by a municipal "re-education-through-labor" committee. The order is No. 910085 of the Management Committee of the Lhasa Municipal Government for Re-education-through-Labor, dated September 26, 1992, TIN Doc 9(ZQ). See "'Counterrevolutionary' Plan to Wear Tibetan Clothes," TIN News Update, February 20, 1992.

2.1 Reasons for Arrest

Estimates of the numbers of people arrested for different offenses, according to unofficial reports concerning 879 cases. Only the most recent and most prominent offense is listed for each case, and second offenses, such as singing songs in prison, are not included in this list. The official reasons given for arrest vary greatly from the reasons given by the prisoners or their families and are not given here.

	Number of Arrests	Percentage of Total Arrests
Protest:	**743**	**(84.53%)**
Demonstrating	574	65.3%
Writing, distributing leaflets	136	15.5%
Investigated for unspecified		
Pro-independence activity	16	2.0%
Possession of Tibetan flags, badges	7	0.8%
Being in an independence group	5	0.6%
Incitement	5	0.6%
(e.g. encouraging others to sing dissident songs)		
Communication:	**71**	**(8.08%)**
Dalai Lama links	29	3.3%
(e.g. spying, communicating or		
having links with the "Dalai clique")		
Possessing pro-independence	22	2.5%
literature or cassettes		
Foreign contact	12	1.4%
(e.g. talking to journalists or exiled Tibetans, passing		
secrets abroad, other than to the Dalai clique)		
Trying to escape or helping people to escape	8	0.9%
Social Protest:	**41**	**(4.47%)**
Social protests	41	4.7%
(protests about taxes, price rises, migrants		
or issues other than independence)		
Violence:	**18**	**(2.05%)**
Violence during a protest	10	1.1%
Allegedly killing policeman	8	0.9%
Others	6	0.7%
Total	879	

Prisons and Detention Centers

The available data reflect, albeit partially, the situation in Lhasa and central Tibet; references to political detentions in areas of ethnic Tibet outside the TAR are largely fortuitous due to the difficulty of collecting and confirming information. Prisons such as Minyag and Kangding in Sichuan province and Xining and Hainan in Qinghai are not sufficiently known about to be accurately represented here; there are also unconfirmed reports that 300 Tibetans are held in labor camps in Xinjiang, although it is not known if these are political prisoners. Even within the TAR, information about where prisoners are being held is incomplete: the place of detention, for example, of 136 of the 604 listed as detained in August 1995 is not known. Of the 196 detained in 1995 and still in custody at the time of writing, the whereabouts of 111 are still unknown.

Our knowledge about the detention facilities in the TAR is relatively complete, at least in the area around Lhasa. Generally, the facilities can be divided into three main categories, which to some extent mirror the procedure applied to detainees. When they are first detained by the Public Security Bureau, prisoners are put in a police lock-up or detention center and held without charge. Their cases are then investigated by the procuracy; this can take three months or longer. Then the prisoner is either:

• released without charge

• sentenced without trial to a *laojiao* (re-education-through-labor center), usually for two or three years, extendable to four years by law, apparently four and a half years in practice in some cases.

• "arrested," i.e. charged with an offense and sent for trial. After the court sentences the prisoner, he or she is then transferred to either a regular prison or a *laogai* (reform-through-labor center) to serve his or her sentence. Over 98 percent of prisoners in China sent for trial are found guilty; the conviction rate in Tibet appears to be higher. Thus the custodial institutions in Tibet can be divided accordingly:

1. Detention Centers (Chinese: *kanshousuo*)

These comprise a variety of institutions where prisoners are held without charge and subject to investigation prior to either judicial or administrative sentencing or release. Gutsa is the detention center for Lhasa prefecture[135] with 138 people listed as detained there in August 1995 for political offenses, seventy of them arrested that year. It is also believed to include a section for detainees held under the "shelter and investigation" regulations (Chinese: *shourong shencha*). This is a practice which in mainland China allows public security departments to hold minor offenders for three months without trial, but in the Tibetan context the distinction between prisoners held under these regulations and in other forms of detention remains to be clarified. Reports from 1990-91 suggest that there was in theory a facility for holding juvenile prisoners at Gutsa, although it is not clear that there has ever been a separate section for this purpose and the distinction seems to have lapsed in 1992. Many of the political detainees at Gutsa were transferred to the newly rebuilt re-education-through-labor center at Trisam in 1992.

Seitru is the detention center for the TAR — that is, it is a regional-level institution — and is located in the Sangyip complex in the northeast suburbs of Lhasa. It is thought to be here that people suspected of more serious political crimes, particularly civilian activists accused of organizing protests or collecting sensitive information, are brought for interrogation, possibly under the unstated supervision of the State Security Bureau. This notion is partly confirmed by the data, which show that about twenty civilians arrested in May and June 1993 during a series of house raids in Lhasa were brought to Seitru and that most were subsequently released without charge after some months; the data also show that nine of the fifteen known to be currently detained there were arrested or rearrested in similar circumstances the following year.

Other prisons in this category include the county-level jails where local protestors are held before being handed over to the prefectural or the Lhasa authorities, and which seem to be in increasing use as protest spreads in rural areas.

---

[135] Technically there is no such place as Lhasa prefecture: (Chinese: *Lasa shi*), literally "Lhasa city" or "Lhasa municipality," to refer to the entire prefecture-sized area administered by Lhasa, most of which is remote rural villages and grazing lands. The term prefecture is used here to clarify the distinction between this largely rural area, which is at the same administrative level as a prefecture, and the urban area of Lhasa, for which the Chinese have no precise term. The word *chengguanqu* is frequently used by the Chinese to describe the metropolitan or inner city area of Lhasa, but even this includes farming communities around the city. Roughly 160,000 of the 400,000 people living in Lhasa prefecture (*Lasa shi*) reside in the urban area, according to 1990 statistics.

County jails in such towns as Taktse, Toelung, Phenpo Lhundrup and Lhokha Gongkar have joined the list of holding centers for Tibetan dissidents; most notable of all is the local jail at Meldrogongkar where thirteen are thought to have been held in connection with a series of nationalist protests by farmers in the nearby Gyama valley over the last three years. As far as we know, these prisoners may still be held in Meldrogongkar, suggesting that at least part of the detention center or a separate local facility is used as a re-education-through-labor center.

In addition, there are at least ten recorded cases of informal detention of suspects in local police stations.[136] There are reported to be other detention centers in occasional use, such as a prison-type compound within the PAP headquarters in Lhasa where the well-known prisoner Tseten Norgye was detained and tortured in 1989, and a facility operated by the State Security Bureau near Drapchi Lamo in north Lhasa. Little is known about these institutions.

2. Re-education-through-labor centers (Chinese: *laojiao*)

These centers are for prisoners sentenced without trial by quasi-judicial government committees. Sentences can be for periods of three years, extendable to four years. There are three such centers in Lhasa: Yizhidui (Section No.1, often written as Yitridu by Tibetans) and Wuzhidui (Section No.5, often written as Outridu), both parts of the Sangyip complex near Drapchi, and the recently established center known as Trisam in Toelung county, ten kilometers west of the city.

Yizhidui may have been adapted from a normal re-education-through-labor center for use as a "forced job placement center," a semi-custodial facility for the employment of discharged prisoners on various pretexts, but it is thought to have at least one current political detainee. Wuzhidui was used to detain many of those arrested during the 1989 uprising but is almost empty of political prisoners today; most were transferred to the new facility at Trisam in 1992. Only fourteen political prisoners are listed as still detained at Trisam — a figure representing lack of confirmed data rather than absence of political prisoners there, since this place seems, if anything, to specialize in political prisoners and may have been built in 1992 specifically in response to the increase in their number. Gutsa prison, nominally a detention center, is believed to incorporate sections which are used as re-education-through-labor centers.

---

[136] See, for example, the case of Damchoe Pemo in May 1993. She is believed to have been abused while in police custody in a Lhasa police station before being moved to the TAR detention center at Seitru.

It seems likely that the six other prefecture-level detention facilities in the TAR also fall into the category of re-education-through-labor centers, although this is unconfirmed. Like Gutsa, they probably also have sections which are used as *kanshousuo* while detainees are being investigated. For example, we know of seventeen political detainees currently held at the center in Tsethang and three in the Chamdo facility; both places seem to be holding long-term detainees arrested in connection with local protests.

3. Prisons (Chinese: *jianyu*)

Chinese authorities acknowledge one prison in Tibet, the TAR Prison No.1 known as Drapchi, after the neighborhood in Lhasa where it is located. Officially, Drapchi is for judicially-sentenced prisoners only. While Chinese authorities have told visitors that the men detained there are those considered "hard-core," serving five years or more, the data show that many prisoners there in fact are serving lighter sentences. All women who have been sentenced judicially in political cases, regardless of the length of their sentences, are sent to Drapchi. There may be a labor camp or camps attached to Drapchi prison.

4. Reform-through-labor centers (Chinese: *laogai*)

These also house prisoners serving judicial sentences. Chinese authorities have said that *laogai* are for male prisoners serving sentences of less than five years. There are officially two *laogai* in the TAR: one is in Lhasa (until the early 1980s part of the Sangyip complex but now believed to be incorporated as part of Drapchi prison), and the Chinese government has recently acknowledged the existence of a second one in or near the town of Tramo, in Powo county, Kongpo-Nyingtri in southeastern Tibet, 500 kilometers east of Lhasa. Powo Tramo, as it is known, is believed to include a number of subsidiary establishments such as Powo Zhungar.[137]

Of the 610 political prisoners listed as being currently in detention, 274 are held in Drapchi, representing 45 percent of the known current political prisoners in Tibet. The number of Drapchi inmates has grown steadily over the last five years and is still growing: most of those detained during 1994-5 have not yet been moved to Drapchi as they have yet to pass through the judicial process. Only nineteen of the 1,276 total cases reported in the study, including those who have been released, are known to have been sent to Powo Tramo, of whom eleven are still held there.

---

[137] Powo Tramo is always referred to by Tibetans as being in Kongpo-Nyingtri, but in fact it lies within the administrative area of Chamdo prefecture, just outside Linzhi prefecture, which is the modern Chinese equivalent of Kongpo-Nyingtri.

The increase in the political prisoner population of Drapchi is the only sound statistic available for strict comparisons, because the availability of figures for the other detention facilities varies from year to year. More or less exact figures for the number of political prisoners at Drapchi, however, have been known from unofficial sources since 1990, when monitoring began and when there were seventy-seven male political prisoners at the prison; it was later learned that by 1991 there were also twenty-three female political prisoners.[138] The figures compiled for this report show an increase of 270 percent over the five years from 1990.

Table 2.2 Political Prisoners in Drapchi

This table shows the number of political prisoners held at Drapchi in different years, according to information made known to TIN between 1990 and January 1996. The Drapchi figures show a number close to the real number of political prisoners held in the prison at each time. The 1994 total for Drapchi includes ten prisoners who are on conditional release, e.g. on medical parole but due to be returned to prison when they recover from their illnesses or if they break their parole terms. Complete figures are not available for the other prisons but the second row shows the total number of prisoners reported in custody each year. The table shows the increase in political prisoners in Drapchi and the much larger increase in prisoners held elsewhere.

Date	09/90	09/91	08/92	08/93	02/94	1/96
Drapchi Prisoners	100	126	198	229	255	274
Total Known Prisoners	100	240	—	450	—	610

[138]   Tibet Information Network, "Drapchi Prison List Shows 14 Year Old Imprisoned," *TIN News Update*, November 5, 1990, and "Convicted Women Political Prisoners in Tibet," February 12, 1992.

Table 2.3 Main Detention Facilities in the TAR

Name in Tibetan	Alternative name	Title in pinyin or probable official name	Type
1) Drapchi*	Dashi	Di yi jianyu ("No.1 Prison") TAR Prison No.1	Prison/*laogai?*

A prison and possibly a *laogai* (reform-through-labor center).

| 2) Sangyip* | Sangyik | PAP No.1 Branch | *Laojiao* |

Sangyip is the term variously used to describe either (a) the complex of buildings including several prisons listed here as (2), (3), (4) and (5), or as (b) Yitridu, one of the prisons within that complex (see below)

| 3) Yitridu | Sangyip | Di yi zhidui ("Section No.1") | *Laojiao*/ Forced Job Placement |

The terms Sangyip or more rarely Yitridu are used for a prison within the Sangyip complex or "forced job placement" center (Tibetan: las-mi-ru-khag Chinese: *jiuye*), which is either a laojiao within the Sangyip complex, or the "forced job placement" center where some prisoners have to work after release, in this case repairing motor vehicles. It is probably situated within the compound officially named "The People's Armed Police Automobile Team" or within the group of compounds named officially as the People's Armed Police (PAP) No.1 Branch.

| 4) Seitru | Sitru | Di si chu ("No. 4 Branch") | Detention Center (*kanshousuo*) |

Seitru is the TAR regional detention center within the Sangyip complex for holding prisoners who have not been "arrested" (i.e. they have not been charged). State Security prisoners are believed to be held here.

| 5) Outridu | Authitu | Di wu zhidui ("Section No.5") | *Laojiao* |

Outridu was formerly a *laogai* (reform-through-labor center) but is now a *laojiao* within the Sangyip complex. Most of the political prisoners were moved from here to Trisam in mid-1992, perhaps because of a brief pro-independence protest by the Sangyip prisoners on May 20, 1991.

| 6) Gutsa* | Gurtsa | Di si ke ("No 4. Unit") | Detention Center (*kanshousuo*) |

Gutsa is the detention center for the prefecture of Lhasa. It holds prisoners who are being investigated. They have been neither "arrested" [i.e. charged] or given administrative sentences. In 1990 it was reported to include a section for holding children after investigations were complete, as a kind of juvenile detention center, and may have included a women's re-education-through-labor section.

7) Trisam*   Toelungdechen   —   *Laojiao*
              Toelung Bridge

Trisam is a new *laojiao*, probably for the Lhasa municipality. It was opened in about February 1992 and received many of the political prisoners from Sangyip. The official name is not known.

8) Powo   Bo'o   Laogai No.2   *Laogai*
   Tramo*   Powo Zhungar

Powo Tramo is a prison run by the regional authorities for sentenced long-term prisoners, situated near Kongpo-Nyingtri (Chinese: Linzhi), about 500 km east of Lhasa. Between five and eleven political prisoners are believed to be held there. it has a number of sub-sections in the neighboring area, of which Powo Zhungar is one.

Note: *This is the Tibetan name for the prison, being the name of the village nearest the prison. It is not the official name for the prison, and the Chinese authorities may refuse to recognize it.

Prefectural Detention Centers and *Laojiao*

There are also prisons in the administrative seat of each prefecture. There are six prefectures in the Tibet Autonomous Region besides Lhasa Municipality:

Tibetan:	Chinese	Administrative seat
Shigatse	Rigaze	Shigatse
Nagchu	Naqu	Nagchu
Ngari	Ali	Ngari
Lhokha	Shannan	Tsethang
Kongpoin-Nygtri	Linzhi	Nyingtri or Bayi
Chamdo	Qamdo	Chamdo

These prisons are probably *laojiao* and *kanshoosuo* (detention centers for prisoners who have not been sentenced). There are also prisons at county level, probably for prisoners who have not been sentenced. We know of one in Meldrogongkar county, which is within Lhasa prefecture.

Administration

It is unclear who actually runs prisons in the TAR. Responsibility for the administration of prisons across China was transferred from the Ministry of Public Security to the Ministry of Justice in 1985, with the exception of such establishments as Beijing's Qincheng prison, where major dissidents and other politically sensitive prisoners are detained.[139] The TAR prisons at Drapchi and Powo Tramo were subject to the same exception for some years and were not handed over to the Ministry of Justice until 1992.[140] Effective control of the prisons apparently remains with the public security department because of the political sensitivity of prison work in this region.[141]

According to new prison laws promulgated in December 1994, prisons are supposed to be run by "the State Council's judicial administration authorities," which in effect means the Ministry of Justice. The "management personnel" within each prison are known as "Prison People's Police"; it is not clear if this term includes administrative personnel as well as those who directly manage the prisoners.[142] Any punishment inflicted by these "Prison People's Police" falls under the supervision of officials from the procuracy — that is to say, the procuracy is designated as the authority which can hear complaints about malpractice within the prisons.[143] The law indicates that People's Armed Police (PAP) are in charge of security around the perimeters of prisons and states specifically that the PAP is responsible in the event of "prison armed alerts," such as escape attempts or

---

[139] Asia Watch, *Detained in China and Tibet*, (New York: Human Rights Watch, 1994).

[140] See report by the Austrian Legal Delegation to Tibet, February 1993.

[141] See interview with released prisoner Palden Gyatso in India, May 1994, TIN Ref 4(RB2). Both the prisons under the Public Security Ministry, and the facilities under the Re-education-through-Labor Bureau were transferred to the Ministry of Justice in 1992, although conditions became worse rather than better, according to the interviewee.

[142] "The management personnel in prisons are the people's police," Article 12 of the "The People's Republic Prison Law," FBIS, May 1995, pp. 21-27. It is followed by the "Explanation" given by Minister of Justice Xiao Yang to the National Peoples' Congress (NPC) on October 21, 1994. The law was adopted by the standing committee of the Eighth NPC on December 29, 1994.

[143] "The people's procuratorate exercises supervision according to law over the legality of prison activities in carrying out punishment" (Article 6).

"prisoners committing any other dangerous acts," and indicates that these armed units are under the authority of the Central Military Affairs Commission.

Accounts of released prisoners often allude to an indistinguishable overlap of different departments in the organization of the prison system. The Prison Law defines as prisons those institutions which hold prisoners sentenced in accordance with the criminal law, thus excluding from its remit re-education-through-labor institutions (*laojiao*) and detention centers (*kanshousuo*). The latter are under the authority of the Ministry of Public Security, with the result that in Lhasa, public security officials are in charge both of detention centers such as Gutsa and Seitru, and of the interrogation which is conducted there. This goes against the official insistence on an institutional separation between those responsible for carrying out arrests and investigations, and those responsible for their custodial detention.

Abuse in Prison

Neither the poor conditions in Tibet's prisons nor the abusive treatment of prisoners, including torture, which have been documented in earlier reports, improved in the period 1994-5.[144] Nearly all prisoners arrested for political protest are beaten extensively at the time of arrest and initial detention. Apart from this routine abuse of new detainees, serious physical maltreatment has been recorded in 208 of 1,276 cases documented in the course of research for this report — 16.3 percent of the total. This figure cannot be taken as absolute, since the study was not designed to look at incidents of abuse, and only the most serious known cases were included in this survey. But it is noteworthy that seventy-eight out of the 208 seriously abused prisoners, or 38 percent of the total, are currently detained, and thirty-one of them were detained in the period 1994-1995, suggesting that abuse is an ongoing problem.

Physical injuries are often the result of torture during interrogation or beatings following an infraction of prison rules. The injuries incurred are often compounded by the lack or deprivation of medical care for political prisoners and

---

[144] See for example reports by Physicians for Human Rights (Boston, 1989), Asia Watch, *Human Rights in Tibet, Evading Scrutiny* and *Merciless Repression*; TIN (UK 1990), TIN jointly with Asia Watch (UK/USA 1992), and Amnesty International (UK 1991, 1992 and 1995). Only one report (Amnesty International 1995) has been issued since 1992, and it covered events before 1994.

by the obligation to fulfil manual labor quotas.[145] Of the thirteen cases from the data of reported deaths in custody, or deaths shortly after release from custody, four occurred in the period 1994-1995; all of these seemed to be the result of physical abuse compounded by lack of medical care. It must be noted that these figures only represent available information on the maltreatment of political prisoners, rather than the actual extent of such treatment, details of which often emerge only after the victims or their fellow prisoners are released or escape from Tibet.

Sentences

The available data on sentencing are incomplete, and virtually none of them pertain to 1994-1995, since details of trials and sentences for this generation of detainees remain largely unknown. They do show, however, that the majority of sentences fall in the three- to five-year range. That range accounts for twenty-three of the fifty sentences recorded in 1990, forty-seven out of sixty-six in 1991, sixty out of 105 in 1992, and fifty out of eighty-four in 1993. It also shows that short sentences (six months to two years) are not handed out to political offenders in the way they were prior to martial law in 1989, when the authorities were using what has been called a "revolving door" policy of short detentions combined with a high incidence of torture. These short detentions fell from fifty-five in that year to fifteen in 1990, ten in 1991, ten in 1992 and twelve in 1993.

There are several examples of very high sentences. These include the seventeen- to nineteen-year sentences imposed on four Drepung monks who formed a pro-democracy group in March-April 1989, sentences of thirteen to fifteen years imposed on five villagers who organized a pro-independence demonstration in the Gyama valley in June 1992 and sentences of twelve to fifteen years for four monks from Chamdo Pasho accused of producing nationalist posters in March 1994. Most sentences over ten years currently being served, however, are the result of extensions imposed for breaches of prison discipline. Our data record thirty such cases, including fourteen nuns whose sentences were extended by an average of six years each in October 1993 for singing songs in praise of the Dalai Lama in their cells at Drapchi prison. In one case a sixty-three-year-old school

---

[145] For example, Gyaltsen Kunsang and Ngawang Rigdrol, both women aged about twenty, are reported to have serious eyesight problems, as does Jigme Zangpo, who is in his sixties. The nun, Ngawang Chendrol, and the monk, Yeshe Khedrup, were both hospitalized in 1994 or 1995 with alleged serious kidney damage, and the doctor Jampa Ngodrup is known to have a severe problem with water retention. See "Prisoners with Alleged Kidney Damage and Chronic Illness" in "Fourth Tibetan Woman Dies After Leaving Jail," *TIN News Update*, April 17, 1995.

teacher, also in Drapchi, had his sentence extended to twenty-eight years as a result of three incidents of shouting nationalist slogans and songs.[146] In 1992 the average sentence being handed out to political offenders in Tibet had gone up to 5.7 years, an increase of 65 percent over the previous year. During 1994 the average sentence for a political offense had increased still further, to nearly six and a half years.

Many of the prisoners in our survey have never been formally charged. For those who have, the charge is almost always "counterrevolutionary incitement," according to court documents which have been smuggled out of Tibet.[147] This a reference to Article 102 of the Chinese Criminal Code, which refers to anyone who "for the purpose of counterrevolution" commits the act of "inciting the masses to resist or sabotage the implementation of the state's laws or decrees" or "through counterrevolutionary slogans, leaflets or other means, propagandizing for and inciting the overthrow of the political power of the dictatorship of the proletariat and the socialist system."[148]

Prisoners

What can the data tell us about the kinds of people who are being detained and imprisoned on political charges in Tibet? Political dissent is synonymous with nationalism in modern Tibet. To some extent this is a creation of Chinese intransigence: it is not impossible, for example, that the food price demonstrations of 1993 or the Shigatse protests against the Panchen Lama denunciation campaign of July 1995 were protests unconnected to a demand for independence. Recently the Chinese authorities, however, have condemned such protests as counterrevolutionary or "splittist," an emotive term which, like the western term

---

[146] Tanak Jigme Zangpo received a fifteen-year sentence for his first offense in 1983; an additional five years for shouting a slogan in Drapchi in 1987; and an additional eight years for shouting a slogan in Drapchi in 1991. He is currently due for release in 2011.

[147] TIN has an archive of about fifty sentencing documents, almost all of which allege counterrevolutionary offenses. The exceptions involve detainees accused of burning vehicles during a protest in 1987 or involvement in the murder of a policeman during a demonstration in 1988. The Chinese authorities have indicated some sensitivity about the use of the term "counterrevolutionary" outside China, and they replaced this term with the word "splittism" or "subversion" in statements to the U.N. in 1990 and 1992 respectively. See *Eastern Express*, August 18, 1995.

[148] Article 102, Chinese Criminal Law, 1980, (English translation) Beijing: Foreign Languages Press, 1984.

"treason," categorizes all such cases as attacks on the integrity of the state, even where the incidents have been relatively minor.

The 1,276 names compiled, including those released from custody, are accordingly those of people who have been accused of or have demonstrated their opposition to Chinese rule and who have almost always been accused of separatist activities or "splittism." The vast majority were detained after they called specifically for Tibetan independence and for the Chinese to leave Tibet. It should also be stressed once more that the numbers presented are only those cases which observers have managed to document; the actual number of political arrests is likely to be higher.

Lay and Religious Prisoners

Of the total figure reported, including those since released, about 44 percent (562) are monks and about 23 percent (289) are nuns. The remaining 33 percent (425) are lay people, of whom at least 81 percent are male. Of the 610 believed to have been in detention at the end of 1995, just over half were monks (346), while a quarter were nuns (156) and the remainder, some 18 percent (108), were lay people.

The age distribution of prisoners shows how young most political detainees are. Of the 978 whose ages have been recorded, a third (324) are aged 18-21, 26 percent (257) are aged between twenty-two and twenty-five, and 17 percent (164) are aged between twenty-six and thirty. There were seventy-one juveniles aged between eleven and seventeen, of whom thirty-seven were still in detention in mid-1995.[149] There are 166 prisoners aged thirty and above, most of them lay men. In other words 83 percent of the prisoners were under thirty years of age.

The disproportionate representation of young people among these detainees reflects the unexpectedly high proportion of youths who identify with Buddhist and indigenous values, as opposed to those of the Chinese socialist society in which they have grown up. This does not mean that their nationalist aspirations are not shared by other sections of Tibetan society: most of these young people have become monks and nuns, and thus have no dependents who will suffer while they are in custody. They are therefore in a better position to carry out public protest, and for that very reason often regard it as their duty to do so on behalf of the lay population. Additionally, for obvious reasons, it is mainly the people who

---

[149] Concerning cases of juvenile political prisoners in Tibet as of December 1994, see Amnesty International Report No. ASA 17\18\95, May 1995 and "Civil Rights of Children in Tibet—A Study of China's Responses to Dissident Activity Amongst Juveniles in Tibet," Tibet Information Network, November 1995.

take part in public protest, who are mainly monks and nuns, who get caught: those involved in underground activities, such as running organizations or printing leaflets, are more likely to survive undetected.

It is hard to assess the character or origins of the nationalism felt by young monks and nuns, but among the young lay people involved in protest, the new nationalism does not seem to be opposed to modernization or to any other benefits which might have come with the Chinese occupation. These protestors are products of modern, and, in some cases, well-educated sectors of the society, and do not seem to be backward looking or even necessarily religious. This raises a serious question for the Communist Party: since few of these young protestors experienced the turmoil of the Cultural Revolution period (1966-76) their dissatisfaction with the Party cannot be reduced to its mistakes in that period, which China has already acknowledged. Their protest is against the reform policies of the Deng Xiaoping era, which in many ways has shown China at its best.

The disproportionate involvement of young women, specifically nuns, in Tibetan protests is even more striking than the involvement of youth. Nuns probably account for no more than a fraction — perhaps around 3-4 percent — of the total monastic population in the TAR, which is put by the authorities at 40,000. They represent, however, 25 percent of the prison population. This confirms earlier reports that young Tibetan women form a significant part of the movement against Chinese rule.[150]

In one respect, however, the pattern of protest changed in 1995: in the second half of the year, at the same time as Chinese authorities began to arrest more senior figures, about half of the political detainees were over thirty years of age, and 40 percent were lay people. This suggest that there was a significant increase in the involvement of older lay people in the protest movement in the latter part of 1995.

The 1995 data show an increase in political arrests since the crushing of large-scale protests in the late 1980s and the imposition of martial law in 1989. Protests have been brief but have increased in frequency since then despite the fact that more sophisticated security and surveillance measures have been introduced. There were sixty-nine political arrests recorded by monitoring organizations in 1990 and 229 in 1995; data for both 1994 and 1995 are incomplete and are likely to rise considerably.

---

[150] See "The Role of Nuns in Tibetan Protest - Preliminary Notes," *TIN News Update*, October 17, 1989; and Hanna Havnevik, "The Role of Nuns in Contemporary Tibet," in Barnett and Akiner, eds. *Resistance and Reform in Tibet*, (Bloomington: Hursts/Indiana University Press, 1994).

Table 2.4 Political Arrests, 1990-1995

Year	1990	1991	1992	1993	1994	1995
Arrests	69	89	180	289	164	229

Rural Arrests

More striking still is the extent to which protest has emerged in rural areas. Of the sixty-nine arrests in 1990, eleven were made in connection with protests outside Lhasa. Thirteen such arrests were made in 1991, forty in 1992 and 108 in 1993, a tenfold increase in three years. The figure dropped to fifty-five in 1994 and rose to 125 in 1995. That is not including the arrests carried out in 1995 in towns other than the capital — the four in Xiahe in Gansu and the forty-six arrests in Shigatse.

Reports of protests in rural monasteries, farming and nomadic communities — almost unheard of between 1987 and 1991 — begin to appear with some frequency in 1992. At that time there were protests by local monks and villagers in Lhokha's Chideshol valley in April and again in November of that year, and by villagers in Meldro Gyama in July. In March and April there was political unrest at monasteries in Rong and Kangmar, which are both in the Tsang, or central southern area of Tibet.[151] In 1993 there was a protest by school students in Nyemo in January, more arrests in Gyama in February, confrontations with the police and army at local monasteries in the Phenpo and Chideshol valleys in June, and widespread protest against Chinese settlers in Sog county and other nomadic areas of Nagchu prefecture in August. The Sog incidents took place much further away from a major urban area than previous rural incidents, which were usually within 200 kilometers of a major city, and were the first reported protest by lay people from a nomadic area.

The year 1994 saw a wave of arrests of political activists much further to the east, in the Drayab and Zogang areas of Chamdo prefecture in January-February. Nearer the capital there were more protests in Lhokha in March, in the Phenpo valley in June and at Taktse Dechen county in December. The next year, 1995, began with a series of protests and police raids at local monasteries in the Drigung, Phenpo, and Nyemo areas, all within 150 kilometers of Lhasa.

In some cases the spread of rural unrest may have some connection to the communication of ideas through affiliated monasteries, and through monks and nuns and their families. Demonstrations in support of Tibetan independence, when

---

[151] "Signs of Rural Unrest in Tibet," *TIN News Update*, June 18, 1992.

they re-emerged in 1987, were initiated by members of the principal Lhasa monasteries, Drepung, Sera, and Ganden, known to TAR authorities as the "Three Troublesome Ones." Since then many of the protests have been led by monks and nuns from institutions affiliated to the three great monasteries, such as Phurbuchok, Kyormolung, and Ratoe, and the nunneries of Chubsang, Garu, Michungri, Tsangkhung, and Shungsep. All of these institutions except Shungsep, which is a Nyingmapa convent some fifty kilometers from Lhasa, are in or near the capital and belong to the Gelugpa sect. Of the 787 monks and nuns detained since 1987 according to the 1995 list, about half (395), are from these monasteries which lie within the Lhasa peripheries. Although monks and nuns from surrounding rural areas such as Phenyul, Meldro, Toelung, Nyemo, and Chushul have also staged demonstrations in Lhasa with some frequency over the same period, and been arrested and detained there for doing so, they were not being arrested for political dissent in their home districts before 1992. But although most of the monks and nuns who were detained before 1991 were in monastic institutions in Lhasa, they were almost all from farming families in surrounding rural areas. Thus, although many of the prisoners come from Phenpo valley, to give one example, there were no recorded political arrests in the valley itself between 1987 and 1991.

That has now changed. In 1992 there were five arrests of monks or nuns in the Phenpo valley itself. The following year there were six, in 1994 there were fifteen, and in 1995 there were eighty-two as of November. Monks from the Gongkar area in Lhokha were demonstrating in Lhasa as early as 1989, but there were no recorded political arrests in the Gongkar area until 1992 when seventeen such arrests were made; in 1993 there were forty-two.

Buddhist Schools

Dissent is not only becoming geographically more dispersed, but it comprises more different groups than before. For example, it can no longer be associated exclusively with the Gelugpa school. The data for 1994 and 1995 show, for example, that ninety monks were arrested from the monasteries of the Sakya school such as Dunphu Choekhor (33), Nalandra (46), and Nyethang Tashigang (11). In late 1994 five monks were detained after an incident at Tsurphu, the main monastery of the Kagyu school, and in early 1995 there were major incidents at Kagyu monasteries such as Taglung, Drigung Terdrom, Drigung Emari, and Phenpo Nakar.[152] Although broadly related, these monasteries belong to different

---

[152] See "Anti-Dalai Lama Campaign Part 2: Provoking Sectarian Divisions," *TIN News Update*, April 7, 1995 and "Demonstrations February and March: Nalandra Monastery Besieged," *TIN News Update*, April 26, 1995. The earlier preponderance of Gelugpa monks

subsects and are unlikely to have been aware of or influenced by the protest in Tsurphu, several hundred kilometers to the west. The Tsurphu incident can be related to the Chinese government making propaganda statements about the patriotism of praising its chief lama, then still a child, which some monks regarded as provocative, but there is no obvious reason for the spread of dissent to other schools besides the existing evidence of an increase in official restrictions on monasteries and religious life.

The arrests of monks from Tashilhunpo monastery in July 1995 show a dramatic escalation in the range of religious dissent. Although a Gelugpa institution, Tashilhunpo was in effect a sub-school of its own, at least in political terms, and had been regarded for decades, certainly since 1923, as broadly accommodating to Chinese aims. It had shown no signs of dissent during the 1959 Uprising and little during the protests of the late 1980s. Its leadership had cracked down aggressively on five monks who were caught listening to the Voice of America's Tibetan-language radio broadcasts in 1993.[153] The arrest in 1995 of forty-six monks and lamas from Tashilhunpo, one of Tibet's most famous institutions, to the list of dissident monasteries and religious schools was perhaps the most significant sign of protest to emerge in Tibet in the decade.

Lay People and Occupations

The 1995 list shows that the largest proportion of lay arrests took place during the popular uprising in 1989, when 111 of the 195 arrests recorded that year were of lay people.[154] In 1993, when large-scale protests returned to the streets of Lhasa, there were 133 arrests of lay people out of a total of 289. Security crackdowns were launched on both occasions and, as suggested earlier, it was then

---

in protests before 1995 is typical of the situation in central Tibet, but it is possible that in other areas of greater Tibet not effectively covered by this study, especially in the eastern areas, protests may have involved monasteries of other schools.

[153] In June and July 1993 five monks were detained from Tashilhunpo, including Sithar Tsering, who was briefly detained for putting up posters calling for Tibetan independence. Two others, Phurbu Tsering and Nyima Phuntsog, were arrested because copies of the Dalai Lama's autobiography were found in their rooms and because they had been listening to the Voice of America.

[154] This figure is given for comparative purposes only: the actual number of arrests was much higher than recorded in the list, but there are no detailed records of detainees at that time. The Chinese authorities have said that at least 400 people were detained after the March demonstrations in 1989 (*Tibet Daily*, December 1, 1989).

the monks and nuns who chose to resume the momentum of protest in the intervening periods.

Among the lay people arrested since 1993 are numbers of Lhasa residents often held for relatively short periods and released without charge. They included, for example, some of the Seitru detainees and others arrested from their homes during May-June 1993 and June 1994; Lobsang Choedrag, "Pa" Phuntsog, Shol Dawa, Trasil and some twenty other lay people arrested in Lhasa in July and August 1995 are believed to be still in custody. These are thought to be suspected members or organizers of underground groups who were taken into custody for interrogation. The purpose may have been to obtain information from them, but it may also have been intended as a means of intimidation and in some cases as a way of enlisting informers.

Occupations are listed for only 199 of the 430 recorded lay arrests. Of these, in decreasing order:

• forty-six are farmers or pastoralists
• thirty-nine are teachers or white collar workers
• thirty-one are artisanal workers
• twenty-seven are students
• thirty are businesspeople and traders.

The remaining twenty-six include security guards, laborers, shop assistants, drivers, cultural entertainers, housewives, and the unemployed. Of all these categories, the two most numerous, farmers and teachers, are particularly interesting in that they have only become active in the period since 1992. The significant increase in the number of farmers can be attributed to the emergence of dissent in rural areas already described.

The increase in the number of teachers is also related to this trend, in that protest incidents in rural communities will tend to implicate and involve the whole community and in particular its natural leaders; in addition, it may be the case, as the authorities may be implying when they speak about dissent spreading along communication lines, that dissident ideas are spread by means of the written word, in which case the teachers are likely to be prominent among the 20 percent of rural Tibetans who can read. Local teachers arrested, for example, at incidents at Lhundrup Nemo in 1993 and Meldro Baglog and Nagchu Sog in 1994 and Katsel in 1995 are likely to have been respected and influential individuals targeted by the police for that reason.

More generally, this increase may represent a greater readiness on the part of the authorities to subject educated and respected members of Tibetan society to arrest and detention. Notable examples which appear on this list of prominent citizens arrested include school headmasters Shabdrung Rinpoche (arrested in Lhasa in March 1994), Samdrup Tsering (arrested in Qinghai Tsolho in July 1993), and Tashi Namgyal (arrested in Katsel in January 1995). This new trend involves religious leaders as well as lay figures; of the nearly 500 monks listed, virtually none are distinguished by seniority or education apart from Yulo Dawa Tsering, the former abbot and philosopher arrested in 1987 apparently in what was then a one-off symbolic gesture of strength by the authorities. But 1995 alone has seen the arrest of several such people, including the Khenpo, or abbot, at Drigung Emari, the chantmaster at Tsurphu, and the abbot of Tashilhunpo, as well as the senior monks expelled from Nalandra. Such moves can be seen as a part of the new climate of assertiveness and intolerance by Party authorities as well as a growing disregard for Tibetan sensibilities, as described in the first part of this report. The arrest of prominent social figures is a change of style which is in keeping with the observation that the Third Forum legitimized the shift of security policy away from notions of caution and cultural sensitivity toward containment and repression.

II. TORTURE

In 1994-1995, Tibetan security forces and prison authorities continued to beat and torture prisoners with impunity. When demonstrators were detained in Lhasa or police raided monasteries and arrested their inhabitants, beatings and electric shock were almost routine. When Tibetans were caught trying to reach or return from India, they, too, were routinely beaten, sometimes to obtain information but often to intimidate and thereby stop the flow of information between Tibetans in India and those in Tibet. Sources in Lhasa have reported that more sophisticated forms of abuse, such as exposure to extremes of temperatures, which leave no visible marks are now being used in place of more evident forms of physical abuse.

Information about beatings and torture is not usually received until a considerable time after the incidents have taken place and usually only becomes known when the victim completes his or her prison sentence, which in Tibet lasts on average five years for political offenders. This is especially true of cases of physical abuse which have occurred during interrogation rather than during arrest. It is routine for detainees to be held incommunicado until about a week before trial, and prisoners who receive administrative sentences often go directly from detention to labor camps without meeting with their families. After they have been sentenced, but before family visits start, prisoners are often warned not to talk about their interrogation experiences, and there are a significant number of cases where prisoners who have revealed information have received further ill-treatment or extended sentences.

As a result, the information thus far available does not indicate the prevalence of torture during interrogation in the period from 1994-1995, and is generally limited to eyewitness accounts of the routine beatings which accompany arrests of demonstrators. These are reportedly more intense when the outlawed Tibetan flag has been displayed. The general practice of prison officials towards beatings and torture described by a former Trisam prisoner in 1992 is probably still current: the prisoner recalled a meeting at which inmates were told by a prison official, "We don't beat needlessly, and we don't beat once the sentence has been fixed." However, there are important qualifications to this remark, notably the prevalence of post-sentence beatings for infringements of prison regulations. These have been very severe in a number of cases, and may even have led to some of the reported fatalities (see, for example, the cases of Phuntsog Yangkyi and Sherab Ngawang).

The kinds of highly detailed reports which describe torture techniques are only obtained from first-hand accounts given by refugees who are themselves released prisoners—in other words, such accounts are almost always received several years after the event. More recent reports are characteristically third-hand accounts which describe the effects of physical abuse as perceived by others, but not the techniques. The most recent accounts indicate an increase in the degree of physical impairment resulting from interrogation in detention centers, notably accounts of people who cannot stand up fully after release. Typical first-hand accounts from the 1990 period give an indication of the probable scenarios which resulted in the forms of visible impairment described in the more recent third-hand accounts.

The following selection of cases of beatings and torture is custody describes typical forms of abuse in different institutional settings.

Police stations

In police stations, where detainees are typically held for a few days, torture is associated with interrogation, and officials are mainly interested in extracting a confession in a short space of time. The most common forms of abuse, apart from kicking and beating, include shocks produced with the aid of small electric generators or from electric batons, the use of self-tightening handcuffs, forcing prisoners to adopt difficult positions; and removing most of a prisoner's clothes, especially in cold weather. The techniques require no skill and on some occasions are extremely violent (notably in the case of Jigme Gyatso in Xiahe), suggesting that the interrogators, presumably police officers, are untrained. A secondary aim of police station torture is to intimidate detainees into keeping silent about the torture and beatings, a factor which may increase the propensity for violence.

• During an interview in India in 1994, Phurbu, a twenty-two-year-old monk from Palhalhupug monastery, detained at the Lhasa Public Security Department because his handwriting resembled that on some pro-independence posters which had circulated in Lhasa in 1989, told about his 1990 detention. The police did not have any convincing evidence against him, so they resorted to torture to force a confession:

They gave me electric shocks in my face, neck and back. My hands were cuffed tightly behind my back in self-tightening handcuffs. I was kicked everywhere. They didn't kick me in my mouth so I didn't lose any teeth. They made me stand on one foot, while the other was tied to a stick which I had to hold in my hands. They made me stand like this for more than an hour. When I fell down, they beat me and forced me into the same position. This torture was given to me only once. Several times they made me stand on my hands with my feet resting against the wall. Each time lasted for at least one hour. One time I was left in the bathroom for about six hours. Except for my underwear, I was naked. My hands were cuffed to the bars in the windows. February is one of the coldest months in Lhasa and I was freezing. After nine days they released me...[and] warned me not to tell anyone I was tortured.

•   A twenty-five-year-old from a farm family in Kham who worked as an unpaid village policeman was detained in a police station in Lhasa for ten days after he took part in a series of price rise protests in May 1993. There is reason to believe he was released in the hope he would lead the police to other activists. As a second wave of arrests began in October-November, he fled to India, arriving in December 1993.

When we were caught, we were handcuffed on the spot. These handcuffs were self-tightening and very painful... [T]hey cuffed my thumbs diagonally behind my back and made me sit down on my knees. I had to sit in this position from sunset (about 6:00 p.m.) until 2:00 a.m... [W]henever I fell down., they beat me with their fists on my ribs, in my stomach and on my thighs... They kicked me so hard on my jaw that I lost two molars. Then I was taken into the courtyard of the police station. Except for my trousers, my clothes were removed. I was given electric shocks on my face, chest, back, hands and palms...At some point, I passed out...

...Then they put self-tightening handcuffs around my wrists and cuffed my legs, I was taken to a cell and put in a kind of iron cage inside the cell. I could not lie down...I was left like this for three days and nights without anything to eat or drink. I got so thirsty I begged the guards...for some water. They replied, "The Dalai Lama will give you water."

•   In January 1995, Public Security Bureau officers arrested three men, Norbu Dondrup and Jamyang Phuntsog, from the same village in Amdo (Chinese: Qinghai) while they were staying in a hotel in Lhasa. Police discovered that the men were planning to escape to India and the three were detained for nine days in the branch police station (Chinese: *paichusuo*) in Kyire neighborhood. They were each interrogated separately. On the first day the interrogators tied wires around their thumbs and administered electric shocks by turning a handle on a small generator. Later the men were tied to a pillar and hit all over their bodies with electric batons, according to statements made by two of the men after they escaped to India.

•   After Jigme Gyatso was arrested on May 19, 1995 for allegedly putting up posters at his monastery, a young Xiahe county policeman who was drunk beat him so badly that he was unable to move his arms or his legs; his mind was also affected. Fearful that he would die in detention, authorities released him but not until his family paid 1,000 renminbi (US$125 approximately) to local police officers.

Detention centers
There is no time pressure on investigators in the detention centers of Gutsa and Seitru, and there is almost no risk that a detainee will be free to speak about his or her treatment for several months or years after it has taken place. Detention center investigators are more interested in obtaining precise information, in particular the names of organizers, rather than in simply obtaining confessions. Interrogations can take a whole day or can be spaced out over a period of several months. Additionally, interrogators can alternate the use of aggressive methods with sympathetic approaches, a technique which seems to be more effective than force alone. Physical techniques include applying electric shocks to sensitive areas such as the mouth, placing heated objects on the skin, and striking with an iron rod on the joints or on the hands. The use of confinement cells, extreme isolation for long periods, sensory deprivation, and standing in cold water are also described.

The techniques used indicate a degree of training or expertise in torture methods and a systematic approach to the extraction of information. Investigation in detention centers in the Chinese system is meant to be carried out by officials from the procuracy, but no Tibetan prisoner has ever described his or her interrogators as procurators, and it remains unclear whether torture in detention centers is carried out by Public Security Bureau officers, prison police, procurators, or, particularly in the case of Seitru, State Security officials who present themselves as members of one or of the other agencies.

• Phurbu, the monk from Palhalhupug referred to above, was re-arrested on April 25, 1990 by a group of PSB officers who came to his room with an arrest warrant. Police had searched his room in the monastery, but found no evidence to incriminate him. This time he was tortured in detention centers. After twenty-two days of torture at Seitru, he was moved to Gutsa where the torture continued.

> ...I was interrogated and tortured every day... They kicked me in the kidneys and hit me with a small iron stick on my elbows, knees, and other joints. After twenty-two days I was taken to Gutsa where I was put in a small cell, all alone. It had no windows, only a small hatch in the door which let in a strip of light. I was kept in this cell for five months and eleven days. Every two to three days I was interrogated. Sometimes I wasn't tortured and they would treat me very sympathetically: 'If you speak the truth you can go back to your monastery...If you throw an egg against a rock, the rock will never break, but the egg will... .'' Most times, I was beaten a lot and tortured...After a month I couldn't bear the torture anymore and confessed that I had put up one poster.

As a result of the forced confession, Phurbu was administratively sentenced to a three-year re-education-through-labor term. He was released in 1993 and reached India in 1994.

• Lobsang Tenzin, a twenty-four-year-old monk from Meldrogongkar interviewed in 1993, talked about having been arrested after a five-minute demonstration on the Barkor on September 14, 1990. Fifteen students and two monks took part: "We were put into two trucks, transporting seven or eight people each. We were dragged into the truck without being handcuffed and beaten with rubber sticks filled with sand. We were driven straight to Gutsa where we were handcuffed." He went on to describe his interrogation and torture over a two-month period in solitary confinement:

> We were made to stand in rows facing each other. One by one we were called to the interrogation room. When I was called in I was asked two basic questions: "Have you organized any earlier demonstration?... Give us the names of those who organized this demonstration"...During this first interrogation I was tortured very badly. I was given electric shocks all over my

body, including my mouth. My thumbs were put in tight cuffs
and I was beaten on my chest until one of my ribs broke.

...I was interrogated once or twice a week for two months. The
very first interrogation was the worst. It took about one whole
day. The subsequent interrogations took about three to four
hours each. During those two months I was tortured frequently.
Sometimes I was made to lie on the floor and my interrogators
would tickle me so long that I lost consciousness. In a way this
treatment was worse than the electric shocks. It was more
humiliating. At other times my interrogators would force me to
undress and burn my skin with a bottle filled with boiling hot
water. Sometimes I had to stand up to my ankles in water which
was electrocuted [sic]...

For two months I was not allowed to receive any visitors. I was
kept in complete isolation in a small cell without windows. The
diagonal length must have been about 1.6 meters since I could
just stretch out if I lay down corner to corner... I felt so isolated
and lonely that I would sometimes knock on the wall hoping to
receive a reply... The guards did not speak to me. I couldn't
make out if they were Tibetan or Chinese. I didn't see them.

After serving a two-year re-education-through-labor term, Lobsang Tenzin escaped
to India.

•   Kunchog Tenzin, a primary school teacher from Sog county arrested in
February 1995, reportedly was beaten so badly in Nagchu prison that his hands are
disfigured and his back permanently injured to the extent that he cannot stand erect.

•   On January 8, 1995, two monks from the Jokhang Temple in Lhasa,
Ngodrup[2] and Pasang[3], were taken to Gutsa detention center and punched, kicked
and trampled on before being quickly released. Pasang reportedly was so badly
beaten that he could not stand up.

•   Lodroe, a security guard at the Public Hospital in Lhasa, arrested in May
1993 after police searched his house and among other "incriminating" evidence
discovered some wall posters, was held for four months in Seitru prison on
suspicion of ties to the exile Tibetan government. During interrogation prison

authorities would ask him to write something so as to compare his handwriting with the posters. But, according to a source in India, Lodroe is "not so literate. He cannot write too well. But they told him, `[You] are purposely not writing well,' and they hit him. As a result, his left hand is permanently disfigured."

Border police
Tibetans detained at the Tibet-Nepal border, either because they have been arrested by the Chinese police or because they have been repatriated by the Nepalese, are almost always beaten at one of the holding centers near the border or at a prison in the nearby towns of Dram (Chinese: Zhangmu) and Tingri. Most accounts refer to beatings rather than to torture, and report as a common feature the use of mockery —the police characteristically taunt the detainees for their belief in the Dalai Lama. There is little interest in extracting information, and there seems to be no official procedure which the officials must follow.

Crossing the border without appropriate documents is a criminal offense in China and can lead to a maximum sentence of one year, but there is no case reported thus far of criminal proceedings being invoked in any of the hundreds of cases of Tibetans caught trying to leave Tibet without papers. Most detainees are held for between two and three months and, typically, they proceed through a series of prisons on their way to freedom either in Lhasa or in towns close to their homes. The physical abuse that detainees describe functions as a form of punishment or as a deterrent and includes elements of humiliation. It almost always occurs in the first one or two places where they are held. It is unclear whether the officials involved are members of the People's Armed Police, the Public Security Bureau, or a border police force, all of which operate in these areas; it seems likely that all three services are involved in such practice.

• A farmer and his thirteen-year-old son from Chamdo in Eastern Tibet, were captured and turned over to Chinese authorities by the Nepalese police after they tried to cross the border at Dram on or about October 24, 1994. They were held for over two months, first in Tingri and then in Shigatse. During the first week in Tingri, prison guards repeatedly told them, "You tried to escape to the Dalai Lama; let's see what the Dalai Lama is going to do for you. Is he going to feed you? Is he going to clothe you?" At the same time the prisoner was beaten. "They beat me with sticks on my legs for one week and all the time they told me to call on the Dalai Lama to help me. My son was beaten and told the same thing," the farmer said.

•   In May 1995, a nineteen-year-old nun from Tingri was arrested by Chinese police at the border crossing in Dram after trying to escape to Nepal. She was interrogated in a prison in Dram for ten days during which she was asked how she had managed to get as far as she did and what route she had traveled. Police officers also asked why she wanted to see the Dalai Lama and told her, "The Dalai Lama will stay where he is and you have to stay where your village is." The policemen pointed guns at her in order to frighten her and took her money. They beat her with iron rods on her legs repeatedly, said the nun, who later escaped to India.

•   Lobsang Choephel, an eighteen-year-old Tibetan student living temporarily in India, was arrested at Dram when he tried to cross from Nepal into Tibet in late December 1994. He was detained for four days by Chinese border guards:

> There was a very high official; he had two stars on his shoulder...He asked me, "Do you love the Dalai Lama? Do you love him politically or religiously?" First I didn't understand. Then I said, "I love him in both ways." Then he beat me on the head with his elbow. Then I fell on the floor, and he picked me up and asked, "Do you really?" And I said, "Yes, I do." He beat me so much and then he called two soldiers into the room and they also beat me so much. They are not good in kung fu but they used kung fu, and they beat me everywhere. It was very painful.

III. COMPULSORY LABOR

The policy change in Tibet described in this report has made a perceptible impact on the extent of civil rights which Tibetans are able to enjoy. It has also brought social and economic changes, including accelerated inflation, unemployment and increased migration of labor, all aspects of the rapid marketization of the Chinese economy. Although analysis of the economic impact of the Third Forum is in many ways beyond the scope of this report, there are implications for civil rights. The rapid increase in indirect forms of local taxation in rural areas of Tibet, for example, has included a growing use of compulsory labor to fulfil the main economic development priorities set by the Third Forum: irrigation, mining, and the construction of buildings and roads.

Many Tibetans interviewed reported widespread use of compulsory labor by Chinese authorities for infrastructure projects such as road construction and digging of ditches and irrigation canals, and building offices and other facilities for Chinese officials. Compulsory labor that constitutes "the normal civic obligations of the citizens of a fully self-governing country" is not forbidden by international labor rights standards, nor are "minor communal services" performed by members of a community "provided that the members of the said community or their direct representative shall have the right to be consulted in regard to the need for such services."[155] The compulsory labor that takes place in Tibet fits neither of these categories.

Forced labor is defined by the International Labor Organization (ILO) in Convention No.29 as "all work or service which is exacted from any person under the menace of any penalty and for which the said person has not offered himself voluntarily."[156] ILO Convention 105, "Convention Concerning the Abolition of Forced Labor," bans forced labor as a means of political coercion or punishment for holding political views; as a method of mobilizing and using labor for purposes of economic development; as a means of labor discipline; as a punishment for having participated in strikes; and as a means of racial, social, national or religious discrimination.

---

[155] International Labor Organization, *International Labor Conventions and Recommendations, 1919-1991, Vol.1,* "Convention No.29, Convention Concerning Forced or Compulsory Labor," (Geneva: International Labor Office, 1992), p.116.

[156] Ibid, p.115.

Although China has not ratified either ILO convention, the provisions of both serve as a standard against which its actions can be measured, and the compulsory labor that takes place in Tibet is in violation of these standards. It is used to mobilize Tibetans for economic development, appears to take place without consultation of those involved, and it is discriminatory: Tibetans, who do the menial labor, are generally not paid, while Chinese laborers appear to receive regular wages.

There are many forms of compulsory labor, or communal labor as it would be termed from a Chinese point of view, and huge variations in the amount of labor demanded in different areas. Although almost all the accounts of such labor come from rural areas, there are important distinctions between labor demanded in nomad areas and that demanded in agricultural areas. Because for much of the year herding work can be carried out by children, officials in nomadic areas appear ready to exact much higher demands in labor from nomads or semi-nomadic families. In agricultural areas some adult workers in each family have to be allowed to remain at home to do farming work, and all adults have to be allowed to return home at harvest time; conscription demands in these areas are therefore more cautious and are proportional to family size.

A second distinction is between those labor demands which are recurrent and those which are one-off projects. In some areas, although the amount may vary from month to month, labor is demanded on an annual basis for work on government fields or in government mines. In other cases, work is demanded for special projects, usually construction work which has in theory a communal value, such as building a school or an irrigation canal. A distinctive characteristic of these projects is that they require labor to be provided directly. The labor is not regarded as a form of taxation, but as a separate form of obligation; fulfilment of labor dues does not lessen people's obligation to pay normal taxes. In some cases, such as the requirement in some areas that each family provide a fixed annual amount of medicinal herbs, these taxes amount to indirect forms of compulsory labor.

The practice of compulsory labor is particularly sensitive in Tibet now and is likely to become more so. First, it has never been openly discussed by the Chinese authorities in the reform era (that is, since 1980) and there is no previous study of it in western literature about contemporary Tibet. Second, it appears at first to contradict China's highly publicized policy of a total tax amnesty for Tibetans in rural and nomadic areas of the TAR. The tax amnesty was declared by Hu Yaobang in 1980 and has been extended until the present day, but it appears to have been circumvented by indirect methods such as quota sales of grain, payment in kind, and communal labor.

Third, although the practice of communal labor is viewed as a positive feature in a socialist society, once it comes to be perceived as a form of compulsion it is associated more with exploitation. This presents a particular difficulty for the Chinese authorities in Tibet, because much of their propaganda justifying their presence in Tibet has been based on the claim that they freed Tibetans from the system of corvée labor which existed under Tibetan rule.

Finally, it is clear from the reports received about this form of labor that rural Tibetans agreed in the past to such demands because they saw the work as a contribution to the community. There are signs, however, that this acceptance may be withdrawn if Chinese migration into rural areas of Tibet is not restricted. Since communal labor is donated by Tibetans for the benefit of the community, any increase in the number of Chinese migrants or settlers in the community tends to exacerbate the resentment of Tibetans towards contributing that labor, even though they may have felt the practice to be acceptable in the recent past.

The amount of labor that individuals or families must contribute varies from area to area and from year to year. In some cases, families are required to contribute labor but are paid for their work. In other cases, particularly construction projects, the required work begins as paid labor and then the payment stops. Demands on time can be as little as three days a year to as much as seven months per year per family. Failure to show up for work can result in a fine or in a doubling of the amount of labor required the next time.

•   In the farming area of Lhakhang in Lhodrak county, southern Tibet, close to the Bhutan border, each family member has to contribute five days of labor a year. This can be increased to six or seven days a year if there is more work which needs to be done. The laborers have to work on government fields making terraced fields for growing apples and vegetables; the products are taken by the government. Villagers who do not perform their work duties have to pay three yuan for every day of work missed. There are some people who are single and who do not have family members who can cover for them at home if they have to leave to do the government work, and they always have to pay the money instead. "There is some kind of resentment [from local officials] if you don't go to do this labor. You will be reprimanded, and they will ask you why you are the only one who is not doing the labor," said two farmers from the area interviewed in India in May 1995.

•   In the rural area of Woka, Sangri county, in Lhokha prefecture, a school was built through collective labor in May 1993. All men between the ages of fifteen and sixty and all women between the ages of fifteen and fifty-five had to contribute their labor in May 1993 to build the new school. The villagers seem to have contributed nineteen days work on the project. They were told they would be fined five yuan a day if they did not take part in the work. They were told the school would benefit the community. "The workers worked without money and you also had to bring your own food," said some Tibetans from the village, interviewed in August 1993. "The leaders sort of ordered us to build it. Nobody paid [the fines]. If somebody couldn't go to work he would ask someone else to go in his place because they didn't have much money... When they started the building the leaders announced that [we] should obey them and do what they said. So we had to follow them."

•   In Yardoe, in Yarlung, Lhokha prefecture, compulsory labor is usually between eight and twelve days per month, nine months a year, for each resident, including monks. Just before the beginning of each month, the authorities fix the number of days of unpaid compulsory labor. It is up to the individual worker whether he or she wants to work the full quota of days at a stretch or break it up and work one day at a time. Towards the end of winter, people are put to work digging irrigation canals; in the summer, when the water from rain and melting snow can cause flooding, the work often consists of building dikes and barricades. During the three coldest months of winter, when the rivers are frozen, there is usually no compulsory labor. Those who do not work have to pay a fine of between three and four yuan for every day missed, which is deducted at harvest time from the cash sum paid by the government for the grain which has to be sold by each farmer to the local authorities.

•   A project using compulsory labor to build an irrigation canal from Risur to Nedong and beyond in Lhokha began in 1990 and was still under way in December 1995. People from the village had to walk about an hour to the work site and work from about 8:00 a.m. to 8:00 p.m. digging the canal and then collecting stones to line the sides. Most of the laborers working on the canal were Chinese, but they received regular wages. "They were doing the same work. The only difference was that for the Tibetans it was compulsory; they were not paid; but the Chinese were paid. If you asked the reason why the Tibetans were not paid they said, "You have land there; this is going to benefit your land...this is going to benefit you," a local resident said. He said that discontent about compulsory work was increasing as more Chinese were moving into the area: "In the past there used to be two irrigation canals; people were happy with those two. But just before I came out of Tibet, they started to dig a new canal and the people were against that. They say it is for the Chinese. Lots of Chinese are coming to the village," he said, in an interview in December 1995.

•   In Tser-we subdistrict (Chinese: *qu*), a semi-nomadic area near Chamdo, a road running from Tser-we district towards Yushu in Qinghai province was being constructed under military guidance by compulsory unpaid local labor during at least 1991-93, according to a twenty-year-old nun from the area. The nun, who left the area in 1993, worked in a team of thirty Tibetans laborers who were supervised by ten Chinese soldiers, who were presumably paid by the army. In her village, ten Chinese soldiers had come door to door, writing down names of family members and instructing all able-bodied individuals between the ages of ten and sixty to report for work. In her family, her mother and the two youngest children did not have to work, but she and her younger brother had to go. The fine was thirty yuan a day for failing to appear to do the work.

        The Tibetan laborers on the road project came from several different districts, and most of those who were from too far away to go home at night slept in tents. The woman, who was interviewed in India in October 1995, had lived under a tree during the two years she spent working unpaid on the project; she got one month off during the year to go home to help with the harvest. Her family brought her food, because she would be fined for leaving, and she had to work from before dawn until after sunset. Her job was to clean away the rock after dynamite had been used. Over the two years, she witnessed one man killed by a dynamite blast and one worker who committed suicide, allegedly to avoid taking part in the labor. Other annual taxes still had to be paid in various forms to the local government irrespective of the amount of compulsory work being done by family members. These included collecting 0.5 kg of *yartsagumbu*, 1.5 kg of *tsur yong*, and 1 kg of *dza yong* (rare plants or insects which have a very high retail value in Chinese medicine) per person per year. The family, which also had to pay a fixed annual quota of butter to the government, survived by living off the produce from its yaks and from its own fields.

•   Villagers in a farming area near Chamdo, in Kham, have to contribute twenty one days' work per year per family in a local mine, according to a thirty-eight-year-old farmer from the area who was interviewed in India in September 1995. Tibetans in his village had to be on call to work as unskilled labor in the mines, about a six-hour walk away. He thought the mine produced iron but had other minerals as well. The workers had no choice about working and were paid about two yuan a day. They were also required to bring their animals to the mine to help carry the ore back to the village, and from there it was transported by truck to Chengdu. There were about 400 Chinese miners, he said, who received between thirty and forty yuan a day, and about two Tibetan conscripts for every Chinese. The Tibetans were "diggers" and the Chinese were "sorters," sifting the rock for ore. Tibetan workers had to bring their own tools. Anyone who refused to work would have his or her labor quota doubled: that is, if a farmer was told to come for a week and said he could not leave his fields at that point, he would have to do two weeks the next time. There was no set work schedule. Villagers could be given a day's notice and told to report the next day, but months could go by without any work at all. No family was supposed to work more than twenty-one days a year, and they could divide it as they chose: one person could do the full twenty-one days, or three people could each work for seven. He himself went to the mines four or five times each year, working from 7:00 a.m. until 12:00 a.m., breaking for lunch, and then working again from 2:00 until 6:00 p.m.

•   A twenty-four-year-old nun from Chushul district, interviewed in January 1994, said that beginning in 1987 many new offices and living quarters for Chinese officials had been built in the district. In many cases, local farmers were moved off their land without compensation so the construction could proceed. The new offices were built by conscripted Tibetan labor, with only the stone-carvers and the carpenters receiving any pay. Those who collected the wood and stones for construction, who dug the foundations and who worked as masons, were not paid. The nun's family worked for weeks at a time without pay, on call from the authorities, while farm work had to be postponed. As no childcare was available, small children often had to be brought to the work site. After the offices were completed, the villagers had to build a school. In 1994 when the interview took place in India, villagers were being conscripted to build grain storage centers.

•   A farmer from Hu Dui (Chinese: Huzhu?) county, an agricultural area of Tsongonpo (Qinghai province), interviewed in June 1995, said compulsory labor was used to level hilly agricultural land in his area. Every year each family in the village was assigned a plot of land and given a certain amount of time to level it, usually a week or ten days. It was up to the family to assign individual members to the work. No one was compensated for their labor, and there was a fine if work was not completed on time. The farmer did not know of anyone who had been fined.

•   In Nyi-shar village in Tingri county, in Shigatse prefecture, villagers were required to provide labor to dig trenches for an irrigation canal continuously for three years starting in 1992. The canal was completed in April 1995. The Tibetan laborers on the project had to dig the trenches and to work as earth removers, carrying the dirt on their backs in order to throw it elsewhere. Families in the area had been visited by officials from the county administration and instructed to provide a certain amount of workers, depending on the size of the family. The workers were unpaid, and food had to be provided by the family. The workers lived in tents provided by the government.

One large family from the area had to provide three male workers. Two of them worked for five months and then they were joined by the third for the remaining seven, so that for every day over a three-year period, at least two of these three were absent from the house, according to member of the family interviewed in October 1995. The men became sore from carrying loads on their backs, and the family's work at home in the fields suffered because the men were away. Because it took two days to get to the work site, the men did not come home at night, sleeping instead in government tents. Twice a year, the sisters and mother took dried tsampa to them to eat. Non-appearance for the work would be punished by a large but unspecified fine. "They will ask for a huge amount of fine; but you cannot pay the fine; so if you cannot pay the fine, then you would be jailed. It's never happened because no one would dare; they have to go," said the source.

• From 1991 to 1993 one out of every eight adults aged between eighteen and sixty in Tingri county had to work on a three-year project to divert about 50 per cent of the water in the Punchu river, known outside Tibet as the Arun. The work involved digging a canal about ten meters wide at the top and four meters deep to provide irrigation for a large agricultural area adjacent to a major military camp at Dramtso, near Tingri. The project remained unfinished in 1993 and was probably a precursor of the project described above, which affected families from Nyi-shar. In 1991 and 1992 most workers on the canal project were paid three to eight mao-zi (about three to nine US cents) per day. If the person was an exemplary worker, he was paid five yuan (about sixty cents) per day for about a month and then paid the same rate as the others. In the last year of the project workers received no pay. The work took place for seven months each year, allowing time off for the four winter months and one month at harvest time.

The average amount of workers that had to be provided was approximately one and a half persons per family. Every family either provided someone to work or hired a deputy or shared the obligation with another family. Monks were included in the numbers available for work, but as a matter of choice families never sent monks to do the work. The cost of hiring a worker to deputize for a conscript was five yuan per day plus food. Provision of workers was obligatory and was enforced by the *xianzhang*, the head of the county.

There were around 200 to 300 Chinese builders on the project, mainly engineers and masons, working in teams of seventy. The Chinese did the skilled work such as construction of concrete sluices and aqueducts, and the Tibetans did the digging and manual work. "Since last year the number of Chinese has dramatically increased... there are more military personnel and secondly, there are more Chinese businesses, shopkeepers... rerouting the river is one of the projects that the Chinese say will make everyone rich... The Chinese are only saying that everybody will get rich, but Tibetans don't get any benefit at all," complained a monk from Tingri interviewed in India in September 1995.

IV. RESTRICTIONS ON RELIGIOUS FREEDOM

As noted in Part 1, all religious expression in Tibet is tightly controlled by the Chinese government. Some of the methods the government uses to limit religious practice in Tibet are described in the following cases and include:[157]

• age limits for novice monks and nuns
• ban on religious education in schools
• vetting of monastic candidates
• limits on the population of monasteries and nunneries
• a limit on the total number of monasteries
• interference in the choice of monastic and religious leaders
• expulsions from their institutions of monks and nuns involved in peaceful demonstrations, pamphleteering or possession of proscribed religious texts
• outlawing of traditional Buddhist rituals
• refusal to permit Tibetan party members to practice religion
• limits to religious practices by non-Party cadres and their families
• restrictions on travel outside the country for religious purposes
• restrictions on monks traveling outside their monasteries
• ongoing political indoctrination in monasteries and nunneries

Cases of Religious Repression

•   A monk from Lhokha, interviewed at the end of 1995, described the monastery where he had resided from 1987-88 until 1994. When he wanted to join the monastery, he had applied first to his work unit, one of several sub-units of his village. That unit, after approval, passed the application up through the bureaucratic hierarchy to the regional government of the TAR. The entire process should have taken between four and five months, but it stretched out another month or two because, he thinks, of his bad class background. The monastery he finally was permitted to join used to have more than 300 monks. Its official cap, as of the time he left, was twenty monks, but despite a great many applications, the ceiling was effectively fifteen. Candidates under eighteen could not apply. Two monks, appointed by the township administration, looked after the religious side of monastery affairs, but the same township administration assumed direct

---

[157] In many cases, names and place names have been omitted to avoid retaliation against informants, their families, and their monasteries or nunneries.

responsibility for discipline and rules. Divination was prohibited, as were trances, consultation of oracles, and certain rituals. Activities with political connotations, such as reciting "Boundless Wisdom" (Tibetan: *tse-me yonten*), a prayer written by the Dalai Lama which refers to the freedom of Tibet, were banned. A monk who had a book containing the prayer was expelled from the monastery. Later, Chinese authorities searched the monks' residences for similar texts. Monks could not listen freely to any broadcasts from India or to the Tibetan language service of the Voice of America. They could not talk privately about the "Chinese invasion of Tibet," and they cannot keep the Dalai Lama's picture. In this small monastery in Lhokha, as in all monasteries and nunneries, Chinese officials conducted periodic political indoctrination sessions. Attendance was mandatory unless the monastery head certified that an absence was legitimate, for instance when a monk was very ill or had to return home. Chinese authorities told monks they could not demonstrate for Tibetan independence and they must oppose those who had demonstrated in the past.

•   On March 3, 1995 after an incident at Nalandra monastery involving pro-independence activity (see Appendix A), a work team took up residence in the monastery. Among other restrictions, the team forbade monks to carry out rituals in private homes even when someone had died. Sixty-four monks who had protested peacefully against the arrest of one of their members for displaying a pro-independence badge were expelled from Nalandra and prohibited from joining any other monastery. They were also banned from leading a "religious life," carrying out private religious ceremonies for lay persons, and traveling without police authorization.

•   By May 1994, Samtenling nunnery in the Golog Dzachukha area in Qinghai province was ordered to reduce its population to 100 nuns. At the time 120 were in residence. The nunnery head tried to delay, but Chinese lay officials threatened to close the entire nunnery if twenty nuns did not leave at once. The nuns' names were placed in a bowl, and the first twenty drawn were expelled. The Chinese further insisted that there could be no new admissions, even if a nun left or died. A secular official came to the nunnery every day, according to a report by nuns who left, to talk with the disciplinarian and check out how the nuns were spending their time. Chinese authorities also conducted political education at Samtenling. Nuns were instructed to study hard, not get involved in politics and, most importantly, to obey the Chinese government. They were required to put their fingerprints to a letter promising that they would not go to Lhasa or to India. Those who disobeyed and traveled to India were fined 600 renminbi (US$85 approximately).

• In 1995 a monk from Sera monastery in Serta county, Sichuan province, described what Chinese officials permitted and proscribed. Within the monastery, the monks were permitted to study and to perform small offering ceremonies (Hindi: *puja*) or rituals and to pray:

> The performance of large puja is not allowed... If someone sponsors a large puja, then the monastery and the sponsor will be punished... the sponsor will have to pay 300 renminbi [US$37] as a fine. If a really big puja is done, the sponsor will go to jail. When a very large puja is done, then the person who takes responsibility, the abbot, goes to jail for one month or for one half a month. This has happened many times. The abbot goes to jail approximately two times a year.
>
> Regarding the rules of the monastery, there cannot be more than 200 monks. The monastery is not rich; the monks get their food from home, from their families. The revenue of the monastery comes from people who make offerings and sometimes from people who have died. The monks have to build their own homes. They have to buy the land from the government. Each monk's family must pay 500 renminbi [US$63] in order that the monks are allowed to build rooms. They build the rooms themselves with the help of friends who know how to build. They use wood, and they need to pay for the wood.
>
> Officials do come to the monastery often to check on what the monks are doing. If somebody even says "Dalai Lama," they will get into trouble and be asked, "Why did you say Dalai Lama?" Regarding rules at the monastery, the discipline is imposed from the Chinese government, from both the subdistrict and the county... They are not allowed to say that China is bad; they have to say that China is good.

In summarizing the causes of the monastery's financial difficulties, the monk noted the prohibition on big sponsors and the withdrawal of its former property from monastic control. He also commented on the intellectual decline, attributable to the dearth of experienced monks and lamas, many of whom have died and have not been replaced.

•   A teacher at a middle school in the Lhasa area reported that in 1994 the TAR government announced that religious teaching in schools and in Lhasa University was henceforth banned. The edict, which prohibited teachers' use of religious language and students' and teachers' possession of pictures of the Dalai Lama and of "blessing cords"— small pieces of string or ribbon, usually red, which have been blessed by a lama — was sent directly to schools and announced in the newspapers. On orders received from the education department, the teacher's own school checked for the outlawed pictures and for other proscribed religious objects.

•   The announcement on February 15, 1996 by the Tibet Nationalities and Religious Affairs Commission that monasteries and nunneries whose residents were involved in political protest would be closed and that religious believers were to "dedicate themselves jointly to the construction cause of socialist modernization," in fact, post-dated actual policy implementation. On November 29, 1995 local officials, on direct orders from Chen Kuiyuan, the secretary of the Tibet Communist Party, informed twenty women from Shongchen nunnery, in Ngamring county, that they were being given five days to demolish the buildings they had constructed as living quarters and to return to their homes. They were further informed that they were prohibited from joining any other nunnery but rather were to resume farming. Chinese authorities permitted the temple the nuns had recently rebuilt with donations from local Tibetans to remain standing, but they ordered the nuns not to use it. It is unclear if nunnery residents were involved in political activity, but according to a local source, Khedrup Gyatso, the lama in charge, "was taken away in a jeep and has disappeared." The nearby monastery of Doglho, with a resident population of ten, was also closed and the monks ordered home.

•   In the past officials have only closed monasteries and nunneries which were allegedly built without any official permission or with only local permission. In March 1994, the Religious Affairs Bureau of Tsetang closed Namrab Samtenling nunnery in Gongkar county and gave the resident population one week to clear out. Although their teacher was allowed to return to his own monastery, the nuns were ordered home. Authorities placed the building itself under the care of a local farmer who planned to use it as a sheep pen.

• In April 1994, a nun discussing the changes that had taken place during the six years that she was at Garu nunnery, starting in 1988, focused on the increased restrictions:

> At first, all Garu nuns were allowed to go to Lhasa whenever there was a religious ceremony. Right now, only very few nuns are allowed to Lhasa for religious purposes. When I joined, there was no restriction on the number of nuns. Now the official maximum is 100. But actually there are only sixty nuns at Garu at the moment and no new nuns are admitted... since 1987 the rules have become stricter and stricter... Under Garu, in a village called Nyare (also called Nyangdren), there is a new police station. It was built in the winter of 1989. This police station was built to check on the movements of the nuns at Garu. It became more and more difficult to get permission to leave the nunnery. We needed a pass from our teacher. We had to show the pass at the police station. If we were lucky, we got permission to leave. Very often we did not get permission.

The nun went on to talk about the "waste of time at political meetings":

> In 1990 the re-education team stayed at the nunnery for a whole year. Every morning and every evening, we had to listen to propaganda lectures. Last summer [1993], the education team stayed for three months... The team consisted of officials from two different offices. There were Chinese PSB officials and Tibetans from the Religious Affairs Bureau. They all carried guns and walkie-talkies... They threatened us that the nunnery would be closed if we didn't do "well."

• In 1994 according to a monk from Ra-nyag monastery, in Jyekundo (Chinese: Yushu prefecture), Qinghai, authorities tightened up again on contacts between the religious communities in Tibet and India. They announced that "lama teachers" returning to Tibet from India, cannot teach in their home monasteries in Tibet and should be given no responsibilities. The same monk went on to describe his monastery's management structure. As with other monasteries in the area, the Religious Affairs Bureau appointed one person, the Turen (Chinese: *zhuren*, leader), to look after the activities of the monks. "If the monks make any kind of trouble, it's [his] duty to quell them. He has the responsibility to make sure that people don't rise up." If anything bad happens in the monastery he has to take the responsibility. In addition to this person, there is one designated to look after the monastery's finances, one to act as secretary, one to look after religious duties, and another in charge when the monastery "has to do something outside the monastery." They are all appointed by the Chinese and have little power. The disciplinarian is traditionally in charge and has about the same power as the Turen. Chinese authorities must give permission for a change of personnel.

• In Shegar monastery in Tingri, special permission must be obtained from lay authorities before ceremonies that were routinely performed in the past can be scheduled. According to a 1995 report from a Shegar monk:

> The Chinese have never given permission for the *tor gya* ceremony — a banishment of evil spirits — because they are afraid it will attract a large crowd and a disturbance might break out. A request to perform the *cham* dances must be made at least fifteen days in advance. When monks' relatives visit from Nepal, they cannot enter the monastery without advance permission from the county administration. If the monastery wants to invite an outside lama to speak, it has to get permission. If the request is granted, on the day of the event PSB men — about thirty of them — "keep an eye on things." It is quite easy to get permission for a lama to come from Lhasa. However, permission for a lama from outside Tibet, for instance Nepal, never comes through.

The monk went on to talk about travel restrictions:

> There are a lot of restrictions during important national days like the first of June, Children's Day and four or five other national days (Army Day, October 1 ["Founding of the Republic"], Chinese New Year)...During these times, the monks cannot go into town for about nine or ten days. The monastery almost becomes like a prison. I have heard from the villagers that during these days there are police around the monastery. I have not seen this...I have heard the police are deployed... outside the wall around the monastery. At 8:00 p.m. the gate is shut and the monks cannot go out...

APPENDICES

Appendix A. Tables and Figures on Political Imprisonment

The table on the following page gives the basic statistics for the 1,276 political prisoners whose cases have been collected and studied by TIN since the end of 1989. Many cases have not been reported to outside monitoring organizations, especially from areas outside the TAR, and this list is therefore not comprehensive. Cases are only included here where there is a primary source or secondary confirmation.

The data give an impression of the situation over the last six years but they do not include cases of people detained and released for political offenses before 1990: there were between 2,000 and 3,000 such cases, and unfortunately it has not been possible to collect adequate data for these cases. In general only the prisoners who received long sentences in Lhasa prisons are included from that period. The Drapchi statistics, included in the totals, are also given separately in the second part of the table because reports from Drapchi prison are more complete than those from other prisons. These numbers therefore may better reflect the male/female and secular/monastic ratios among prisoners.

For similar logistical reasons the hundreds of cases of people detained for crossing or attempting to cross the Tibet-Nepal border, or repatriated by the Nepalese authorities, have not been included. There were at least 200 such cases in 1995, most of whom are believed to have been detained for two to three months in various prisons.

Note: there are some discrepancies in the totals because of prisoners who were imprisoned before 1987, or whose year of arrest is uncertain. An asterisk indicates that figures for these twenty cases have been added into the total. Seven prisoners who are on conditional release (usually because of a serious medical condition) and eighty prisoners whose current status is unknown are not included in the figures given here for current detainees. The term "all status" means all former detainees are included, those who have been released or have escaped as well as those still in custody.

121

Tibetan Political Prisoners by Year of Arrest

YEAR DETAINED	1987	1988	1989	1990	1991	1992	1993	1994[158]
Known Detainees: Year Detained	25	71	195	69	89	180	289	113
Currently Detained	1	8	26	15	18	81	161	104
Status Unknown	—	—	—	1	2	18	59	—
Nuns Currently Detained	0	0	3	10	0	29	50	26
Lay Women Currently Detained	0	0	1	0	0	2	7	6
Monks Currently Detained	0	6	20	4	20	26	5	58
Lay Men Currently Detained	2	3	7	3	5	15	83	14
Deceased	1	1	6	0	0	2	2	—
Monks and Nuns (all status)	15	48	84	50	70	149	156	89
Lay Persons (male & female)	10	23	111	19	19	31	133	26
Female Prisoners	7	30	38	39	31	49	73	33
Nuns (all status)	4	21	25	32	28	45	59	26
Number of Nunneries	0	4	4	4	4	5	11	6
Lay Women (all status)	3	9	13	7	3	4	14	7
Male Prisoners (all status)	18	41	157	30	58	131	216	79

[158] Figures for 1994 and 1995 are not complete.

YEAR DETAINED	1987	1988	1989	1990	1991	1992	1993	1994[159]
Monks (all status)	11	27	59	18	42	104	97	63
Number of Monasteries	5	5	17	10	6	20	23	12
Lay Men (all status)	7	14	98	12	16	27	119	17
Sentences Total	46	210	787	308	269	655	394	163
Known Cases with Sentences	14	62	187	64	73	115	86	26
Average Sentence	3.29	3.39	4.21	4.8	3.7	5.7	4.58	6.3

[159] Figures for 1994 and 1995 are not complete.

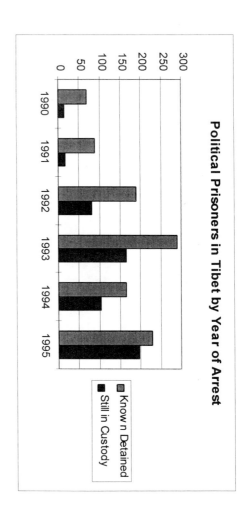

Political Prisoners in Tibet by Year of Arrest

Drapchi Prison, Lhasa (TAR Prison No.1)

YEAR DETANIED	1987	1988	1989	1990	1991	1992	1993	1994[160]
Total Drapchi Prisoners	4	15	70	31	34	109	64	18
Currently Detained Drapchi	1	7	33	18	28	97	62	18
Total Drapchi men	4	15	64	11	34	76	43	15
Current Drapchi Men	1	7	29	5	28	68	43	15
Total Drapchi Women	0	0	6	20	0	33	21	3
Current Drapchi Women	0	0	4	13	0	29	19	3
Current Drapchi Monks	0	4	21	3	23	62	37	15
Current Drapchi Nuns	0	0	3	13	0	28	17	3
Current Drapchi lay Men	1	3	8	2	5	6	6	0
Current Drapchi Lay Women	0	0	1	0	0	1	2	0
Released or Deceased Men	3	8	35	6	6	6	0	0
Released or Deceased Women	0	0	2	7	0	4	2	0
Drapchi Sentence Total	29	120	513	217	175	614	319	71
Number of Cases	3	15	70	31	34	107	64	15
Average Drapchi Sentence	9.67	8.0	7.3	7.0	5.2	5.7	4.98	4.73

[160] Figures for 1994 and 1995 are incomplete

Political Prisoners Known to Have Been Detained Since 1987

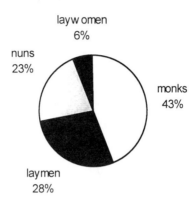

laywomen
6%

nuns
23%

monks
43%

laymen
28%

Prisoners Still in Custody in March 1996

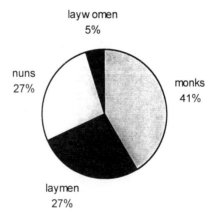

laywomen
5%

nuns
27%

monks
41%

laymen
27%

Number of Monasteries and Nunneries Involved in Protest

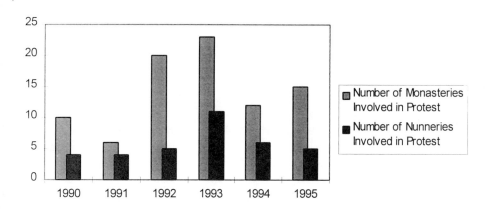

Number of Men and Women Prisoners

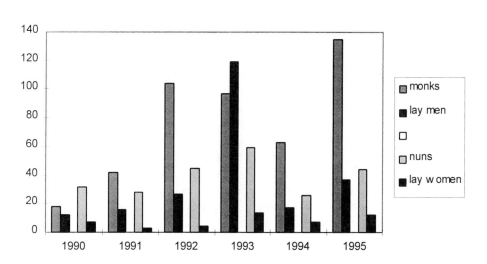

Appendix B: Arrests and Prison Related Deaths in 1995

Arrests[161]

Emari Monastery

•   On December 15, 1994 three posters or leaflets reading "Chinese quit Tibet" and "Tibet for Tibetans" circulated in the village of Yangri Gon (Yangrigang), adjacent to Yangri monastery. Another leaflet was found on the door of Emari monastery, a small hermitage east of Yangri. As a result, police first interrogated villagers, then on January 8, 1995 over 100 men in eleven police cars and three trucks descended on Emari and seized **CHOEDE**, a twenty-year-old monk whose handwriting, they claimed, matched that on the leaflets. Three days later, on January 11, an even larger Public Security Bureau and People's Armed Police contingent returned and arrested three more monks, **NORBU³**, and **SONAM TSERING**, both twenty years old, and another whose name is unknown. On March 29, local officials with a military escort came to announce that the abbot and one lama had been expelled, the first time since serious monitoring began in 1987 that a serving abbot has been forced out for political reasons. Twenty-four unregistered novices were ordered to leave the monastery.

There were reports that local authorities suspected the Emari monks, as well as monks in Katsel monastery and lay residents of Meldrogongkar — some forty people altogether — of reading a copy of a book smuggled to the area from Dharamsala. The book, *Tenpa Ratroe* (Literally "Exposing the Truth," published in English in June 1993 as *Tibet: Proving Truth from Facts*), was written by the Tibetan government-in-exile as a response to a document produced by the Chinese authorities in September 1992 called "Tibet — Its Ownership and the Human Rights Situation." The paper was produced as a "White Paper" by the State Council on September 22, 1992. Quotations from the book were pasted on the wall in Drigung, and when one of the monks from Emari was tortured, apparently with electric batons, he gave the names of others who had read the book or passed it on.

In late January, after a Tibetan flag was found in the home of **TENPA YESHE**, he and another middle school teacher, **DAWA²**, twenty-six years old, were detained. After extensive interrogation, Dawa reported that two Tibetan policemen, **TSEWANG**, who was taken into custody in Lhasa, and another whose name and whereabouts are unknown, had given him the flag.

---

[161] Individuals with the same name have been differentiated with a number in superscript that appears after their names, as in Dawa, Dawa² and Dawa³.

The discovery of a Tibetan flag drawn on the wall at Katsel also led to a police raid similar to the ones at Emari, Nalandra and other monasteries. About 100 soldiers from Lhasa, equipped with tear gas, surrounded the monastery at Katsel and detained two monks, **DORJE**, aged twenty, and **KUNCHOG TRINLEY**, aged forty. The night before the raid, the troops had gone higher up the mountain to an affiliated retreat center or hermitage where a young lama, **TRINLEY DONDRUP** (also known as Tulku Trinley Dondrup), twenty-three; and one other monk were detained. Others arrested in connection with similar independence initiatives in the area included **TASHI NAMGYAL**, headmaster of the "Swedish school" near Katsel (who may have already been released); three unnamed persons, a monk from Bumsumdo monastery, and **TASHI DONDRUP**, believed to be a lay person. As of mid-July 1995 all those arrested were thought to be in the prison in Meldrogongkar.

Ganden Monastery

•   According to an unconfirmed account by a Human Rights Watch/Asia source, **BADO LOBSANG LEGTSOG**, a twenty-eight-year-old monk responsible for blowing the trumpet at Ganden monastery ceremonies, was arrested on August 23, 1995 for chanting independence slogans in front of the Jokhang Temple in Lhasa.

•   According to exile government reports, **NGAWANG THONGLAM** (lay name **Lobsang Choejor**), a twenty-three-year-old Ganden monk from Meldrogongkar, Dro village where his family farms, was "suddenly and arbitrarily" re-arrested in February 1995. It is believed Ngawang Thonglam's latest arrest was related to his political activities, as his earlier one had been. His sister, Ngawang Tsepak, a Chubsang nun, also was politically involved. She completed a two-year prison sentence on September 2, 1991, then fled to India where she gave a detailed account of torture in prison. Originally detained on October 10, 1989 in connection with a planned demonstration during which he carried a Tibetan flag, Ngawang Thonglam was sentenced to a three-year term, sent to Sangyip prison, and expelled from his monastery. The sentence was extended by another year and a half after a prison protest on May 20, 1991, three days before the fortieth anniversary of the Seventeen-Point Agreement, the formal surrender of the Tibetan government to the Chinese and their acceptance of Chinese authority. At least twelve political prisoners, who delivered a petition to prison authorities describing the agreement as having been imposed by force on an independent Tibet, were placed in isolation cells for a minimum of three weeks. Seven were given new sentences, among them

Ngawang Thonglam, who was moved to Drapchi prison on September 28, 1991. Despite the extended sentence, Ngawang Thonglam reportedly was released in 1993.

Labrang Monastery

• In May 1995 police in southern Gansu began the "Striking a Powerful Blow" campaign in response to March and May displays of pro-independence posters and the scattering of leaflets in Ngulra, Xiahe, and Labrang monastery in Xiahe. The campaign led to increased surveillance in the monastery, including the installation of undercover police, and to harassment of local people who spoke foreign languages. In some cases, police reportedly beat or briefly detained people on the street after midnight. *Ganlho Sanggyur*, the Tibet-language edition of *Gannan Xinwen*, an official newspaper, declared the campaign a success on September 1, reporting that it accomplished its goal of "exposing organizations [and] strongly overthrowing cases of underground activity... The Xiahe county police," it continued, "made great strides in achieving social stability." By the end of August at least five people reportedly were arrested, one of whom is said to have received a seven-year sentence, one of whom is still missing, and one of whom, **JIGME GYATSO**, a monk, is partially paralyzed as a result of police brutality.

Xiahe county police arrested Jigme Gyatso on May 19 for putting up pro-independence posters at the monastery. According to one source, "a young policeman who was drunk" beat him very badly... After the beating, he couldn't move his arms and legs. When police suspected he was going to die, they demanded 5,000 renminbi (approximately US$675) from his parents before they would release him." He reportedly was finally freed in exchange for 1,000 renminbi. "When he came out of prison, his mind wasn't clear and he still couldn't move his limbs," the source continued. Doctors at the Xiahe County Hospital refused to treat Jigme Gyatso because of his political involvement and he was finally admitted to the Traditional Tibetan Medical Hospital. Local authorities reportedly dropped their case against him because the only evidence they had to connect him to the posters, a copy of a speech by the Dalai Lama found in his room, was insufficient.

DROLKAR GYAP (Zhong Gejia in Chinese), a twenty-six-year-old from Machu county (Maqu in Chinese), in Ganlho (Gannan in Chinese) Tibetan Autonomous Prefecture in southern Gansu province, detained for "political reasons" in June 1995, was sentenced to a seven-year term. After studying for two years in India, he taught at a primary school for Tibetan exiles, then returned in

March 1994 to study Tibetan language at the North-West Minorities Institute in Lanzhou.

Police arrested **KUNCHOG JIGME**, from Ngulra and a member of the administration of Labrang, in June 1995, on suspicion of putting up posters in Ngulra in March. When his room was searched in June, Xiahe police allegedly found a video tape and some books connected to the Dalai Lama. He reportedly has been badly beaten. **KUNCHOG CHOEPHEL**, probably another Labrang monk, has also been detained, but no details are available.

BENZA TRINLEY (also known as **Badza Trinley**), a twenty-six-year-old monk from Labrang Tashikhyil monastery was arrested in November 1994 and his current whereabouts are unknown. Some reports suggest that he might be in custody in Tsoe. Just before Benza Trinley was seized, he had returned from Lhasa where he reportedly had been searching unsuccessfully for his brother, a layman, who had earlier run away from Labrang. One report said that it was the Public Security Bureau that had sent Benza Trinley on the errand, but by the time he reached Lhasa, his brother had gone on to India. The police then accused him of sending his brother on a "political mission." Benza Trinley had been forbidden to leave Labrang and required to report to the police whenever summoned after he spent July-August 1993 in detention on suspicion of "counterrevolutionary activity." At the time, pro-independence posters had been found on the monastery's walls and in shops and government offices in the county capital. However, there was no evidence to tie him directly to the posters. Benza Trinley was arrested again in April 1994 after police intercepted a letter he allegedly wrote to a former classmate at the Gansu Buddhist Institute, from which he had graduated in 1993. The letter referred to a "Free Tibet." It was his brother who succeeded in getting him released at that time. There are two other names associated with the case. **JAMYANG** and **TSULTRIM**, but it is unclear if these represent additional cases or are lay names of monks already reported in detention.

Nalandra Monastery

• A day or two after the county government set up a reorganization committee at Nalandra monastery on February 20, 1995, **THONGMOM** and another monk went to a local football field near Ganden Choekhor with small Tibetan independence badges pinned to their robes. The next day, the two were detained in Lhundrup county. When police searched their rooms, probably on February 23, they found more badges. Some time following the search, the monks reportedly staged a protest march to the town of Phenpo. A few days later, on or about February 28, 1995, some seventy People's Armed Police troops, traveling in one truck and thirteen jeeps, raided the monastery. As monks threw stones, the troops fired tear gas into the monastery, then entered the monastery buildings, threatening to open fire if the monks did not surrender. According to reports, the troops beat up "all" the monks, immediately detaining thirty-two and subsequently seizing eight more, among them the monastery's chant-master, discipline master, accountant and other senior officials. Initially held in Lhundrup prison, all those arrested were transferred either to Gutsa detention center or to Sangyip prison.

During a second raid probably on March 1, during which the monks again threw stones, troops searching the chapels, storerooms, kitchens, and dormitories found wooden printing blocks, reactionary documents, and song lyrics as well as hundreds of newly printed pro-independence leaflets and two large Tibetan flags, leading to speculation that a demonstration had been planned. Tibetan television broadcast a videotape of the search.

By March 3 a work team had taken up residence in the monastery. All remaining monks were required to spend entire days listening to political speeches, confessing "guilt," criticizing other monks, and declaring support for official policy. All monastic activity was suspended, and all visits from outside were banned. On March 15 the "reorganization of Nalandra affairs meeting" was held in the monastery with leaders of Lhasa municipality and the county district participating. The effort was extended to all monasteries and nunneries in Phenpo county, and warnings were issued that in the event of any further protest, all would be shut down. Monks were forbidden to carry out rituals in private houses even when someone had died. In addition to banning all further construction, Chinese authorities expelled sixty-four monks, forbidding them from joining any other monastery, leading a "religious life," carrying out private religious ceremonies for lay persons, and traveling without police authorization. According to one source:

> There was no reason -- like shouting slogans or sticking up posters -- for doing that. The only reason the Chinese gave was that they were harming the reputation of the monastery and making trouble. On top of that, they announced on the radio that the monks were not behaving according to ethics and spoke rubbish about them. Now Nalandra monastery is a mere name; it is just an empty building.

Before the arrests and expulsion order, the official limit on registered residents at Nalandra numbered 140. Those arrested included:[162]

---

[162] Note that some of these names may refer to the same person.

Place	Ordination name	Lay name
Langthang		DAWA
	JAMPA TSULTRIM	Penpa
	NGAWANG DAMCHOE (?)	Norbu
	RINCHEN GYATSO	Penpa[2]
	(Rinchen Gyalpo)	
Dayal		JAMPELCHOEJOR
Khartse	JAMPEL PENPA	Migmar
	LEGSHE PENDAR	Kelsang Bagdro
	LEGSHE YESHE	Lhagchung
	LOBSANG PHUNTSOG	Sonam Dondrup
	LEGSHE LODEN	Loden
Phugyaron	JAMPEL THARCHIN	Chungtag
Dendrong	LEGSHE THUBTEN	Paljor Wangyal
		CHOEZANG
Dangga	LEGSHE DRUGDRAG	Phurbu Jamyang
	LEGSHE LHARAG	Tenpa Gyaltsen
Shideng	LEGSHE THUPKE	Penpa Wangdu
Karkong	LEGSHE GELEG	Dondrup Choephel
Pennang	LEGSHE NGAWANG	Buchung
		LOSEL (Lobsel)
		TENGYE
Drangga		THARCHIN
Drugu	LEGSHE NYIMA	Namgyal
	LEGSHE TSERING	Lobsang Samdrup
Nagchu	LEGSHE SAMTEN	Gyagtob
Bodrong Gang	LEGSHE TENZIN	Tsewang Sonam
Nubna	LEGSHE THAPYE	Norsang
Thumong	LEGSHE TSERING[2]	Dondrup
		NYIMA KELSANG
		RINCHEN
		GYALPO[2]
		TSERING
		SAMDRUP
		YENLUNG
Sonam Gang	LOBSANG GYALCHE	Lhagpa Wangyal
	NGAWANG DAMCHOE[2] (?)	Norbu[2]
Ngagrong		TSERING
		SAMDRUP[2]
unknown	JAMPEL CHOEJOR[2]	Nangchung
	(or Jamyang Choejor)	
	LEGSHE CHOESANG	Tashi Loyag
		NORBU JAMYANG

LEGSHE GYATSO	Tsering Sangpo
LEGSHE KUNGA	Jigme Tashi
LEGSHE LODROE	
LEGSHE TENGYA	Phuntsog
LOBSANG GYALTSEN	
RINCHEN DONDRUP	Penchung

• Seven prisoners, including three monks from Nalandra monastery, **JAMPA DRADUL, TENPA RABGYAL** and **THUBTEN LOBSANG**; and four from Nagchu prefecture, **CHOEDRAG, NYIMA SANGPO, THUBTEN CHOEDRAG** and **TSETEN SANGPO**, escaped from custody on January 6, 1995 during transfer to Lhasa. The four from Nagchu had been arrested for holding a demonstration in Ngachu.

Sera Monastery

• **THUBTEN TSERING**, seventy-three, has been arrested again, this time during June 1995 when he tried to flee Tibet by walking across the mountains in the company of two other former prisoners, Gyaltsen Oezer (also known as Ratoe Dawa) and **TSEWANG PALDEN**. All three were seized on the Nepal side of the border because they did not have legitimate travel documents. Gyaltsen Oezer jumped out of the truck carrying them back to the border and managed to escape. The two others were handed over to Chinese police officers; their whereabouts are unknown.

The earlier charges against Thubten Tsering, a native of Damshung county, stemmed from remarks he and a well-known monk, Yulo Dawa Tsering, allegedly made to two visitors from Italy, one an exiled Tibetan monk and the other an Italian tourist, Dr. Stefano Dallari, who videotaped the conversation. Formerly treasurer at Sera monastery, Thubten Tsering was arrested on December 16, 1987, sentenced to a six-year term in January 1989, and sent to Drapchi prison. By the time he was released, his health reportedly had seriously deteriorated.

According to a March 1988 Radio Lhasa broadcast, "...on the afternoon of July 26, 1987, (they) spread reactionary views, such as Tibetan independence, to foreign reactionary elements who came to Tibet as tourists and viciously vilified the policies adopted by the Chinese Communist Party and the people's government." Both monks were charged under Article 102(2) of China's Criminal Law for spreading "counterrevolutionary propaganda."

In an official 1992 report to the U.N. Working Group on Arbitrary Detention, the Chinese government acknowledged Thubten Tsering's detention for "engaging in unlawful activities advocating Tibetan independence." He was one of thirty-nine political prisoners whose release the Working Group requested. On December 6, 1991 Tsewang Palden, a sixty-four-year-old retired carpenter, was arrested somewhere between Lhatse and Dingri in central Tibet while visiting relatives, for "trying to split the country." The charges were reportedly fabricated out of official anger over the political activities and subsequent escape to India of his daughter, Sonam Drolkar, whom he was hoping to join. After having served almost three years of a five-year sentence, Tsewang Palden's conditional release was one of four officially announced by Xinhua on November 7, 1994. Under the terms he was liable to rearrest at any time.

Taglung Monastery

• After monks from Taglung monastery and its affiliate Barilbu monastery (also known as Dre'ulung) traveled to Lhasa to stage pro-independence protests, a total of thirteen monks were arrested and reportedly taken to Gutsa detention center. The incidents took place on or around February 11 and again on February 15, 1995. Those arrested after the first demonstration included **BUCHUNG**[3] and **PASANG**, both twenty; **DARGYE**, twenty-four; **JIGME**, twenty-three; **LOBSANG TSONDRU, TENZIN CHOEDRON**[2]**, TENZIN GYALTSEN**, all twenty-eight; all from Phenpo Lhundrup. **NORBU**[4]**, NORDI**, and **SANG SANG**, also from Phenpo Lhundrup, were among those detained after the second incident. Several monks reportedly were badly injured after they were seized. On February 17, when police came to the monastery, more injuries occurred, this time to monks who resisted the incursion. Officials subjected resident monks to a period of intense political re-education, warning that the monastery would be completely closed in the wake of renewed independence activities.

Tashilhunpo Monastery

• **CHADREL RINPOCHE (Jampa Trinley)**, the fifty-five-year-old abbot of Tashilhunpo monastery who headed the Chinese-authorized search party for the reincarnation of the Panchen Lama, is believed to have been taken into custody in Chengdu on May 17, 1995, three days after the Dalai Lama announced the choice of **GENDUN CHOEKYI NYIMA**, a six-year-old from Nagchu. He probably was held first under some form of "residential surveillance" or house arrest. For six months, Chinese authorities refused to admit that the abbot was being detained, despite the fact that on July 11 the TAR's two top leaders, Gyaltsen Norbu, chairman of the TAR government, and Ragdi, executive deputy secretary of the

TAR, were present when a fifteen-page report condemning him was read to assembled Tashilhunpo monks. On July 14 Chadrel Rinpoche was formally replaced as head of the monastery's management committee by a pro-Beijing hardliner. On August 21 Chinese authorities finally reported that the abbot was ill and hospitalized for treatment. No public accusation against Chadrel Rinpoche had been made before November 4, when an article in *Tibet Daily* referred to unnamed people in responsible positions at Tashilhunpo who had co-operated in a conspiracy with the Dalai clique to undermine the Panchen Lama selection process. Chadrel Rinpoche was named for the first time in an article in Xinhua on November 30, which described him as a "criminal" involved in a "conspiracy." By December, the campaign to denounce him was in full swing.

Others have disappeared in relation to the case, including Gendun Choekyi Nyima and his family, reportedly in a government "guesthouse" in Beijing. Chinese officials deny that he is either missing or in custody, but insist that he "should be wherever he was born." On March 8, 1996 Chinese authorities announced in a Xinhua statement that Gendun Choekyi Nyima was at home with his parents but gave no further details. Chadrel Rinpoche's assistant, **JAMPA CHUNG**, (**Jampa**[2], Chinese: Jing-la), about fifty, who was arrested with the abbot and accused of assisting him to communicate with the Dalai Lama, reportedly was returned to Shigatse in leg irons and handcuffs at the beginning of June and was at that time held in custody there. Placed under pressure at a denunciation meeting in Shigatse to make statements incriminating Chadrel Rinpoche, Jampa Chung initially refused, claiming he alone and on his own initiative had carried out all contacts with the Dalai Lama. Later, under duress and possible torture, he may have made a full "confession."

SAMDRUP, described as being in his thirties or forties, manager of the Dram (Chinese: *Zhangmu*) office of the Gang-gyen Development Corporation, was taken into custody at a police checkpost in Tingri on May 30, 1995. During the course of business travel between Beijing, Lhasa, Shigatse and Dram, he allegedly facilitated communication between the Dalai Lama in India and Chadrel Rinpoche, the nominal head of Gang-gyen. Two other businessmen associated with Gang-gyen were released in late August: **GONPO**, the Tashilhunpo representative in Lhasa, detained on June 10, and **TOPYGAL**, the manager of the Lhasa office, also arrested in June. The tenth Panchen Lama organized the Gang-gyen Development Corporation in 1987 to spearhead the development of Tibetan trade and industry.

More arrests resulted when over 100 monks disrupted a July 11, 1995 meeting which regional-level officials had organized to officially denounce Chadrel Rinpoche. Despite the presence of a seven-man video crew, and despite the fact that the monks had been instructed not to move their heads, they hissed and spat, began to chant "Long live Chadrel Rinpoche," and threw handfuls of dirt at departing officials' cars. Three trucks, carrying some sixty People's Armed Police troops, were called to the scene, but Ragdi ordered that there be no arrests while officials were present. The troops and trucks remained in the monastery courtyard through the night.

The following day the monks boycotted a major religious ceremony, the unfurling of a scroll painting of the Buddha for public viewing. Security forces were moved to the monastery; tourists were ordered to leave the area immediately; and Tashilhunpo was sealed off. Monks reportedly shouted to the Tibetans waiting outside to join them in the monastery. Five lay women approached the gate looking to gain entry and were arrested. It is unclear if they are the same five as the five heads of women's associations who, according to an unconfirmed report issued by the Tibetan government-in-exile, were detained in connection with the events at Tashilhunpo. They included **RALPA**, head of the Shigatse Women's Association, second neighborhood committee; **LHAKYI**. who headed the association in Panam district; **MIGMAR DROLMA** and **PENPA DROLMA**, joint heads of the association in Shetongmon; and the head of the Shigatse Women's Association, fourth neighborhood (name unknown). All five are said to have been detained in Tashikyitsel in Shigatse.

For at least a few hours on July 12, thousands of Tibetans from the countryside who had come to Shigatse for the three-day festival were forbidden to perform the "korwa," a ritual of walking around the outside of the monastery considered particularly auspicious at this festival time. The route, which winds through the hills above Tashilhunpo, provides a clear view of the monastery's walled courtyard.

By 5:30 p.m., some one hundred monks had gathered in the courtyard, shouting slogans at officials and at the police. They called out in support of the Dalai Lama's candidate for Panchen Lama, for the release of Chadrel Rinpoche, and for an end to the cordon around the monastery. On July 13 at 1:30 a.m., a number of trucks, carrying prisoners escorted by armed police drove out of the monastery. Included among the thirty-two arrested Tashilhunpo monks, some of whom were beaten, are twenty-four known by name:

GYALTRUL RINPOCHE (Jampa Tenzin), over fifty years old, a lama and former member of the monastery's management committee, who was in charge of writing the biography of the ninth Panchen Lama. There have been reports Gyaltrul Rinpoche was severely tortured.

SHEPA KELSANG (Thubten Kelsang), over fifty years old, a senior monk and former secretary to the tenth Panchen Lama.

LHAGPA TSERING and **RINGKAR NGAWANG**, both over fifty years old, senior monks.

NGODRUP, known as Cham-pon (dance master) Ngodrup, under thirty years old, in charge of monastic dance rituals.

TENZIN, TENDOR, SHERAB, TASHI DONDRUP², **TSERING PHUNTSOG, CHUNGDAG, PEMA, PENPA TSERING,** **BUCHUNG², SONAM PHUNTSOG (Soephun), LOBSANG TSETEN,** **WANGCHUG, PEMA DORJE, LHAGPA TSERING², LOBSANG DAWA,** and **TSERING GONPO**, all junior monks under thirty years old.

TENZIN², known as **Ngag-khang Tenzin**, under thirty years old, in charge of the Ngag-khang or Tantric Temple dance rituals.

GENDUN, known as **Amdo Gendun** because he comes from the area of northeastern China known as Amdo to Tibetans, under thirty years old.

DORJE GYALTSEN, from Shigatse, under thirty years old, whose spleen was ruptured as a result of severe beatings during and/or after his arrest, reportedly was coughing blood and had to be hospitalized. According to one source, it was "the monks who would not admit they committed any error [who were] badly beaten in prison and forced to admit they did something wrong."

Three more monks were arrested on July 22. And on July 12 in Lhasa, two monks were arrested during a demonstration on the Barkor which reportedly was related to events at Tashilhunpo. Eight other monks arrested on July 13 were released within a week.

One other monk, twenty-six-year-old **WANGDU**, a caretaker of the ninth Panchen Lama's mausoleum and stupa, committed suicide on July 24, reportedly because he did not want to denounce the incarnation of the Panchen Lama recognized by the Dalai Lama.

On November 4 six more monks were arrested for demonstrating outside Tashilhunpo and two lay women from a carpet factory run by the monastery also have been detained in connection with the Panchen Lama dispute.

Toelung Tadrag Monastery

•   **PASANG²**, a nineteen-year-old monk affiliated with Toelung Tadrag monastery, was detained on January 20, 1995. He is from Yamdrog Nakartse.

Tsurphu Monastery

•   Six monks from Tsurphu monastery, which is composed of two distinct colleges. one associated with Gyaltsab Rinpoche and the other with the Karmapa, were arrested on January 29, 1995 in Saga, having fled their monastery on January 24 or 25. Along with at least one other monk, they had been expelled for throwing stones at a Chinese political re-education work team vehicle during a demonstration in late November or early December 1994. They had also put up a poster which allegedly contained pro-independence slogans and was critical of the head of their monastery's Democratic Management Committee. Notes left in the monks' rooms reportedly found fault with Chinese manipulation of the Karmapa and condemned the anti-Dalai Lama campaign. The captured monks were taken first to a prison in Shigatse, then to Gutsa detention center and from there to Toelung County Prison. Three of the five were senior monks, **KYIGEN** (or **Kyergen**), twenty-seven, from Toelung Dangoma, who was the monastery's main chant master; a second chant master, **TSOME**, aged twenty-six, from Toelung Tsome; and the deputy disciplinarian, **GEYOK**; a fourth monk, **LODROE**, a twenty-two-year-old from Toelung Nambar, worked in the monastery's print shop. There is no additional information about two other detainees, **KARMA RINCHEN**, a twenty-two-year-old from Toelung Nagar, and **DRADUL**, twenty-three, from Toelung Gyata.

Unnamed monasteries

• Between five and seven monks were arrested on April 14, 1995 for demonstrating on the Barkor and shouting for a free Tibet. All those who took part reportedly were badly beaten and removed to Gutsa detention center. The monks, from an unnamed monastery in or near Damshung, left for a Buddhist shrine dedicated to the Protective Deities and Female Protectors on April 11, where they made a vow concerning their plan to stage a demonstration; they then proceeded to Lhasa. Those apprehended included **CHOEPHEL LOBSANG, CHOEPHEL SAMTEN, GELEG TENZIN, TENPHEL CHOEYANG**, from Drongkar village in Damshung; **TENZIN CHOEDRAG**, from Toeling village, also in Damshung; **LOBSANG GELEG**, from Yarlung village, Damshung; and **TENZIN CHOEPHEL**. The last two names may be alternate names for two of the other five. All the monks were described as "about twenty years old."

• Two monks, **LOBSANG GAWA**, a fifty-two-year-old teacher, and his pupil **TENZIN YESHE**, aged thirty-four, were arrested in December 1995 for putting up posters in Toelung Tsome about the Panchen Lama controversy. On January 22, 1996 during transport from Lhasa to a prison in Kongpo where they were to start their three-year terms, both men escaped. Eight other prisoners also escaped; the Chinese driver died in the incident.

Chubsang Nunnery

•   Five Chubsang nuns, **NGAWANG TSERING, PEMA[2], PENPA[3],** **YANGDROL[2],** and **ZANGMO,** all from Meldrogongkar, demonstrated briefly on the Barkor in Lhasa on February 2 or 3, 1995 before being seized and taken away in a closed van. They reportedly continued to shout pro-independence slogans calling on the Chinese to leave Tibet as they were removed. It is believed the nuns are held in Gutsa detention center.

•   Five nuns from Chubsang nunnery, arrested for demonstrating near the Jokhang Temple in Lhasa on February 8, 1995, reportedly were beaten at the time they were detained. The names of four are known. **KHETSUL** and **YESHE** **PEMA** are from Phenpo Lhundrup; **NGAWANG DROLZER** (also known as Ngawang), and **GYALTSEN WANGMO** are from Lhoka. All reportedly were taken to Gutsa detention center after their arrests.

•   Three other nuns from Chubsang nunnery, **DORJE TSOMO, KELSANG** and **PASANG LHAMO,** were arrested for demonstrating on the Barkor in February 1995 on either February 10, 16 or 25. They are believed held in Gutsa detention center.

Gyabdrag Nunnery

•   Between thirteen and nineteen nuns from Gyabdrag nunnery were arrested on February 15, 1995 after a protest in Lhasa. People's Armed Police reportedly came to the village adjoining the nunnery and offered to release the detainees in return for payment of 2,000 renminbi (approximately US$250 or about four years' average income in the area) for each of the detained nuns. Those reportedly in custody in connection with the two events include **CHE-CHE, JAMPA,** **NGAWANG TSOMO,** and **YANG-GA,** all twenty-two; **CHIME DROLKAR,** **PAL-CHIN,** and **SHERAB CHOEPHEL,** all twenty; **CHOEKYI** and **NAMGYAL[2],** both eighteen; **CHOGDRUP DROLMA** and **CHAMDRON,** both twenty-three; **DEKYI, LODROE TENZIN, NGAWANG TENZIN,** all twenty-eight; **NGAWANG ZOEPA,** thirty-five; **RIGZIN** and **TSERING** **CHOEKYI,** both nineteen; **TENZIN CHOEDRON,** thirty-two; and **YANGDROL,** nineteen, all from Phenpo Lhundrup. All were initially held in Gutsa detention center.

Michungri Nunnery

• **LODROE CHOEZOM** (lay name **Sil-zhi**), a thirty-five-year-old nun from Michungri nunnery, was arrested for the third time before the September 1, 1995 anniversary "celebrations" to mark the founding of the TAR, probably on or about August 12 and probably in the Tsomonling area. There are reports that she "had a connection" with Chadrel Rinpoche. Her whereabouts are unknown. Lodroe Choezom was first arrested on September 27, 1987 after taking part in a demonstration in Lhasa. Released after four or five days, she was detained again soon afterward and taken to Gutsa detention center where she was held for between five and six months. Police also detained Lodroe Choezom for a few days in February or March 1994.

Shar Bumpa Nunnery

• Eight or nine nuns from Shar Bumpa nunnery were arrested on February 28, 1995 for taking part in a demonstration in Lhasa, among them **CHOEKYI**[2], **CHOEYANG KUNSANG, DAMCHOE DROLMA, LOBSANG TSOMO, NAMDROL WANGMO, PENPA LHAKYI, PHUNTSOG CHOEKA, TENZIN DROLMA**, all from Phenpo Lhundrup. No additional information is available.

Shongchen Nunnery

• On November 29, 1995 after local officials gave residents of Shongchen nunnery in Ngamring county, west of Shigatse, five days to clear out and to demolish their residences, **KHEDRUP GYATSO**, the lama in charge, "was taken away in a jeep and has disappeared." It is not clear if the arrest followed suspected political activity in the nunnery or because officials claimed it had been constructed without permission.

Toelung Chimelung Nunnery

• Four nuns from Toelung Chimelung nunnery were arrested, probably on March 9, 1995 after they demonstrated on the Barkor. **CHANGCHUB DROLMA**, aged twenty-two; **NGAWANG CHOEZOM**, twenty-three, and **YESHE CHOEDRON**, twenty-two, both from Yangchen; and **NGAWANG YESHE**, twenty-nine, reportedly were taken to Gutsa detention center after they were seized.

An alternate report lists the nunnery as Chulung or Chuglung and the date of arrest as November 11, 1994.

Lay persons

•   **KUNCHOG TENZIN**, arrested on February 17, 1995 (or possibly February 7), reportedly was beaten so badly after his detention in Nagchu prison that his hands are disfigured and his back permanently injured to the extent that he cannot stand erect. The authorities had allegedly identified him as the author of a pro-independence poster or pamphlet by matching his handwriting to the confiscated material. To avoid the risk of a protest on his behalf in Sog county, the popular primary school teacher was asked to come to the office of the education department in the prefectural town of Nagchu where he was promptly arrested. Among the reasons suspicion was directed at Kunchog Tenzin was the fact that he made no secret of his belief that Tibetan language and culture should be given priority within the school syllabus,

•   **MIGMAR TSERING**, a nineteen-year-old from Lhasa, and an unidentified twenty-year-old, returning from a two-and-a-half-year stay in India at the Bir School, were detained in late January 1995 or early February. According to one account, Chinese security seized them after the two crossed illegally from Nepal to Dram. While awaiting transfer to a facility in Shigatse, they managed to escape back to Nepal, but were picked up again by Nepali police who handed them back to Chinese officers in Dram. At least one of the two detentions in Dram lasted several weeks; and during at least one, they were held in a very small crowded detention center. Hundreds of Tibetans traveling between India and Tibet have had similar experiences.

•   **LOBSANG CHOEDRAG**, a forty-one-year-old trader, was arrested at his home during the night of July 6-7, 1995, reportedly on suspicion of involvement in a bomb explosion in early July at the site of a Chinese memorial plaque. Police thoroughly searched his home but reportedly found nothing to substantiate his involvement in the bomb plot. A member of a politically active family — his father, Choezed Tenpa Choephel died one day after he was transferred to a hospital from Drapchi prison; his mother was arrested twice; and a sister at least once — Lobsang Choedrag served a four-year term beginning in 1980, the last year of which he spent in Powo Nyingri, a notorious labor camp. During that year, his jaw was broken as a result of beatings. According to some sources, he was shot and injured during a demonstration in December 1988.

Detained again on June 17, 1993, just days after he returned from Sikkim where he attended the Kalachakra Initiation at which the Dalai Lama officiated, he was released in 1994.

• NGAWANG CHOEPHEL, a thirty-year-old Tibetan who had studied and taught ethnomusicology as a Fulbright scholar at Middlebury College, reportedly was detained in Tibet where he had gone to make an amateur documentary film about traditional Tibetan music. He had been expected to return to India, where he lived with his family, in November or December 1995 and then to proceed to the U.S. to complete the film. The arrest occurred after an American photographer traveling with Ngawang Choephel during the early part of his trip, left Lhasa on August 22. She said he had planned to continue on to Shigatse to look for traditional musicians. He did make the trip and was seized in the Shigatse marketplace and taken to Nyari prison sometime before September 16. Police confiscated his camera and videotapes. As of October 8, he was still being held. As a refugee, Ngawang Choephel has no passport but traveled to the U.S. on an Indian Identity Certificate. The Chinese government does not recognize the certificates which designate the holder as a "Tibetan refugee"; instead it requires Tibetans to use the designation "overseas Chinese."

• Twenty people were arrested in July, August, and September 1995 after the discovery of a protest document found in the home of **PHUNTSOG**[2], a fifty-year-old living at the Lhasa Granary in Tsomonling. The document was about protest against the planned Chinese celebration of the thirtieth anniversary of the founding of the TAR. A native of Drayab in Kham, Phuntsog began his career as a young novice monk in Ratoe monastery, then during the Cultural Revolution was employed as a stone cutter, and later worked sporadically as a petty businessman. At the time of his arrest in July, he was employed at the Vehicle Assembly and Repair Unit, reportedly a forced job placement unit. It has been reported that Phuntsog is being held at Gutsa Detention center.

Among those detained as a result of the document's discovery were two well-known pro-independence activists. One, Yulo Dawa Tsering (see below), was held for several days in Drapchi prison after a student of his, who had been associated in some capacity with the protest document, disappeared. The other was **DAWA**[3], fifty-five, also known as **Shol Dawa** because he lives in the Shol District of Lhasa. He was taken to Sangyip from a house in Tsomonling on or about August 12, 1995 and reportedly accused, along with the other dissidents, of planning to raise a Tibetan flag in Shol and of distributing pictures of Gendun Choekyi Nyima, the six-year-old whom the Dalai Lama recognized as the reincarnation of the

Panchen Lama. Dawa has a long history of political involvement. In 1975-76, he was deprived of his political rights for unknown reasons. Then, on September 29, 1981, he was arrested and subsequently sentenced to a two-year term and one year's deprivation of political rights for first plotting with two others to "write a circular on the independence of Tibet," then copying and distributing the pamphlet, "Twenty Years of Tragic Experience." After his release, Dawa worked for one year in forced job placement at a brick-kiln in Nyethang. He was arrested again on November 8, 1985 and, according to court documents, sentenced to four years in Sangyip prison with suspension of political rights for an additional year for "writing with his own hand, some ten copies of a circular denouncing the deteriorating living conditions of six million Tibetans...and the foreign (Chinese) invasion of Tibet... He also wrote thirty copies of pro-independence posters and...stuck up all of them in front of the TAR Song and Dance Society, Lhasa Cathedral Ground, schools, TAR Second Reception Center, road crossings, Lukhang lake site, crossroads, Gate No.10 of Barkor Southwest Meru Street, and other newly established schools and their premises." Eight others were charged in connection with the distribution. After his release, Shol Dawa worked as a private tailor. He had previously been employed as a construction worker.

Others arrested in connection with the discovery of the document in Phuntsog's house or from associated groups in Lhasa included:

TARCHEN, a forty-six-year-old from Kantse (Chinese: Ganzi), who had been associated with Dargye Monastery in Tehor, arrested in September 1995;

two laywomen from Lhasa, **PENCHUNG**[2]; and **TRASIL**, in her fifties, arrested in August; and **THAGCHOE**, from the south Lhasa area, also arrested in August;

TSEWANG[2], from Shol, formerly a sedan chair carrier for the Dalai Lama; and **MARPOG** (a nickname), from eastern Lhasa, once a bodyguard for the Dalai Lama;

RIGZIN WANGGYAL, from Lhasa, the former groom for the Phunkhang family; and his brother **WANGCHUG**[2] who was detained in September;

PHURBU TSERING, arrested in August;

BU GA-GA, from Tsomonling, a pharmacist working in Outhridu prison;

DAWA[4], a teacher at Lhasa Agricultural College; and one of his colleagues;

DARDRUG;

TAPCHE TENZIN or **TASHI TENZIN**, in his fifties, arrested on or about August 10.

• During the night of July 12, 1995, **TENZIN**, a fifty-eight-year-old from the Drapchi area of Lhasa, was forcibly removed from his house and accused of engaging in counterrevolutionary activities possibly in connection with the run up to the thirtieth anniversary celebrations. Police thoroughly searched his home as well as the room of his son, Sonam Tsering, a monk at Sera monastery Tenzin was first arrested in 1988 and accused of contacting foreigners. He was released after spending one year in Gutsa detention center. Before 1959 Tenzin was a monk at Sera. He later worked as a treasurer-accountant in the Work Brigade of the North Lhasa Tsang-Relshang Red Flag People's Commune (re-named Drapchi Neighborhood Committee), and in 1990 began work for the restoration of Tsangpa House, a part of Sera.

Sentence extended

• **LODROE GYATSO**, a thirty-three-year-old member of a dance troupe from Sog county, who was serving a sentence in Drapchi prison for murder, had six years added to his fifteen-year sentence for his prison protest on March 4, 1994 which included shouting political slogans, calling for Tibetan independence, praising the Dalai Lama, and handing out political slogans he had written. Lodroe Gyatso's leaflets cited a prophecy which claimed that the Dalai Lama would triumph if he reached his sixtieth birthday on July 6, 1995. According to unofficial reports from Tibet, prison authorities who ordered Lodroe Gyatso removed to a punishment cell where he was severely beaten had originally recommended that he be executed for "instigating unrest in order to overthrow the government and split the motherland."

Arrests and releases

• **DORJE RINCHEN**, a businessman, was arrested on suspicion of spying on August 14, 1995 and held for twenty-seven days in the Tenkhye District Detention Center, then moved to Nyari prison in Shigatse and held for another twenty-seven days. He was released on October 8, 1995.

• On January 8, 1995 two monks from the Jokhang Temple in Lhasa, **NGODRUP**[2], a twenty-two-year-old from Meldrogongkar, and **PASANG** , a[3] twenty-year-old from Toelung, were detained "on suspicion" and punched, kicked and trampled on, reportedly at Gutsa detention center, before being released. Pasang reportedly was so badly beaten that he could not stand up and had severe back pain. Both monks were threatened with further punishment if they spoke of the incident.

House arrests

•   In August 1995 as part of a series of arrests connected to the case of Phuntosg[2] (see above), **YULO DAWA TSERING**, sixty-six, Tibet's most famous supporter of Tibetan independence, was held in police custody for a few days. He had been conditionally released from Drapchi prison on November 6, 1994, where he had been serving a ten-year sentence for telling two Italian tourists that he believed in a free Tibet (see Thubten Tsering above). But by May 25, 1995 he had been ordered to report to the police every two days and to inform them of everything he had done since their previous meeting. At that same time, police confiscated the identity card issued to him at his release, effectively preventing him from traveling outside Lhasa.

In November 1994, three weeks after his release, Yulo Dawa Tsering told the U.N. Special Rapporteur on Religious Intolerance who was visiting Tibet, that he had been arrested for "political reasons," and that he did not accept official statements that he had been released "for good conduct, submission to prison rules and recognition of his guilt." He went on to tell the special rapporteur that since his release he had been "forbidden to join any monastery, just like other clergy who had demonstrated and put up posters calling for Tibetan independence"; and he criticized the treatment of prisoners in Tibet, including their ill-treatment if caught praying.

A senior Ganden monk, well-known theologian and former member of the Political Consultative Conference, Yulo Dawa Tsering, from Dushi Taktse county, had been arrested on December 16, 1987 and sentenced some thirteen months later, on January 19, 1989, to a ten-year term for supporting Tibetan independence. In 1959 he had been sentenced to life imprisonment for a similar offense, but he was released under an amnesty in 1979. The 1987 charges stemmed from remarks made to two visitors from Italy, one an exiled Tibetan monk and the other an Italian tourist, Dr. Stefano Dallari, who videotaped the conversation. Yulo Dawa Tsering reportedly suggested that foreign journalists should be permitted to enter Tibet and the Dalai Lama should not return until "everything had been changed."

During a November 1990 visit to Tibet, diplomats from four Scandinavian countries met Yulo Dawa Tsering in Drapchi prison. According to their report, he appeared in fairly good health and was able to walk across the prison courtyard to meet them. Former U.S. Ambassador to China James Lilley also met with him but indicated that no genuine conversation was possible; and after an October 1993 meeting, U.S. Assistant Secretary of State John Shattuck reported that the carefully controlled circumstances prevented any serious discussion.

Deaths

•   **GYALTSEN KELSANG**, (lay name **Kelsang Drolma**), twenty-four, a Tibetan nun held as a political prisoner, died at home on February 20, 1995 apparently as a result of mistreatment or prison conditions. She had served seventeen months of a two-year jail sentence on charges of separatist activities when she was permitted to temporarily return to her village in Nyangdren township for medical treatment. When her body was prepared for traditional Tibetan sky burial, evidence of severe anemia, internal adhesions around the lungs and ribs, a ruptured liver and gall bladder, and wasting of the musculature around the heart was revealed. Gyaltsen Kelsang was in good health when she entered the prison system.

After being badly beaten when she was first arrested and then again on transfer to Drapchi prison, Gyaltsen Kelsang was assigned to hard labor. Her health deteriorated to the point that she was bedridden for twenty days, but she received no medical treatment until she was removed to the Police Hospital in Lhasa in late November 1994, where she was diagnosed as having severe kidney problems. During her hospital stay, she lost movement and feeling in her lower limbs, her speech became impaired, and she stopped eating. After a month with no improvement, the authorities sent her home. Gyaltsen Kelsang's parents then arranged for her to be admitted to a Tibetan hospital where she spent nine weeks. She died seven days after returning home for the second time.

With eleven other nuns from Garu nunnery, Gyaltsen Kelsang was detained on June 14, 1993 for allegedly taking part in a pro-independence demonstration. However, there are no reports of protests that day, and the nuns are thought to have been arrested even before they began to demonstrate. That the arrests took place on the first day of the World Conference on Human Rights in Vienna was construed by some in Lhasa as a "symbol of official contempt for the UN Conference." The detentions were also part of a "crackdown" on Garu nuns who had always been an active presence and often took leadership roles within the pro-independence movement. The 1993 crackdown at Garu was to include a "re-education campaign" scheduled to begin in July.

• **SHERAB NGAWANG,** formerly a novice nun at Michungri nunnery and reportedly the youngest political prisoner in Tibet, died on May 15, 1995. Twelve years old when she was arrested for taking part in a political demonstration on the Barkor in Lhasa in February 1992, she was fifteen when she completed her sentence in February 1995. At her release, she was treated unsuccessfully in various hospitals in Lhasa and then in a rural hospital near her parents' home in Meldrogongkar. According to a Tibetan undertaker, Sherab Ngawang's kidneys showed signs of acute damage, and there were adhesions on her lungs. During her imprisonment in the Trisam "re-education-through-labor" camp, prison guards reportedly beat her with electric batons and with a plastic tube filled with sand because she allegedly made a face at them when they were closing the cell doors one evening. She also was trampled on or kicked. One source reported, "They beat her until she was so covered with bruises that you could hardly recognize her."

When she was arrested on the morning of February 3, 1992, Sherab Ngawang told police she was already fifteen because she did not want to be separated from the nuns with whom she had protested. However, most of her friends, four Michungri nuns and a monk from Nyemo Gyalche monastery, received longer sentences and went to Drapchi prison while she served out her term in Trisam. Their protest had only lasted a few minutes, but particularly upset Chinese authorities because it interrupted a New Year visit to the Barkor police station by the governor of Tibet, the vice-mayor of Lhasa, and fifteen other officials.

Another of the nuns involved in the protest, Phuntsog Yangkyi, has also died. On June 4, 1994, only a few days after her transfer from Drapchi prison to a police hospital in Lhasa, she died from prison-related injuries and illness. Chinese authorities later said she died from cerebral tuberculosis, a diagnosis consistent with prison mal-treatment.

• **TASHI TSERING,** fifty-nine, from Ngabring county, Shigatse, died on January 17, 1995, possibly from severe punishment and lack of medical treatment during his years in Drapchi prison. In 1993, it was reported that he was ill with heart problems and had been briefly admitted to the prison clinic in April 1991. He was released in September 1993 under conditions which remain unknown.

A prominent public figure and member of the Chinese People's Political Consultative Conference, Shigatse Prefecture before his detention, Tashi Tsering was arrested on November 18, 1989. Charged with "counterrevolutionary propaganda" and "inflammatory delusion," according to Radio Lhasa, on December 1, 1989, he was sentenced to a seven year term. His case was described in detail in a Radio Lhasa (November 29, 1989) report: "For a long time (Tashi

Tsering) has been slack in remolding his ideology, showing great discontent against the party and about the reality. He wrote a total of seventy-three slogans and leaflets supporting independence for Tibet this year and put them into complaint letter boxes at the central airport of the prefecture...the general office of the CPPCC Prefectural Committee and the head office of the Shigatse City Party Committee. These slogans and leaflets, venomously slandering the Chinese Communist Party and the socialist system, reflected his very reactionary thinking. They have had extremely bad influence among the public and have seriously undermined political stability and unity..." Tashi Tsering was also a monk at Drongtse monastery and had worked at the middle school in Shigatse Prefecture.

Appendix C: Document No. 5 of the Sixth Enlarged Plenary Session of the Standing Committee [of the Fourth Congress of the Tibet Autonomous Regional Branch of the Chinese Communist Party (excerpted)

On September 5, 1994, at the annual meeting of the TAR Communist Party Committee, the delegates gathered to hear in detail what decisions had been made by the Third Forum on Work in Tibet, which had met in Beijing six weeks earlier. The meeting was chaired by Regional Party Secretary Chen Kuiyuan and attended by all the main deputy secretaries. Phagpalha Geleg Namgyal was given a special honorary invitation to attend, in his capacity as a vice-chairman of the standing committee of the National People's Congress. The main speech, "Seize the 'The Third Forum on Work in Tibet as a Good Opportunity to Achieve a New Situation for Work in Tibet in an All-Round Way," was given by Ragdi who had attended the Third Forum, along with Regional Party Secretary Chen. With the exception of the first five paragraphs, the excerpts translated here are taken from the full internally circulated version, not the official public summary printed in the Chinese-language edition of Tibet Daily the day after the meeting and published in English translation by SWB on September 26, 1994. The passages from the internal version which were omitted from the public version are marked in bold. They include the sections on cutting off the serpent's head, encouraging migration, closing monasteries, intensifying political education, and punishing people who sing counterrevolutionary songs.

The Third Forum on Work in Tibet helped by the Party Central Committee and the State Council was a meeting on important strategic policy to rejuvenate Tibet, convened by the third generation of the collective central leadership with Comrade Jiang Zemin at its core—a generation that has inherited the tradition of the first and second generations of collective leadership in attaching importance and paying attention to work in Tibet. It was an important meeting for promoting stability and development in Tibet in the new period. It will have an extremely important and far-reaching effect on work in Tibet in the future.

The central authorities are paying a great deal of attention to Tibet, and the entire country is providing energetic support to Tibet. In such a situation, what should we do in Tibet? To answer this question, there are three very important things to do: One is to thoroughly comprehend the guidelines and seriously achieve ideological unity; next is to have a clear concept and formulate concrete measures; and the third is to work hard in unity and perform actual deeds.

The sixth enlarged plenary session of the Fourth Tibet Autonomous Regional CCP Committee will adhere to Comrade Deng Xiaoping's theory on building socialism with Chinese characteristics, follow the guidelines of the Third Forum on Work in Tibet, as well as the principles for work in Tibet in the new period, and consider both the overall situation and Tibet's reality. After thoroughly comprehending the guidelines, unifying thinking, and clarifying the tasks, the plenary session will discuss how to comprehensively implement the tasks set by the Third Forum on Work in Tibet, seize the opportunity to accelerate development and maintain stability, and strive to create a new situation for work in Tibet with a new mental attitude, a new concept and new measures.

1. *It is Necessary to Seriously Study and Thoroughly Understand the Central Guidelines and Identify our Thinking with Them.*

The Third Forum on Work in Tibet discussed Tibet's stability and development in light of the changes in the international situation and Tibet's new situation and new problems in the course of China's establishment of a socialist market economic structure. After summing up experience and increasing the conferees' understanding, the forum clarified the guiding principles and major policies for work in Tibet for a time to come and put forward Tibet's development objectives and concept for the period extending from the latter part of the century to the early part of the next century, as well as the strategic principle of safeguarding the motherland's unification, opposing splittism and maintaining social stability. It helped Tibet overcome specific difficulties and solve specific problems and mobilized the entire country to support Tibet.

The important decisions made by the Central Committee and by the State Council during the Forum constitute the general strategy of our Party to administer Tibet in this new historic period. They are the basic principles for every level of our region's Party and government organizations together with the people of various nationalities to follow for a time to come. They indicate that from this point onwards we have entered a new phase of the modernization and development of our region.

(1) Seeking unity of thinking means, first of all, that we must seek unity of thinking concerning the five basic experiences. The five basic experiences summed up by the central authorities are not only a summary of experiences and lessons from the past, but what is most important is that they are also guidelines and principles for us to recognize and follow in the future. **General Secretary Jiang Zemin said**

that the Central Committee is responsible for some errors in Tibet work in the past. This is a reflection of the kind concern of the central authorities, which is to sum up our experiences and lessons from the positive point of view. This should be understood as a guideline laid down by the central authorities for us to look up to. It does not mean that we do not have to consider the past, and above all it does not mean that things which proved to be wrong in the past should be preserved now. We must seek unity of thinking according to the spirit of the Central Committee.

(2) We must clearly understand that the we must do our work well in Tibet not only for the sake of our own region's stability and development, not only for the interests of our people, but also for the sake of the whole nation's stability and development.

(3) We must understand well that to obtain stability is the prerequisite, and to develop is the basis. The relationship between these two should be handled correctly.

(4) The central authorities have decided that the speed of Tibet's development should be higher than the average growth rate of the whole country so as to enable the living standard of the majority of the masses to reach the middle standard of wealth. This decision is an important strategic decision and it has created a historic and significant new opportunity for Tibet's social and economic development.

(5) The focal points for the widening of Tibet's open door are to put the stress on mutual economic support and the exchange of different goods with the inner part [of China], which should build an inseparable economic relationship between Tibet and the whole nation.

(6) In the process of building a socialist market economy, co-operation and interchange between Tibet and the inner part of our country should be expanded more than ever before.

(7) We should seek unity of understanding concerning the fact that the Dalai clique is the root of Tibet's instability, and the fact that the nature of the struggle between us and this clique is one of contradiction between us and an enemy. The struggle between us and the Dalai clique is not a matter of religious freedom or of rights to autonomy, but one of safeguarding the unification of our nation, a matter of opposing splittist activities among our nationalities, and of securing the achievements of the democratic [land] reforms [of 1959 onwards]. The essential

point of ensuring stability and gaining victory in the struggle against splittism lies in carrying out our own construction in Tibet and doing our tasks well.

(8) Dealing well with nationalities work at this present juncture means placing emphasis on speeding up economic development and encouraging the development of the society to achieve prosperity together. This is our main task in this field. **On the basis of law we should enhance administrative work in the field of religion, and guide religion to become an appropriate practice according to the socialist system.**

(9) [We] should have a deep understanding of the principle of "the two inseparables" [the minority nationalities are inseparable from the Han nationality; the Han nationality is inseparable from the minority nationalities] which is a policy that also applies to cadres, and is also a fundamental principle for resolving relationships between different nationalities. In Tibet, to persevere with "the two inseparables" is essential for the development of economy, culture, science, and technology, and is also an urgent need for safeguarding the unification of the motherland, enhancing the solidarity of the nationalities, and bringing stability to Tibetan society .

We must fully understand the spirit of the Third Forum correctly. We should neither take a one-sided approach nor bring an outdated way of thinking and point of view to our understanding of the spirit of the Forum.

2. *[We Must Get Our Ideas into Shape, Strengthen Our Confidence, and Bring about Unconventional Economic Development in Tibet.]*

The units dealing with propaganda, ideology, culture, theoretical studies, and broadcasting must consider their work of publicizing the spirit of the Third Forum as their foremost task in this and the following year [1994 and 1995]. They must carry out propaganda about this widely and deeply.

The Party Committee of the TAR has decided to hold a wide-ranging discussion throughout our region on the subject of "Change the way of thinking, seek unity of thinking, and emancipate the mind," and the Propaganda departments should organize this well.

The Propaganda Department of the TAR Party Committee should organize and focus its attention on publishing propaganda materials appropriate for the

masses in agricultural and husbandry areas, appropriate for people in towns and cities, and appropriate for external propaganda.

[In the year 2000] every county should have a middle school, every village should have a primary school with a complete set of classes, and eighty percent of school-age children should be at school. Conditions of medical treatment should improve noticeably. Radio and television broadcasts should cover more areas.

If we speed up Tibet's development at a rate faster than the usual speed, then we will be able to transform the poor backward aspect of our region, minimize the gap between Tibet and other parts of the country, and catch up with the strategy of the Three Steps plan. We could then improve the living standards of the vast numbers of masses to obtain a middle standard of wealth along with the whole people, and then we also could make some contribution to the whole nation and guarantee the stability and development of the whole nation.

The focal point of the policy of opening the door wider in Tibet should be towards the inner part of the country. While depending on our region's own good aspects of policy and production resources, we should combine these with the good aspects of the inner part of the country, its intellectuals, technicians, management personnel, and communications. Mutual economical support and exchange in every field should be broadened. We should encourage traders, investment, economic units, and individuals to enter our region to run different sorts of enterprises. We should turn our good production resources into economic [advantages] and join our region's economy with the nation's vast market. We should build an inseparable relationship with the whole nation.

While practicing the open door policy, we should pay attention to take precautions against things that damage our stability, and if these things occur we should get rid of them. We should consider our economic interests, but we should also consider the stability and security of our nation.

It is very important to develop our agriculture and husbandry, as stability in these areas is an important factor in developing and stabilizing the entire region.

With respect to giving aid to the poor, we should practice excellent methods to solve the most difficult cases, so that 480,000 poor people in eighteen counties may reach a living standard above the poverty line.

The middle schools and Tibetan classes for our region which are being run in inner parts of the country should continue and should be administered well. We should pay attention to Tibetan language education. We should put effort into developing education both in Chinese and Tibetan language so that both languages are learned and we should even provide the conditions to learn a foreign language.

The Central Committee, the State Council, and other provinces are helping us to accomplish sixty-two construction projects with a value of up to 2.3 billion *yuan*.

All leading cadres of different levels should keep up their spirits and make efforts to improve. They should not despair because of the backwardness and lack of speed in developing the society. They should not be scared of disturbances and damage caused by the enemy.

3. *We Must Improve Our Understanding, Clearly Define Measures, and Bring about Long-term Political Stability in Tibet.*

The main reason why Tibet could not be made stable is the Dalai clique's splittist activities. The Dalai clique hopes to gain "Tibetan independence" by relying on the hostile forces of western countries, and those western hostile forces use the Dalai clique's demand for "Tibetan independence" to cause disturbances in the hope of splitting our country. To secure stability in Tibet is not only to obtain a peaceful situation in Tibet, but, far more important, is to secure the unity of the whole nation, to safeguard the integrity of our sovereignty, to oppose western hostile forces so that their hopes of "westernizing" China and splitting China disappear into thin air. From this point on we should recognize the importance of opposing splittism in Tibet and should have a better understanding of the necessity and significance of this struggle.

We must be able to reveal the true colors of the Dalai clique. Due to the traditional religion, Dalai has a certain prestige among monks, nuns, and devotees. But Dalai and the Dalai clique have defected and escaped to a foreign country, and have turned into a splittist political clique hoping to gain Tibet's independence and have become a tool of international hostile forces. Its true nature of what Dalai is shouting about when he says "Tibetan independence," "a high standard of autonomy" and "Greater Tibet" is to oppose communism, to deny socialism, to overthrow the dictatorship of the people, to split the motherland, to destroy the solidarity of nationalities, and to restore his own authority in Tibet. **Although he sometimes says some nice words to deceive the masses, he has never ceased his splittist actions aimed at dividing our motherland.** Up to now his standpoint on Tibet's independence has never changed, and we must reveal his double-faced true color. The focal point in our region in the struggle against splittism is to oppose the Dalai clique. **As the saying goes, to kill a serpent, one must first cut off its head.** If we do not do that, we cannot succeed in the struggle against splittism.

The struggle between ourselves and the Dalai clique is not a matter of religious belief nor a matter of the question of autonomy, it is a matter of securing the unity of our country and opposing splittism. It is a matter of antagonistic contradiction with the enemy, and it represents the concentrated form of the class struggle in Tibet at the present time. This struggle is the continuing struggle between ourselves and the imperialists since they invaded Tibet a hundred years ago. We must safeguard the achievements of the democratic reforms and of the Open Reform Policy. As long as Dalai does not change his splittist standpoint, we have nothing else to do but to continue this struggle right up till the time we achieve victory.

The guidelines and principles of our struggle against the Dalai clique are these: we must persevere [in stating] that Tibet is a part of China and by holding this banner high and clear, we must wage a tit-for-tat struggle against them. We must prepare for a long-term struggle, but at the same time, according to our present situation, we must work hard and grasp things well. Work in our region must be done seriously, and the international struggle must also be solved well. In this argument we should hit the nail on the head, and make more foreign friends in order to smash the Dalai clique into pieces. The Central Committee's policy towards Dalai is this: If Dalai admits that Tibet is a part of China and is inseparable from China, if he changes his mind and gives up Tibet being independent, and stops all his splittist actions to divide the motherland, then we welcome him back to the motherland from exile as soon as possible. But he cannot claim independence, semi-independence or independence in a disguised form. On the question of safeguarding the unification of the motherland there is nothing to bargain about.

The Dalai clique is the reason why Tibet has not achieved stability. But securing stability in Tibet must depend on us ourselves doing our work well. The focal point of our work is not outside but inside our country; it is not outside but within our Party and it is not with the masses but with the cadres. This should be understood clearly. If we have a Party of great courage and strength, if we have a contingent of cadres with pure hearts and souls, then we will be able to lead the vast masses, and make friends with patriotic personages of different nationalities and different walks of life, and achieve victory in this struggle. If we deal well with our work within our country, then there will not be a market left for the Dalai clique, and their international activities would achieve nothing. We must enhance our own construction and solve problems by laying emphasis on key points. We must focus on key districts and key problems and use good methods to solve bravely and promptly the problems and to handle the persons who have those problems as soon as they appear.

Cadres at all levels, especially leading cadres above the county level, should have a clear understanding of the nature of this struggle and of the principles, guidelines, policies, and methods of this struggle, and should have a correct and clear attitude towards it. No one should be careless about it. This is a life-and-death struggle, and of course it is not an ordinary issue but an important issue.

(1) We Should Enhance the Administration of Monasteries, Monks, and Nuns Within the Law.

We must acknowledge that most of the monasteries, monks, and nuns are patriotic and obey the law. At the same time we also should observe that the reality is that the Dalai clique is using religion for its splittist activities. Recently there have been no limitations on the development of monasteries, and the numbers of monks and nuns have increased by a great amount. Some monasteries have become a basic place for the Dalai clique to practice splittism in our region and they have sneaked into these monasteries. A handful of unlawful monks and nuns have become the vanguard of disturbances. Monasteries are the places where monks and nuns live and practice their religion, but if these monasteries do not do any study of religion, do not develop Buddhism, do not obey religious rules, but instead carry out splittist actions, then their monastery has lost its justification, and they have gone beyond the range of religion. The Dalai clique assumes that "getting hold of a monastery is equivalent to [getting hold of] a district of the Communist

Party," so our prefectures, cities and counties should seriously consolidate [re-organize] the monasteries which have problems. Those monasteries which take sides with the splittists and which are always causing trouble in order to stir up disturbances should be reorganized within a certain time, and if necessary their doors can be closed in order to do so. Those monks and nuns who joined the splittists to cause disturbances and who could not be persuaded to change their attitudes should be punished severely according to the law. This wind of building monasteries and of recruiting new monks and nuns just as they wish should be stopped entirely. In future to build a new monastery, permission must be received from the Religious Affairs Bureau of the TAR. No monastery is allowed to be built without its permission. Those monasteries where the numbers of monks have already been set still need to be limited as much as possible, and are not allowed to go beyond that limit. The excess monks should be expelled, and those monasteries which have not set a stipulated number of monks and nuns should set a number as soon as possible.

(2) By Enhancing Knowledge in the Fight Against "Corrosive Influence" and by Enhancing the Internal Administration, We Should Screen and Purify our Cadre Contingent.

In recent years the Dalai clique had a corrosive influence on some of our region's cadre contingent and intellectuals, and were looking for their supporters to rebel against us. Some of our Party members believe in religion and have participated in religious activities. Some cadres and leaders put up religious symbols inside or outside their locations and have prayer rooms and altars in their houses, and hang up pictures of the Dalai.

Some cadres were hoodwinked by the propaganda of the Dalai clique about nationalism, and they see people and events from the viewpoint of nationalism. Some cadres act as secret enemy agents and have joined counterrevolutionary organizations. They collect confidential information for the Dalai clique and participate in splittist activities. Some teachers use their class room as a platform to spread the idea of "Tibetan independence" without hesitation. Some cadres do not have a firm standpoint and when splittists cause disturbances they do not dare to fight against them. Some cadres and leading members have sent their children abroad to be educated in schools run by the Dalai clique to leave a leeway for themselves. All these things mean that if it is not an ordinary problem of ideology recognition, then it is a problem of nationalism and religion. What it reflects is that some of the cadres in our region do not have a firm standpoint and that the cadre contingent is not pure. Although the Party Committee of TAR has carried out internal consolidation this year the achievement was uneven. Some Party organizations were not serious enough and their consolidation work was carried out just for show. The purification of our cadre contingent and our region's development is directly connected to the fight against splittism, and the size of the victory relies on them, so much so that every Party and government organization at each level must carry out this investigation and purification work well. The Discipline Inspection Commission should enhance its work on building a good Party work style and should carry out the task of taking authority honestly in organizations at every level. While striking at economic criminals we should focus on purifying the cadre contingent and on observing political discipline. All Party members, especially leading members, are forbidden to put up religious symbols, Dalai photos or altars in their house and should not have prayer rooms. Their children are not allowed to be sent abroad to study in schools run by the Dalai clique. Those cadres who do not correct the above mistakes immediately after this meeting should never be promoted. Those who are leaders and who are in important positions should be transferred to other places without hesitation. Those who have serious problems should be punished according to the Party's constitution and government regulations. Those who have opposed the Party or have defected from our country by escaping abroad and have surrendered themselves to the Dalai clique should be expelled from the Party. Those who were involved in splittist and counterrevolutionary activities should be dealt with by the law. Those who have gone abroad to visit their relatives and have not returned in time should be dealt with as if they have tendered their own resignation.

(3) Enhance Work in Schools and the Education of Teenagers.

The Dalai clique has enrolled lots of teenagers in their schools abroad to imbue them with the idea of "Tibetan independence" and splittist ideas. They are trying lots of methods to train successors to the cause of "Tibetan independence." In our region there are students in schools who wear the red scarf [indicating that they belong to the Young Pioneers, the junior wing of the Communist Youth League] but go to monasteries to feed the butter lamps, and what's more, some have even been deceived by the counterrevolutionary propaganda of the Dalai clique, so that they sympathize with them and take part in splittist activities. What will happen after some decades? Will our teenagers grow up as successors to the cause of socialism or to the cause of splittism? This is an important issue that we ought to consider seriously. If we want to have successors to the cause of socialism in Tibet, then we must enhance the education of teenagers continuously. This is a strategic task which we must confront, and the whole society must create an environment for teenagers to grow up well. The Communist Youth League should contribute their work on uniting and educating the teenagers. Relevant organizations, especially the educational organizations, should put great effort into training our successors. They should practice different methods to help Tibet's teenagers to grow up healthily. By using the method of recalling past suffering and considering the source of present happiness, and by comparing the old society and the new society, we should let the young generation acquire an understanding of the dark serf system and see the true colors of the Dalai clique. Those teachers who spread the "Tibetan independence" idea from the platform of their classroom should be reasoned with, and should be cleared away. As for those who have sent their children abroad to be educated in schools run by the Dalai clique, if the parents are citizens, peasants or herdsmen we should enhance our work on educating them, but if they are Party members in government departments or are cadres, then we should let them call back their children within a specified period. Those who do not call back their children should be dealt with seriously, and their children's residence cards should be cancelled. Those graduates from schools of the Dalai clique who have come to work in Tibet should be controlled strictly; they should not be allowed to work in the Party or the government or in other important departments. Those who are already working in Tibet should be checked, and they should be dealt with in different ways according to the different cases.

(4) Resolutely Screen and Abolish Counterrevolutionary Documents and Propaganda Materials.

In recent years some people have sung counterrevolutionary songs in public. Some people have been selling Dalai photographs and badges. Some people bring from abroad published counterrevolutionary materials and materials such as cassettes and tapes and then they record them or make copies of them in great numbers for distribution. The Public Security Bureau, the Commercial and Cultural Departments, etc. should check up on these things seriously and confiscate them as soon as they appear, without any hesitation. They should cancel the licenses of those who sell these things and fine them. Those who encourage teenagers to sing counterrevolutionary songs should be punished severely according to the law. Those who make, put up or distribute counterrevolutionary publications, and those who shout counterrevolutionary slogans should be punished severely and in a timely manner, according to the relevant stipulations in the law. We must strike back at them through the mass media and reinforce this struggle in the ideological field.

(5) Enhance our Work in Establishing Laws and Regulations.

The Standing Committee of the TAR Congress and the judicial organs should carry out thorough investigations in order to find out problems in the ways we deal with our struggle against splittism, and seriously analyze those problems in the law. If there is anything not yet mentioned in the law, the judicial administrations should give their views quickly and establish laws and regulations to fight against the splittists so that the laws and regulations become more effective. By educating the people about the laws and regulations we will enable the people to act according to the limits set by the laws and regulations.

(6) Strengthen Public Security through Comprehensive Management.

The focal point of the system of Comprehensive Management of Public Security is to puncture [the pride of] the splittists. On this premise we should construct our methods and direct our basic organizations in order to crack down on the criminals by establishing a responsibility system for the leaders in the Comprehensive Management of Public Security which must be assured by guarantees. The document named "Some Decisions about Assuring a Responsibility System for Leaders in Public Security" published by five committees has been dispatched by the Central Committee, and a document named "Detailed Implementation" has also been dispatched by the government of our region. Now our task is to implement these measures seriously. Every level, including those of the region, the prefectures, the municipality, the counties, the departments, and other units should make their own regulations to implement the responsibilities of public security leaders at the primary level and with each individual. To those leaders whose organizations always have problems which are hard to solve, we should exercise "Power to Make Unilateral Decisions" without any hesitation. As "striking relentless blows" [.ie. carrying out a crackdown] is one of the important elements of the Comprehensive Management of Public Security, the judicial organs should organize local public security organizations to solve their own main problems by having focal places to deal with and focal points to solve. We must rely both on the relevant public security offices and on the vast numbers of masses in dealing with public security work. We must exercise well our authority at the grassroots [in primary] levels and organize the masses to oppose splittism as much as possible. We must give credit and hand out bonuses to people and groups who are outstanding in the struggle against splittism so that they will be encouraged. We must weaken the enemy's social base, and let the splittists come under the influence of the surrounding society, so that they find themselves in an isolated position without any friends.

(7) Strengthen Judicial Work and Let the Pillar of Dictatorship Stand Stronger than Ever.

All the judicial departments, the military command in Tibet and the armed security forces, etc. should contribute to maintaining stability, developing the economy, safeguarding the people, striking the enemy, and in punishing [and cracking down on] criminals. We must strengthen undercover work and strike relentless blows at splittists who have been sent into our region [by the Dalai clique] and at counterrevolutionary organizations which operate underground movements. We must enhance our investigation of focal districts, focal bases, and focal points and speed up our gaining of control over them. We must take great caution against the revival of armed rebellion by the splittists. By putting more effort into construction along the borders and by tightening control along the borders, we must block the way for Dalai infiltrators to sneak into our region. Any disturbances and sabotage activities should be immediately and effectively dealt with. We must guard against plots from the beginning and attack them as soon as they occur. We must put more effort into building up the judicial administration contingent, and improve political and professional standards in order to collect as much intelligence as possible so that cases can be dealt with immediately and effectively. The funds and materials needed to improve the efficiency of the judicial organs should be ensured.

(8) Strengthen **the Work of Dividing and Demoralizing the Enemy**, and Unite All the Forces that Can Be United.

Although the hostile forces in the West are using the Dalai clique, because of their all-round future policy and interests they will not at present dare to take any crucial steps. The Dalai clique has its own unavoidable difficulties and has lots of contradictions among themselves. We must use all their contradictions and by every means we must divide and demoralise those forces controlled by the Dalai clique so that the splittist forces who claim "Tibetan independence" will be isolated without any friends, and we will gain more supporters for ourselves.

(9) [We] Must Handle Well Diplomatic and Propaganda Work Abroad.

We must do propaganda work abroad with enthusiasm and on our own initiative. When carrying out propaganda work we must consider our audience and persevere in telling the facts in a reasoned way and we must strengthen our propaganda work according to the various different circumstances in which we find ourselves. By attacking the Dalai clique we must try to gain more support throughout space and in people's hearts. By publicizing the positive side we must let people know about the truth and we must take the initiative in attacking the Dalai clique by targeting their activities. By raising the standard of planning and anticipation, by improving the efficiency of propaganda work abroad, by using well our policies and tactics, and by improving our ability to carry out propaganda work abroad, we must gradually change the international point of view. We must boldly do propaganda work showing that Tibet is a part of China, and do propaganda work about social development and achievements. We must reveal the true colors of the Dalai clique and the dark side of the serf system of old Tibet by using archives and the real development [since the end of the serf system]. The Western countries are supporting and encouraging the Dalai clique and using the so-called Tibet issue to interfere with our country's internal affairs. We must deal with this diplomatic struggle in a reasoned way, with interest and within limits so that we can gain more international understanding and support. By working hard we must defeat their hope of internationalizing the Tibet issue.

(10) By Paying Attention to Hot Social Problems, We Must Promptly Solve Contradictions Among the People.

Because of the reforms there will be different problems of social opinion about the change in traditions and the adjustment in [people's] interests, and we must pay attention to these, and in due course handle well ideology work among the people. We must be alert to the fact that the hostile forces and the splittists may deliberately cause disturbances and incite [discontent with] the contradictions in order to gain their chance to sneak in.

In our struggle against splittism we have the leadership of the Central Committee and its correct policies and strategies, we have the firm foundation of communism since Tibet's peaceful liberation, we have a contingent of cadres of different nationalities who have proved to be reliable, we have the firm base of the masses, we have the respect of people of all the nationalities and from all walks of life, we have the support of the different nationalities of the whole nation and we have the authority of the people and the people's mighty army. These essential conditions which we have as a base are our strength, so that although the Dalai clique insists on splittism it can only end with its defeat. The twelve hundred million people of China, including the Tibetan people, will never let Tibet depart from its great motherland, and no one is allowed to invade China's territorial sovereignty.

4. *[We Should Uphold the Banner of Patriotism, Comprehensively and Correctly Implement the Policies on Nationalities and Religion, and Continually Consolidate and Expand the Patriotic United Front.]*

We should wholeheartedly take care and believe patriotic personages and show concern about them more than ever. **As for those few who do not have a firm standpoint, whose attitudes are not clear and who are not close to the Party, and who are trying to have it both ways, we must teach them to correct their mistakes and help them to change their hopeless standpoint. Those who insist on the wrong road will be deserted by history.**

The most important thing is that it does not only mean that the Party is concerned about the patriotic personages of the various different nationalities, it also means that all the patriotic personages are greatly enthusiastic about putting themselves forward for the sake of Tibet's development and stability.

Patriotic personages of the different nationalities and personalities from **various circles should wholeheartedly hold the same standpoint with the Party, and work fearlessly in the struggle against the splittists. By persevering with one's brave attitude in this struggle one should be able to prove oneself as a worthy and proud member of the patriotic United Front Line.** We must continue to expand and consolidate the patriotic United Front Line.

In this new historical period we must develop the patriotic United Front line more than ever. Under the leadership of the CCP we must form an alliance with the vast masses of laboring people, with the people of different nationalities, different religions, different economic standards and different intellectual circles, and with our brothers and sisters of various circles who live abroad but who support the unification of our motherland. We must work hard to form this great alliance with all walks of life and all kinds of people.

We must train and bring up successors to the patriotic personalities of various circles in the new generation and we must deal well with our work concerning our brothers and sisters abroad and try our best to win over most of them to take the side of the motherland.

The nature of exercising autonomy in nationality areas is different from the Dalai clique's shouting about "a high level of autonomy" and a "Greater Tibet." They are plotting to pass off fish eyes as pearls and we must be on our guard. While different areas and nationalities have personal contacts and economic exchanges, it is certain that all sorts of problems will appear, but they are all contradictions within the people and we must not view these problems as a nationality issue. If there are matters damaging the unification of the nationalities, then we should expose them and resolve them at once. We must carry out criticism and if necessary we should take measures to punish them under the law. Our Party's cadres should not have any difference between nationalities, should reject nationalism and selfish departmentalism and should stand on the same ground with the Party in the understanding that safeguarding the solidarity of the nationalities is the top priority. Now our region has decided to hold a Nationalities Unification Commendatory Conference every second year.

The Dalai clique made use of religion to exercise its splittist mischief with the result that the religious issue in Tibet became more complicated. We must teach and guide Tibet Buddhism to reform itself. All those religious laws and rituals must be reformed in order to fit in with the needs of development and stability in Tibet, and they should be reformed so that they become appropriate to a society under socialism. [Such a process of adaptation] is in accordance with the nature of the development of religion.

The government guarantees the rights of the law-abiding religious masses by guaranteeing the rights of people not to believe in religion. This religious

freedom policy does not include Party members - no Party member is allowed to believe in religion. Although the Communist Party respects the religious beliefs of the masses of non-Party members, every Party member should persevere with his or her proletarian world outlook of materialism and atheism.

(3) The Dalai clique is making use of religion in its aim to carry out splittist mischief and we must be able to perceive this reality. We must reveal the true political face of the Dalai hidden behind the religious mask, and prevent by all means and ways the monks and nuns in the monasteries of our region from being affected by the influence of the Dalai clique. The Communist cadres and the vast masses of monks and nuns in the monasteries should demonstrate their determination to differentiate themselves from the Dalai clique in the political field.

(4) All the monasteries, monks, and nuns must voluntarily submit to the authorities at every level. The religious rituals must be practiced within the limits of the state laws... Religion is not allowed to interfere in politics, law or in school education. Especially, it is strictly prohibited for teenagers within the restricted age to join the monasteries; it is strictly prohibited for monasteries and lama reincarnations to make use of religion to exploit the people: it is prohibited for them to accept money and materials from the masses thus adding to their burden: and it is strictly prohibited for them to make use of religion to arouse the masses to cause trouble and create social disturbances.

In the struggle against splittism, we have to acknowledge that there are a few religious personalities who do not have a firm standpoint, and a few monks and nuns who participate in splittist activities... At present our main task in the field of religion is to enhance the administration of monasteries, monks, and nuns under the law.

The Democratic Management Committees in [all] monasteries are the grass-roots units of our administration, and they assist the government in administering the monasteries. We must choose well the members of the Democratic Management Committees so that those who have authority over the monasteries are patriotic devotees who act according to the civil and religious laws. We must enhance the understanding of the monks and nuns about patriotism and law. In recognizing the reincarnations of the trulkus [re-incarnated lamas] of Tibetan Buddhism, we must follow the relevant decisions of the state and implement them according to the real conditions in our region and make them more practical as soon as possible. We must do this work earnestly in order to gain the initiative. We must take precautions against the Dalai clique - they are interfering in the recognition of trulkus in order to manipulate the monasteries, and this situation must be reversed. [one page of the original document is missing here]

5. *[We Should Strengthen Self-development, Improve the Party's Leadership, and Shoulder a Major Historic Responsibility to Create New Conditions for Our Work in Tibet.]*

If we cannot state our position on matters of political principles, then these problems will increase and the influence of splittism might spread to the grassroots and to agricultural and husbandry areas. We must be alert and pay great attention to the possibility of losing the masses to the splittist side. This would shake us by our foundations.

Gyantse county and Shol neighbourhood under the Lhasa Metropolitan Committee have made achievements in their grassroots works which we should give credit to, and we should introduce their experience [to others] so they can learn further. Those who do mischief to our cadres at the grassroots by hurting and retaliating against them must be punished severely under the law. Recently there has been a period during which we have been careless and have neglected our work at grassroots level... Those primary organizations which are not well qualified should be helped to reorganize them by sending work teams to the relevant villages and towns in order to investigate and improve their work.

By learning from the experiences of the past we must practice good methods and take effective measures to obtain a contingent of cadres from different nationalities which will work in Tibet permanently. We must use all means to keep the intellectuals [who are now in Tibet] to go on working in Tibet. We must continue the system of sending cadres to Tibet from inner parts of the country. The policies towards those cadres who were sent and went home must be carried out well, and when assigning cadres from the inner parts to work in Tibet we should be farsighted and strive to have cadres living and working long-term in Tibet. We should enroll students by deciding that their future professional work [will be] in Tibet. Universities in the inner areas should enroll those students at [their] own expense. The TAR Military Command and the People's Armed Police should transfer their outstanding officers and soldiers to civilian work [in Tibet] when their military service is over. In these ways we should strive to have a permanent contingent of cadres in Tibet. The Central Committee has divided the tasks and responsibilities among other provinces within set time limits to support Tibet with people from all walks of life as we have requested. This is a new strategy corresponding to a new era in which we need to sum up our past experiences and find ways to perfect our work.

Those leading cadres who have not held to a firm standpoint when they have been confronted by problems, who do not have an appropriate political ideology, who do not move forward, who do not do much work for a long time and who do not play a leading role, and so forth, should be dismissed without hesitation. We should have a system both for promoting and dismissing a cadre from his position. We must raise the salaries and benefits of cadres in Tibet by practising special salary methods in Tibet.

Within the leadership we should exercise mutual support, trust, understanding, friendship, and concern. We should never create bad air among ourselves. All leading cadres at every level should remember this and practice it as good political behavior.

We should emphasize the principles of centralism more than ever, that is, the lower level is subordinate to the higher level, and the entire Party is subordinate to the Central Committee.

Appendix D. Nalandra Monastery

On March 25, 1995, the Chinese authorities released a public report about a raid on the monastery of Nalandra in the Phenpo valley, north of Lhasa. Printed in the little-known Lhasa Evening News and not seen outside Tibet until nearly a year later, this was the only public description of Tibetan unrest given by officials that year, as far as we know. It describes the police operation at the monastery, which led to the highest number of arrests from a single monastery since 1987, and suggests that pro-independence activity by the monks had been widespread for at least three years. The role of the Work Team in screening and re-educating the monks is emphasized, and the article gives the first indication that the unrest may have been triggered by the arrival of such a team in the monastery. Although the article begins by describing a police raid on Nalandra on February 23, it says that a Work Team had been established in the monastery three days earlier. It is understood from unofficial sources that the first arrests at Nalandra took place on about February 21, and it now seems likely that the Nalandra unrest was a response to the official attempts to "overhaul and consolidate" the institution. None of the officials referred to here was previously known, and this is the first time that it was known that the Party Secretary in Lhasa and the head of Public Security in Lhasa are both Chinese officials.

What Has Been Heard and Seen about Overhauling and Consolidating Nalandra Monastery

Lhasa Evening News (lha-sa 'i dgong dro 'i tshags par)
March 25, 1995

Nalandra Monastery is situated about ninety kilometers north of Lhasa in the valley of Khartse village, Lhundrup county. Its history goes back more than 560 years, and it is the biggest monastery of the Sakya school in Lhasa municipality. After the Third Plenary of the Eleventh Party Congress, the Party and the state appropriated 140,000 *yuan* to the monastery for its renovation. Since then it has been full of butter lamps and juniper smoke offered by the masses of devotees who came for pilgrimage every day. But a small number of monks, manipulated and instigated by splittists, had the bad conduct of splitting the motherland and sabotaging the unity of the nationalities. In August 1992 they not only spread quantities of reactionary leaflets and posters [*log spyod bsgrags yig*] within Lhundrup county, but even put up reactionary posters [*log spyod byar yig*] on the hillside next to the entrance to the county government offices. As Nalandra monastery became a den [*nag tshang*] of splittist forces, which sabotaged public security, unity and stability [their activities] had a bad impact on the masses.

On February 23, 1995, members of the public security discovered huge amounts of reactionary documents and wooden blocks for printing reactionary song lyrics. While the security members were carrying out their official duties, about ten monks gathered in the grand meeting hall of the monastery, and some monks were stirred up to attack the security members who were on duty by shouting, throwing stones, and spitting at them. They also sang reactionary songs. The police showed extreme forbearance, which the monks in an act of madness misunderstood as weakness and as being easily [susceptible] to bullying, and they not only insulted and shouted at those police, they also called them "running dogs of the Chinese [*rgya-mi'l rgyug khyi*]," "beggars" and " dirt eaters" [*mi gisang ba za mkhan*].

In order for the vast mass of the peasants and the monks to gain a better understanding of the monastery's real situation and to celebrate the coming Tibetan Year of the Wood Pig in a peaceful, harmonious way, the Party committee and the government of Lhundrup county immediately started to overhaul and consolidate [*bcos-sgrigs* - literally, reorganize] the monastery by sending a work team on February 20, [1995].

Since 1992, the few splittists had used loopholes in the monastery's management to conduct very many evil splittist activities; therefore, it was time to reorganize the monastery to solve the following problems:

[1] The regulations of the monastery have turned out to be blank sheets of paper, and the Democratic Management Committee has been existing in name only.

[2] The masses complained that some young monks broke their religious vows and came to the town to play basketball and mahjong. What's more, they even stole things belonging to the masses, fought in the streets, and caused disturbances in the marketplace.

[3] During the past years and months the Democratic Management Committee neglected to educate the monks to love their country and religion, and to abide by the law. They were careless and showed no concern about the monks' illegal activities.

[4] Some old monks irresponsibly accepted students, so that even some under-age boys were registered as monks. The number of monks exceeded the quota fixed by the government.

[5] Since August 1992, there have been many incidents in the monastery. The number of reactionary leaflets [and] posters published by the few splittists and distributed or stuck up by so many people over such a wide area and [over such a long] period has been unprecedented in recent years.

The Work Team stayed in the monastery and explained the Party's policies on nationality and religious affairs, the law, and the constitution to the monks. They raised the level of understanding of the monks and pinpointed unlawful activities. They helped the Democratic Management Committee make regulations for the monastery and spent eighteen days with them in overhauling and consolidating the monastery. They interrogated and expelled from the monastery those few who were involved in counterrevolutionary activities and who had obstructed the police from carrying out their official duties and had broken their religious vows. Those monks who entered the monastery without permission were sent back, and the underage monks were given advice and persuaded.

On March 15, 1995 the Work Team of Nalandra monastery held a large meeting, attended by the leaders of the city and the county. They were Zhao Lanji, [?kra'o lan ci], Wang Huaisheng [kha'i hrang], Lhasum, and Tashi Tenpa. At the meeting, Lobsang, from the Democratic Management Committee, declared the monastery's regulations to be as follows: the vast [numbers of] monks must follow the leadership and administration of the Party and the government on their [own] initiative; must respect the socialist system; must be determined to oppose any activity that sabotages the unity of the nationalities and splits the motherland; must seriously observe all the relevant management regulations. The vast majority of the monks must carry out their normal religious rituals under the administration of the Democratic Management Committee and the village authority; and must punish with determination all those unlawful activities which aim at splitting the motherland under the mask of religious rituals, etc. The monastery's regulations also call on each individual monk to love the country, cherish religion and abide by the law. Besides this, decisions about administration and about the preservation of cultural relics were made [at the meeting].

At this meeting there were agreements between the Khartse village authorities and the Democratic Management Committee together with the prayer leader; between the prayer leader and monks who lived in the monastery; and between the monks in the monastery and their families, to take responsibility for loving the country, cherishing religion, and abiding by the law. In this way it was made clear that in the future all religious rituals must be in compliance with what was ratified by the unified administration of the Khartse village people's government; and if not in accord with the law and regulations, they [the monks] would be severely punished in accordance with the law. It also meant that the Democratic Management Committee has the duty to advise the monks to love the country, cherish religion, and abide by the law all the time.

The vast majority of the Nalandra monks were very angry with the few monks who were involved in the evil deeds of splitting the country and requested that the government punish them severely. [At the meeting,] the deputy-chairman of the monastery's Democratic Management Committee, Tenzin, said:

> The serious problems of our monastery have brought discredit to our monastery's name, so that in future we must enhance the administration of the monastery and of the monks. We will pay great attention to educating the monks to love the country, cherish religion, and abide by the law continuously. According to the different levels of crimes committed by the few monks, the government has detained and expelled or ordered them to leave the monastery, etc. I wholeheartedly support and comply with all these decisions.

After this reorganization meeting was over, Lama Legshe Zoepa told the reporter, "Due to the few monks who unlawfully carried out evil deeds it was timely to overhaul and consolidate the monastery. We resolutely complied with the government's decisions, and exposed those who sabotaged public security and condemned those who brought discredit to holy and pure Buddhism." Those monks who were expelled from the monastery and sent away, were taken home by their village leaders and their families in order to have adequate arrangements made.

Zhao Lanji, the secretary of the Municipal Party Committee [*grong aud kyi hru'u ci*], and Wang Huaisheng [*kha'i hrang*], the deputy director of the region's security department [*sbyi bde thing gi thing-krang gzhon-pa*], who concurrently holds the post of Director of the Lhasa Municipal Public Security Department [*grong-khyer lha-sa sbyi de cus kyi cus-krang*], and other leaders spoke highly of the achievements in overhauling and consolidating the monastery. They emphasized that in future the administration and the regulations of the monastery should be enhanced, and the families and relatives of those monks who were expelled or sent away from the monastery should be given more ideological education so that by having a better understanding of the situation and of the present state of affairs they would put their efforts into the economic construction of their homeland with securing social stability.

To split the motherland, to sabotage the unity of the nationalities, and to act against the essence of religion will never conform to the wishes of the people. If the people achieve stability in their thinking, the conspiracy of the few evil doers will never succeed. By overhauling and consolidating Nalandra monastery, we once more understood the importance of government at all levels working to enhance the administration and regulations of the monasteries, the important role of the Democratic Management Committee of each monastery in educating the vast majority of the monks to love the country, to cherish religion, and to abide by the law, so that society can achieve long-term stability and the people can enjoy their life by concentrating on their daily work in a peaceful environment.

[At the end] the vice chairman of the monastery's Democratic Management Committee, Tenzin, said to us, "The monks of Nalandra monastery welcome all monks and laymen devotees to come to the monastery on pilgrimage."

Appendix E. Nun Describes Protest in Trisam[163]

Introduction
Lobsang Choedron, from the village of Lhokha Dranang Gyaling, was a sixteen-year-old nun at Michungri Nunnery near Lhasa when she was arrested for taking part in a demonstration with four other nuns and a monk in the Barkor on the eve of Chinese New Year, 1992. The protest lasted a few minutes but disturbed a visit by the top regional official to the local police station.

Three of the nuns and the monk were tried and sentenced to between five and seven years each; the other two nuns, Lobsang Choedron and Sherab Ngawang, were each sentenced without trial to three years imprisonment because they were under eighteen. Sherab said that she was fifteen years old but is believed to have been only twelve at the time of arrest. The two girls spent eighteen months in Gutsa detention center awaiting sentencing and were then sent to Trisam re-education-through-labor camp to serve out their sentences.

In April 1995 Sherab died just after being released from Trisam, apparently from beatings in the prison. Phuntsog Yangkyi, one of the nuns sentenced to five years, died in prison, apparently from beatings, in 1994.

This is the most recent account of conditions in Trisam and the first direct account of the severe beatings in Trisam that led to the death of Sherab Ngawang. It describes a protest by nuns inside Trisam prison, which led to beatings and solitary confinement in tiny punishment cells.

Lobsang Choedron escaped from Tibet on October 14, 1995 and gave this account of her experience in prison after arriving in India [TIN ref: R24(RM2)].

Lobsang Choedron: Background
I have been a nun for seven years [since 1988]. I was ordained by Gen Ngawang Phuntsog in Drepung and then stayed in Michungri nunnery, just outside Lhasa. At that time there was a teacher in Michungri; but she was very old and later she fell sick and had to go back to Lhasa. But I remained at the nunnery.

I went to the Barkor to demonstrate on March [error for February] 3, 1992. I shouted slogans calling for independence. It was the first time I had taken part in a demonstration. I was with four other Michungri nuns and a Sera monk:

---

[163] First published in "Documents and Statements from Tibet, 1995," *TIN Background Briefing Paper No.26*, December 1995.

- Lobsang Drolma, twenty-two years old at the time of arrest; sentence: seven years. As of January 1996 in Drapchi. *[Given the longest sentence at a trial on August 3, 1992 because, as the oldest, she was regarded as the "ringleader."]*

- Trinley Choezom, seventeen years old when arrested; sentence: five years. As of January 1996 in Drapchi. *[Usually said to be eighteen years old when arrested; convicted on August 3, 1992.]*

- Phuntsog Yangkyi, seventeen when arrested; sentence: five years. Died in Drapchi on June 4, 1994. *[Usually said to be nineteen years old when arrested; convicted on August 3, 1992; death attributed to brain and other internal injuries.]*

- Sherab Ngawang, fifteen when arrested; sentence: three years. On April 18 or May 15, about three months after her release from Trisam, she died in Meldrogongkar County Hospital. *[Usually said to have been twelve years old when arrested, sentenced without trial in mid-1993 to three years re-education-through-labor, death attributed to internal injuries.]*

- Lobsang Choedrag, eighteen when arrested; sentence: five years. From Nyemo, but he stayed a few months in Sera monastery before his arrest. As of January 1996 in Drapchi. *[A monk at Nyemo Gyalche monastery, and affiliated to Sera monastery; convicted on August 3, 1992.]*

1992 Demonstration
The demonstration took place on a special day in the Chinese official calendar [Chinese New Year]. We arrived very early in the morning at the Barkor and first went to the Tsuglhakhang [the Jokhang Temple] to pay homage and receive blessing. Then we started to make a circuit of the Barkor while shouting independence slogans. Walking from the northwest corner, in two rows of three each, we were arrested in front of the police station situated in the southwest corner of the circle. They had phoned for many cars to be sent and about thirty policemen were ready. There were no Tibetans at all. They arrested some of us by catching us from behind; three were arrested first and the other group after. They took us in the vehicles while holding tightly our arms in our backs. We were not handcuffed. Locked in the vehicle we couldn't see anything, but they took us to the *gong an* [public security] office on the east side of the Lingkor.

Gutsa Detention Center: Beatings

The first group went directly to Gutsa [detention center]. I was with Lobsang Drolma and Sherab Ngawang. We were asked questions together by a policeman who probably came from Amdo judging from his accent; he had Chinese assistants. They asked where we had come from and why we did the demonstration. They didn't beat us at all, just asked question. We didn't stay long, maybe twenty minutes. Then they took us to Gutsa.

There is a big space of grass and we stood there with a space of a few meters between each other. "Trang chuzhang" [Department Leader Zhang, the head of Gutsa] arrived and a Chinese man came to take us. We ran away but they brought us back and told us to get on our knees. One came and took me into a room where I had to undress completely; they searched in each item of clothing. I dressed again and went to another room. All of us had to do the same. Zhang Chuzhang, a Chinese man, and Liu Chuzhang [Department Leader Liu], his deputy, a half Chinese-half Tibetan man who could speak both languages, were in the room where we were ill-treated and were shouted at.

"Why did you demonstrate in Barkor? There is no hope for an independent Tibet. Do you think that a few persons shouting will be able to change something? Be careful, if you don't answer properly you will really be ill-treated," they said.

They beat me. I was screaming. One of them would write at a table (Leader Zhang) while another (Leader Liu) would beat me with his hands and kick me with his big boots. This lasted for two hours. Then we had to stand against a wall from about 2:00 p.m. to 9:00 p.m. without being allowed to sit for a moment.

Each of us had the same treatment. Then they put each of us in a separate room. We stayed three days there without being questioned. Each evening I received a cup of black tea and a *tin-momo* [steamed dumpling] and was sent to the toilet twice a day. Then they resumed the questioning, but without ill-treatment. Only Phuntsog Yangkyi said she had been threatened with a knife, but she was able to stop them using it. They asked about the reason why we demonstrated. I said that there were no human rights in Tibet and as an example I said that we were not allowed to go freely from the nunnery to Lhasa.

Also they wanted to know if somebody had encouraged us or helped us to do it. I said it was my own idea. They also told me that if I would agree to say I made a mistake it would improve my situation. I answered that I had not made any mistakes and did not have to apologize for anything. They also said that when Tibet was independent the people had suffered greatly, that I was young and had been misled, that I should ask older persons. I answered that I never heard an old person say that the past was a better time than now.

This happened about six times, with them trying more and more to convince us and spending less and less time asking questions. Then I had to go three times to another office called *jianchayuan* [the procuracy] where we were asked the same questions. They said they would decide where we would have to go.

After six months, Lobsang Drolma, Trinley Choezom, Phuntsog Yangkyi, and Lobsang Choedrag went to the court for their trial; after ten days, they received their sentences and were sent to Drapchi. During one month and eighteen days following our arrest, each of us stayed alone in a room. Then we had to work and shared a room with others: bringing water to water trees, sweeping, cleaning the toilets, houses and windows, growing vegetables, and so on.

For the first six months no visit was allowed but we could receive some food sent from outside. After this, visits were allowed on the fourteenth day of each month. The permit to visit a prisoner is very difficult to get, especially for us villagers. One member of the family has to go to his *xian* [county government offices] or *chu* [sub-district government offices] and ask for it. It is much easier for criminal prisoners to get visits. If there is a special event in the prison they don't allow visits. On the twentieth day of the first Tibetan month 1993 [March 12, 1993], three nuns from Michungri arrived after having been arrested for staging a demonstration: Ngawang Drolma, from Toelung, seventeen years old at that time; Tenzin Dekyong, from Meldrogongkar, seventeen years old; and Jampa Dedrol, from Meldrogongkar, seventeen years old. They had the same treatment as us: they had been questioned and beaten, three days solitary confinement, questioned again and then, after some time, sent to work. They also spent one year and a half in Gutsa before being sentenced (to three years) and being sent to serve the remainder in Trisam.

Daily life, discipline and visits

We were not allowed to talk too much to each other, nor allowed to sing or to pray. When Chinese guards were talking to us, we could not understand; Tibetan ones had to say that we were not allowed to pray or recite mantras.

Before a visit we were completely searched, and when we returned from seeing the visitors too. They would check thoroughly each thing that we had been given, for example, open each packet of instant noodles soup, look at each parcel of food. Three days after the visit the rooms were searched: we were not allowed to keep mirrors, a thermos flask, or cups - all of them would be confiscated. It was the same for prayers books or books.

During the time we were there we had to attend meetings where they would tell us to do well and behave properly. At the same time our rooms would also be completely searched. When we got back [from the meeting] we would find sheets and blankets upside down, objects which had been confiscated or taken way to be burnt would be missing. Wearing a belt was not allowed. We had to make one from a piece of cloth we would tear up, as we were wearing *chubas* [Tibetan gowns]. After some time these would be confiscated again and we had to make other ones.

Because Sherab Ngawang and I were to young to be sentenced, they kept us in Gutsa, working every day. We asked again and again that they decide something about us. We stayed there for one year and half from the time of our arrest. We didn't go to the court; a three- year sentence was decided in Trisam while we were still in Gutsa and the papers were sent to Gutsa. After a week we were transferred to Trisam.

Trisam: Prison Protest

On August 10, 1994 there was some trouble and twelve of us were deprived of visits as a result. We used to work outside watering plants; we had to bring the water from a water tank. A guard saw a Chinese man taking some of it and asked us why this happened. We said we didn't know, but he said we must have some special reason for letting this happen. They asked us a lot of questions. Afterwards we went back to the work and talked about it. The guards came again asking what we were talking about, what we were planning. One Chinese man was particularly rude and nasty to us. Two of us were deprived of visits; but we said that nobody would go to the next visit if any of us were prevented from seeing their relatives. On the day of the visit we all refused to go. They called us again and again but we were firm. It lasted a long time; our relatives were asking the guards to send us out and they had to say they were helpless because we were refusing to come.

Singing pro-independence songs was forbidden. We were staying in three different rooms and one evening we sang, from each room at the same time. The guards heard, came, and asked us to come out. All the thirteen nuns that were there at that time said we had been imprisoned for no reason and started to shout slogans and to say there are no human rights in Tibet. Some prisoners from the other *rukag* [unit] heard and shouted too. Guards started beating us with electric prods and sticks, or kicking us, pulling and pushing our head by our hair, which was very long because we were not allowed to cut it in prison. We were handcuffed or our hands were tied behind our backs with rope. We were separated but all received the same ill-treatment. We could hardly breathe and could not stand. There was a lot of *gong an* [public security], maybe fifty of them, all Chinese. It lasted from 11:00 p.m. to 5:00 a.m. the next day. They asked us to stay kneeling on the hard cement, saying: "You shouted independence slogans; if you don't apologize and say you made a mistake, you will have to kneel until this evening". We refused, and said that we had not made any mistake. After some time some of us fell over. The guards said we were pretending to be sick.

Each of us was put in an isolation cell: a very tiny bare room without any window; only from a small slit on the door could I guess if it was night or day. There was no blanket and I could not sleep, because it was so cold at night and I was freezing. I stayed there for four days, without food, and using a part of the room as a toilet. Then they took me out and I was asked more questions, beaten, with my hands tied behind my back with rope. They asked me to apologize but I always refused. They slapped me, pulled my hair and ears, beat me with a round plastic stick [or truncheon]. I was bleeding. Before sending me outside the room, they carefully washed all traces of blood, because they were afraid that other prisoners would see it. We stayed seven days in isolation cells without leaving. We were not allowed any visit then - that period included the fifteenth day of the month, the visiting day.

When we were released from the cell, all of us were sick, unable to stand up, some vomiting. They wanted us to work and didn't allow any rest to recover. While carrying the water I was feeling dizzy and I had no strength. They said we were lying and pretending to feel sick. Going to the hospital was useless as the doctor and medicine were no help. I was so sick that I didn't eat for five days. They took me to the Military Hospital where I was supposed to stay only seven days (usually we were not allowed to stay more than that) but because my health didn't improve (I had an abscess in my back), I stayed seventeen days in all before going back to Trisam. Doctors were not good at healing me and for the next two months I stayed lying down, sleeping all the time, unable to urinate. I don't remember exactly this period. The other nuns were worried for me.

They would always tell us that Trisam is not a prison but a school; but the discipline and treatment you receive there are really those of a jail. They were always repeating that one should never tell anyone that there had been a demonstration in the prison or that we had been sick. They said we should answer any questions by saying that Trisam was fine.

They never put meat or oil in the food but only boiled vegetables. Praying, reciting mantras or prostrating was completely forbidden. We would be questioned and beaten if they would find a *mala* [rosary] or a picture of His Holiness in our room.

Re-education and work

We worked full-time in the summer, spreading what they called fertilizer —excrement from toilets—bringing water, planting and picking vegetables. Usually we worked from 9:30 a.m. to 12:30 p.m. and from 3:00 to 7:00 or 8:00 p.m. Sunday was free for the prison workers so we would stay inside, cleaning the prison. In winter there is a two month-long re-education meeting. The *wu jing* [People's Armed Police] organize it. They all speak Chinese and as most of us can't understand Chinese, we were again ill-treated. At 5 a.m. we would wake up very early and then we had to study until to 9:00 a.m. After a quick meal we would study again until 12:30 p.m. We would start again at 1:30 p.m. and do more study until 7:00 p.m. This lasted two months during the winter period.

During this period they were extremely rough with us, beating and slapping us, taking off their belts and beating us with them. They said we were not allowed to tell anyone outside that we had been beaten. We had to write about what we had studied during the meetings, and we used to answer that we had not understood whatever we had been taught. They said that these studies would be very helpful to us in future, after our release, and they would shout at us if we could not remember what had been said. Once a year we had to write a letter that was supposed to be sent to the United Nations and this was the most difficult and the most important thing to write.

If some leaders were coming to visit the prison, we had to clean everything before they came, and wear clean clothes. I don't know which offices they belonged to; they were wearing either plain clothes or *gong an* uniforms.

I was released on February 2, 1995. They gave me some papers showing my sentence and the time I had been sentenced to in prison. They sometimes reduce the sentence of criminal prisoners by some months, or increase them according to their behavior. Reducing the sentence of a political prisoner is very rare; the most would be few weeks.

At the time I was in Trisam there were thirteen of us nuns who were political prisoners. We were in *rukag* [unit] No.3. There were about 100 boys, both political and non-political prisoners, in *rukag* Nos.1 and 2. We didn't have any contact with them, except for meetings which we would have together. Work, meals, and visits were separate. There are no children of fourteen or under in the prison; the youngest must be fifteen. When I left there were seven nuns still in Trisam.

Appendix F. Security Preparations for the Anniversary

In March 1994, a year and a half before the thirtieth anniversary of the founding of the TAR, the Lhasa Party Committee decided, through its Political-Legal Committee (PLC), to set up a "leading group" to coordinate a survey of its security apparatus in the run-up to the anniversary. This document was written on March 30, 1994 and sent out to all the committees and offices involved in security work (which in Party terms comes under "political-legal" work) instructing them to carry out a survey of their security operations. The document shows how systematic Chinese officials are in their approach to administration, and especially in preparing for major public events. The document is an order issued by a Party committee, the Lhasa Political-Legal Committee, in conjunction with a subsidiary Party committee, the Lhasa Comprehensive Management of Public Security (CMPS) Committee, to a wide number of government officials, as well as to lower-level Party committees. Since the Party and the government are in theory different bodies, this document provides a good example of how the government is used as the inferior administrative arm of the Party. The document describes this relationship as "unified leadership."

The second and third sections of the document deal with administrative issues involved in establishing a new "leading group," the term used to describe a high-level Party committee established to "shadow" and direct the work of a government body or bodies in particular fields. Details of such groups are not usually publicized. The leaders of this group are Chinese officials who are deputy leaders in other, more public areas. For example, Hou Jianguo is deputy-secretary of the Lhasa Political-Legal Committee, and Wang Huaisheng is a deputy director in the Regional Public Security, which is a government post. The group includes at least eight Tibetans and five Chinese and is under the leadership of a Chinese official (who, unusually, uses his own name as the issuing authority at the head of the document) and its office is also run by a Chinese official.

The questionnaire confirms that Chinese officials in Tibet regard the campaign against the pro-independence movement as the outstanding political and security issue in the region. Unlike western questionnaires, which generally proceed from the general to the specific, this document starts with what are apparently the central issues and then addresses secondary matters. The central premise appears to be that the major security threat is nationalist activity stirred up by monks and nuns. The document lists questions about sixteen issues, of which the first is "splittist" activity, and the second is activity in monasteries and nunneries. The spread of nationalist ideas to the countryside, which is addressed as a potential threat rather than as a process that has already happened, is presented as the fifth issue in the questionnaire—effectively the third most pressing concern on the list, since items three and four are administrative. The question of the migrant or "floating" population, which is usually presented in Chinese documents as the main security problem, is listed here as item No.11; corruption is mentioned briefly as item No.7. There is no explicit reference to conventional security concerns, such as crime, which many Tibetans say has increased dramatically in Lhasa in the last three years, although the issue is covered in more general questions about "recent criminal cases" and "pressing social concerns."

The document [TIN ref.: 20(WN)], issued in March 1994, consists of eight pages printed in Chinese, except for one line printed in Tibetan at the top of page one: *srid khrims u-yon lhan-khang yig-cha* (Political-Law Committee document). A star is printed at the center of page one to indicate that it is a Party document, and the names of the two issuing authorities—the Lhasa Political-Legal Committee and the Lhasa CMPS committee—on page seven are overstamped by two circular stamps each with hammer and sickle inside. It was not previously clear that the CMPS committee is a Party rather than a government organ.

The distribution order attached to the document shows that only sixty copies were printed, each one of them numbered individually. The text follows.

A Document from the Political-Legal Committee (PLC) of Lhasa Municipality

Lhasa Municipality Political-Legal Committee: Document No.2 (1994)
Lhasa Municipality Comprehensive Management of Public Security (CMPS) Committee Document: No.4 (1994)

Issued by: Hou Jianguo

[Title:] A Notice Concerning Advancing the Work of the Political-Legal Committee and Emphasizing the Comprehensive Management of Public Security [*guanyu jiaqiao zheng fa he zong zhi qiaoyan gongzuo de tongzhi*]

To: The Political-Legal Committee of Counties ([and] Sub-districts [*qu*]), CMPS Committees, to All Departments of the Municipal Political-Legal Committee and the [Municipal] CMPS Committee, to [Party] Committees to which Members of CMPS Committees Belong

In the spirit of the Regional Political-Legal Committee Conference and the document [entitled] "Notice About Strengthening Political-Legal Committees'

Investigation and Research" dispatched by the Regional Political-Legal Committee of the Party Committee, we should enhance the Political-Legal Committees' and CMPS committees' investigation and research by connecting them with the reality of our city's stability, and provide them with first hand material about basic issues. To make our reform measures more scientific, more systematic, more reliable and better directed, we should summarize our experiences and guide our efforts in advance to meet our targets. We should provide the Party committee and government with reliable and systematic information so that they can make decisive policies to obtain stability, to promote the improvement of society and the economy, and to celebrate the thirtieth anniversary of the TAR government.

Therefore, the following questions for investigation and research, which have been ratified by the Party Committee of the city, must be answered seriously.

First: Questions for Investigation and Research

1. What are the present characteristic movements aiming to split the nation? What are the means and forms of infiltration by the international forces who are hostile and in favor of splittism? How do they appear? How should we enhance the leadership of anti-splittism? Furthermore, how should we carry out anti-splittism more efficiently? How should we safeguard the unity of our nation and nationality, and guarantee a stable political situation? (The State Security Bureau must specifically investigate the above questions.)

2. How many monasteries (including retreat centers and temples) are there in the cities and countryside? [Where are they] located and [what is] the number of nunneries plus monasteries? How many monasteries and nunneries have been renovated or newly built, both with and without permission from the government? How many monks and nuns in the monasteries and nunneries were approved by the government, and how many are there today? Did they participate in the 1959 rebellion and the 1987 demonstrations of the splittists? How many times did they participate and how many of them participated? How many of them have been detained, interrogated, sentenced, and re-educated through labor? How many of them have escaped to foreign countries and how many of them have been checked upon? What are the most pressing problems in the monasteries and nunneries at the moment, and what are the causes? How many reincarnations are there, and how many of them have come from abroad? Are the hostile forces interfering or using religion for their splittist activities? Are they interfering in governmental affairs, in the work of the Political-Legal Committees, or in educational matters, etc? How should we legally strengthen the administration of the Party and government over

the monasteries and over religious affairs? (The [Lhasa] Municipal United Front Department, [and the] Civil and Religious Department [of the] counties and sub-districts should investigate the above-mentioned matters within their own areas of jurisdiction.)

3. Under the jurisdiction of the [Lhasa] municipal government, what is the population of each town, neighborhood, and village? How many basic level mass organizations are related to public security work? What are the conditions of these organizations and how many members do they have? How many work efficiently and how many are ineffective? Why are they ineffective? What about their salaries and funds? What are the problems and how should we solve them? (Counties and sub-districts should investigate the above and the following matters.)

4. How should the CMPS correctly combine the work of specific organizations with the goals of the mass line of the Party and how should it successfully manage the relationship between the specific organizations and the general mass organizations of the Party related to public security work? What has been the results of experience in relying on general mass organizations of the Party to gain stability and public order? How should we implement all the measures of the CMPS at the basic levels? What the plans and measures are [which will define] the responsibilities of CMPS leaders?

5. What are the pressing public security problems in the agricultural and nomadic areas at the moment? What are the causes? How should we successfully perform CMPS work in these rural areas, and take precautions against the infiltration and expansion of splittism in the agricultural and nomadic areas? How should we safeguard political stability there?

6. What are the characteristics of recent criminal cases in our city and what are the most common crimes? What are the new trends? How should we further continue "to strike relentlessly" [carry out a crackdown against crime]? What are the weak links and what are the reasons for them? How should we improve and solve the problems? (The Public Security [Bureau], the CMPS committees, and the procuratorial department must specifically investigate the above mentioned matters.)

7. What are the present characteristics and methods of the criminal offenders? How should we take further steps in our struggle against corruption? How can we strike

relentless blows at crimes in the economic field? (Procuratorial organizations must specifically investigate the above mentioned matters.)

8. What are the pressing problems in our municipal public security [work]? Under the new circumstances of reform and construction of a socialist market economy, how should we enforce public security and safeguard social order and security? What suggestions do you have? (Counties, including sub-districts and departments of the municipal government, should investigate these matters.)

9. How many special trades and service trades are there in our city, counties, and sub-districts (counties and sub-districts under city jurisdiction)? Among them, how many are owned by the state, how many are collective, and how many are private? Do the legal persons [officials with PLC responsibilities?] and managers have any political problems? Are there any weaknesses in our administration, and how should we enhance the management of these trades? (These matters should be specifically investigated by the Municipal Commercial Department, by counties, and by sub-districts.)

10. What are the names of newly-constructed or expanded roads and resident areas in Lhasa? What is their condition and the condition of the house number plates and grassroots organizations? (These organizations should be investigated by the Inner City District [chengguanqu], Public Security Bureau, and by the City Construction Department.)

11. How is the floating population from outside our region living in our city? What is the population of these temporary residents? How many are from within and how many are from outside our region? How many of them live in government departments, in residential areas, in private houses or in houses rented by organizations? What are their problems? What are the main issues for those people who stay on in our city? What is their income and their condition? Do they have any problems? Are there any problems in the administration of the floating population? How should we administer [them]? (The Metropolitan District and the Public Security [should address these matters.])

12. How many houses for rent have been occupied under our jurisdiction? How many departments and private [organizations] have houses for rent and have been occupied? How many people without residence cards have bought or built private houses in our city? Are there any loopholes in our administration and how should

we close them? (The Metropolitan [*chengguanqu* or Inner City] District [should address these matters.])

13. As reform has strengthened, there has been a change in people's interests. Therefore, what types of unstable elements exist? How do they appear, what are the reasons for them and by what method should we deal with them? How should we correctly understand and deal with contradictions among the people and prevent the contradictions from intensifying? (The Department of the Municipal Government [should address these matters.])

14. How should we regulate the market economy through legal means? What are the working conditions of the Regulator Office at the basic level? (The Municipal Intermediate People's Court [should address these matters.])

15. What is the general situation regarding popularizing common knowledge of the law? How should the law generally serve and guarantee the construction and development of the socialist market economy structure? (The Municipal Judicial Department [should address these matters.])

16. How should the Party strengthen its leadership over Political-Legal Committee work? Analyze the situation of Political-Legal Committee improvement and its problems and offer your ideas and suggestions about reform and about the Political-Legal Committees' self-improvement. (The municipal government and its counties [should address these matters.])

Second: To Organize Leadership

The Political-Legal Committee and CMPS Committee of the Municipal Government should establish a group of leaders to be responsible for the work of all the investigation groups under the unified leadership of the Municipal Party Committee (MPC) and the government. Hou Jianguo, the deputy secretary of the MPC, is appointed as the leader of this leading group. Jiacuo [Gyatso], the Deputy Mayor; Wang Huaisheng, [who is] the deputy director of the Regional Public Security and the Director of the Municipal Public Security Office; and Lasung [Tibetan: Lhasum?], will be the deputy leaders. A-deng Gong-po [?], Hu Duliang [or Hu Yuliang], Ou-zhu [Ngodrup], Lawang Ou-zhu [Ngodrup], Pu-dawa [Bu-dawa], Dengzeng Ou-zhu [Tenzin? Ngodrup], Yuan Chengquan, Leicuo [Legtsog], and Kang Yuquan will be members of this leading group.

The office of the leading group will be located in the Office of the Municipal Political-Legal Committee headed by comrade Bi Quanzhuan [or Jinzhuan?]. Some well-read people should be transferred to this Office from different units of the Political-Legal Committee to be staff-members of the leading group. These staff members should deal with concrete matters, examine and verify investigation materials, and compile [reports? from] them.

As a result of necessity, the Municipal Political-Legal Committee and the CMPS Committee have decided to transfer some people from the Municipal Public Security, the Civil and Nationality Affairs Department, the Inner City District, the Political-Legal Committee, and the CMPS offices to form different groups to conduct investigations. These groups should vigorously conduct thorough investigations to answer the relevant questions.

The Political-Legal Committee and CMPS Committee of the counties and sub-districts, and the Municipal Political-Legal Committee and its departments should organize competent cadres into different investigation groups to infiltrate the masses and the grass roots units, and to thoroughly conduct investigations to answer the relevant questions by combining the facts from the field with departmental observations. All of this should be done under the unified leadership of the Party Committee and the government.

Third: Requirements

1. After receiving this notice, the Political-Legal Committees of the counties and sub-districts should immediately report it to the Party Committee and government to obtain their leadership and attention. The Political-Legal Committees at all levels should discuss and plan their work well. There should be plans to carry it out and focal points to investigate by combining them with the facts. They should organize investigation groups and submit a report about them to the Office of the Municipal Political-Legal Committee before May 1[1994].

The investigation groups of the counties should carry out their work as soon as they are organized and the Municipal Political-Legal Committee will send working groups to carry out inspection of their implementation. After accomplishing their tasks as set out in the notice, they can also use the method of "dissecting a sparrow" to analyze the status of grassroots administration, to investigate pressing problems, to discover weak, negligent, and incompetent areas of work, and to discover good ways to strengthen grassroots administration.

2. All the departments of the Municipal Political-Legal Committee and the Inner City District should decide on their investigating person as soon as possible

according to the requirements of the Municipal Leading Group. At the same time, they should seriously carry out their own departmental investigations. Those relevant departments and units should coordinate and support the work of the investigation group.

This order is hereby pronounced.
[with the stamps of:]
The Political-Legal Committee of the Lhasa Municipal Party Committee
The Lhasa Municipal CMPS Committee

March 30, 1994

INDEX OF NAMES

189